GIANT BLUEFIN

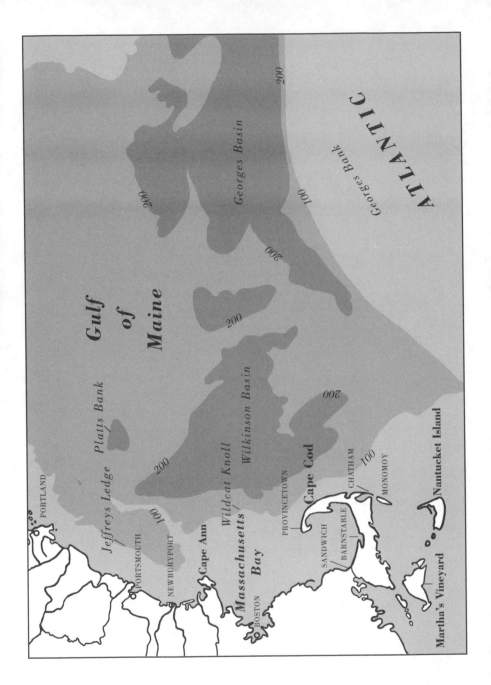

GIANT BLUEFIN

DOUGLAS
WHYNOTT

NORTH POINT PRESS
Farrar, Straus and Giroux
New York

Published in Canada by HarperCollins*CanadaLtd*
Printed in the United States of America
DESIGNED BY FRITZ METSCH
First published in 1995 by Farrar, Straus and Giroux
This edition first published in 1996 by North Point Press

LIBRARY OF CONGRESS CATALOGING-IN-PUBLICATION DATA
Whynott, Douglas.
Giant bluefin / Douglas Whynott.—1st ed.
p. cm.
1. Bluefin tuna fisheries—New England. 2. Bluefin tuna—New
England. I. Title.
SH351.B56W48   1995
639.2'758—dc20   95-4089 CIP

North Point Press
A division of Farrar, Straus and Giroux
New York

For my daughters, Isha and Elizabeth,
and for my grandfather, Sam Thacher

CONTENTS

ix

CONTENTS

x

PART ONE

The 1992 Season

THE SHOW

T H I S   W O U L D   be an afternoon show, Brad Sampson figured. At least it had been so far, with the bluefin rising to the surface with the slack tide in the warmer part of the day. Bluefin tuna were an epipelagic species, meaning they ranged far and lived in the upper waters of the ocean. Bluefin liked to get close to the heat of the day, to cruise with their dorsal fins above water, like sharks or dolphins. "Making water," trailing wakes, by triangular aspect revealing their courses, a purple shade moving along, that was what the bluefin harpooners looked for. That was the show.

Just three days ago, July 4, the last good-weather day, Brad Sampson, a harpoon fisherman, had been near Outer Kettle off Portland when he got a call from Eric Hesse, another tuna fisherman who'd come from Cape Cod to Maine to chase the first fish of the season. Eric told Brad that fish were only "five boats," or 250 feet, away. Brad had stopped the boat and was working on the engine. When he looked up, he saw four wakes coming his way. His mate took the wheel of the *Scratcher*, and Brad got on the stand, and they circled around behind the school—it's much more difficult to approach bluefin by going straight at them. The boat got close, but the school settled and Brad couldn't make a throw. That was a hard opportunity to miss. You didn't see fish up like that very often.

Atlantic bluefin tuna seemed to show up first off the coast of Maine, or at least that was where the first fish were usually caught. Sixteen to twenty bluefin had been taken so far this season. Strangely, some bluefin arrived in Maine fat, while most came in lean. The fish taken on June 11 weighed over 500 pounds "round," 370 pounds "dressed," and brought $16 a pound in Japan. Another tuna brought $25 a pound, and a third $43, but most of the others were not good enough—not fat enough—to merit a trip to the Japanese markets. These "domestic" fish were bringing about $3 a pound and went primarily to New England fish markets and restaurants.

In Japan, red tuna meat, *maguro*, is an essential component of a good meal, and bluefin is the quintessential *maguro*—the food of perfection. Served raw in thin slices as sushi or sashimi, a two-ounce serving could cost as much as $75 in Tokyo. The Japanese consumed 400,000 tons of raw fish yearly, about 35 percent of it imported, and the raw market was the only niche for American fishermen. Bluefin tuna had the highest status among imports—3 percent by volume, but 10 percent by value. Of the many sources—Australia, California, Spain, the Canary Islands—the "jumbo bluefin" of New England, because of its size, oil content, and color, was most often the bluefin with the highest status on the Japanese market.

The early arrivals in the Gulf of Maine (some called them "marauders," others called them "racers") had migrated to feed on the abundant mackerel and herring. They had come days or weeks ahead of the big schools now making their way north off the Atlantic coast, or heading in from eastern waters. And in concert with their prey, the fishermen working in Maine, harpoon fishermen generally, were also in the vanguard—ahead of other harpooners, and ahead of the fleets of rod-and-reel fishermen soon to drop their lines along the underwater ledges and hills, and ahead of the purse seiners, who would begin setting their nets in August. Fish and fishermen, scouts and hunters, testing the northern waters, following instinct, following leads.

Brad Sampson, twenty-two years old, a college student, son of perhaps the best tuna fisherman in New England, thought these Maine fish were "squirrelly." Moving along in singles, pairs, foursomes, they weren't "acting right"—staying still long enough to be good harpoon targets. They were skittish, and shy, and they screwed too easy. But Maine was the only game in town right now, until schools of tuna

4

showed up off the Cape and in Massachusetts Bay, and the way to succeed in tuna fishing was to be out there when it happened, to get on the fish, to make the throws, to work the percentages.

T H E   S A M P S O N S , and those like them, were the true sons of the whalers of old. In body and spirit, in style and confidence, speech and manner, sense and intuition, intent and determination, the fishermen who harpooned bluefin tuna in the waters of Cape Cod and the Gulf of Maine were the inheritors of the New England whaling tradition. The harpooners of the nineteenth century inherited the tradition from the Danes and Basques and the British before them, from the Native American hunters, from the fishermen who'd dried and traded their salt cod—New England's first currency. The bluefin tuna fishermen had the whaler's harpoon, the cod fisherman's persistence, and the lobsterman's boat, and in this last decade of the twentieth century, they had loran navigation systems and radios with scramblers and descramblers, and they had spotter planes. They had fax reports from Tsukiji market—like their seafaring ancestors, some had gone off to the Orient to trade. They had an international regulatory system subject to diverse contention.

The bluefin tuna harpoon fishery in New England was technically advanced, and yet in its tool, that bronze harpoon head riding off the prow, it was also the most primitive, so ancient in aspect it spoke of the toggled Indian harpoon made of bone, spoke of the Eskimo hunters, spoke of the African or South American tribesman working the edge of a river a hundred thousand years ago, spoke of a preternatural tool hardened in the first fires over which the first languages drifted.

Transposed whalers, then, riding the pulpit in the swell, in Nantucket Sound and Cape Cod Bay and the Gulf of Maine. Their prey was also at a kind of apex. *Thunnus thynnus* (the rushingest of the rushing) was the largest of the finfish (a torpedo, ten feet long, a thousand pounds), and among the fastest (a hummingbird's response, a bumblebee's musculature, fifty-mile-per-hour bursts), and the most highly migratory (transoceanic, a tropical fish evolved to feed in subpolar waters), the most valuable (a $5,000 fish, a $50,000 fish), among the most fertile, and by the hue of its opalescent skin, its ovoid form, its lunate tail, perhaps the most beautiful. Bluefin swam with whales and dolphins, swam in phalanxes, shot into the air to chase bluefish or to escape killer whales. No one who had ever seen them charging along in formation, a bank of three, say, making water, would ever forget their shouldering mastery and grace.

Since the bluefin was one of the most intensively sought fish, some people claimed it was the most endangered. Fishermen at government hearings, arguing against proposed decreases in U.S. quotas, talked of the balance of trade, of how they were sending product to Japan, of how their New England bluefin tuna were equivalent to Japanese automobiles—a tuna for a Toyota. The stocks, they claimed, were abundant, and the government assessments were inaccurate. As they saw it, the fishery, not the fish, was endangered.

THE FIRST time I saw the tuna fishermen at work was not on a Sampson boat but with a charter captain. He ran a million-dollar boat for a retired businessman and I had come along for the day. Heading out of Cape Cod Bay, he gave me the wheel, said he was going to make some coffee, and told me to look out for tuna. If you see a fin like a shark's, he said, yell. Soon I did see fins, and I shouted below. The captain came up the ladder but by then, after a pair of the animals had soared out of the water in crossing arcs, I knew they were dolphins. (I had a good eye for them, since at one time I'd blown whistles at trained dolphins, shouted orders at them to jump through hoops, spit out fires, wave bye-bye, and pluck pieces of paper out of my mouth at ten feet above the water.) This dolphin school, this day, loosely moving along, looked like a tribe of hunters and gatherers migrating to ancient feeding grounds.

The captain crossed the tip of Provincetown and went about six miles off the Cape. Soon we saw a wake, and the flash of a tuna's side as it turned to go down. Then we saw whales feeding, dozens of them. They were finbacks and humpbacks eating sand eels, fish the size of sardines. Some whales crashed to their sides to stun the fish. Others slapped their tails or bobbed up and down, pitchpoling side by side, mouths open. The cleverest among them went below and spun circles, blowing bubble rings. When the sand eels bunched into the center, the whales coursed up with open mouths. Some whales even worked together, making communal bubble rings.

Cruising among the whales were the tuna boats. Occasionally someone would run out on a pulpit, the stand projecting from the bow, but we didn't see anyone make a throw. The tuna were below the whales, snapping at the sand eels, and they weren't making themselves available, they weren't acting right. Meanwhile, two spotter planes worked the air.

It seemed odd that the whales were no longer the prey, the point of the hunt in this place. Time, progress, had passed them by. They were no longer the source of food and light and bone. Only two decades earlier, the bluefin tuna, the "horse mackerel," was worth five cents a pound and served as cat food. Now this prime sushi fish was airfreighted, fresh on ice, to Japan.

Standing in the tower above the wheelhouse that day, the captain said, "Catching's bad, but the fishing's good." And it was true. The bubble rings, the flapping tails, the breaching and pitchpoling, the boats with dipping pulpits and nodding towers, the drone overhead, seemed a strange dance, a confluent motion, a technological and natural spectacle, on a sunlit day, with the water soft and blue, and a view of the Wellfleet sand cliffs off to the west.

N O   B U B B L E   feeding, not a whale in sight in the Gulf of Maine on this day. Brad Sampson and I and the first mate, St. John Laughlin, were huddled up in the tower of the *Scratcher*, heading away from Portland Harbor. "We should get a good charge of fish today," Brad said. "It should be an afternoon show. Conditions should be right."

Though it was calm and clear, we were riding into the air, cruising along at eight knots. It was a hot day, in the eighties. Brad had smeared his sunburned nose and face with sunblock. He and his mate were wearing long-sleeve shirts, jackets, hats, and polarized sunglasses with leather side shields that cut the glare and gave a better view down into the water. Days of wearing this binocularized getup left harpooners with pale foreheads and burned cheeks—tuna tans.

Brad pulled a chart out from a cabinet in the tower and unfolded it. He pointed out the areas they'd been working—a twenty-mile path from Murray Hole to Outer Kettle to Mistaken Ground, and another twenty miles to the east, over to Toothaker Ridge, in water 200 to 250 feet deep.

We were crossing the Pasture on a course for Outer Kettle, headed for a meeting with "Brooksie"—Fred Brooks, the Sampsons' spotter pilot. Brooksie usually flew for Continental Airlines, but he had recently begun a leave of absence. For the rest of the summer he would function as the Sampsons' eyes, from 900 feet.

"So far we've been looking for them by sight," Brad said. "That's a lot harder. You have to stay intense all day, eight hours, looking on the water. It can get to your eyes."

The *Scratcher* was a "stick boat," and you could spot a stick boat a long ways off. Crossing the horizon, they looked a bit like mounted knights carrying lances, with their towers perched over the wheelhouses and the long pulpits leading the way. Some towers looked like old-style mastheads with crow's nests, but others (such as the *Scratcher*'s) were four-legged structures modeled on power-line towers. Three people could stand in the tower and ride comfortably. Climbing a tower on a moving sea was like scaling a metronome, a real test of the wrists.

The *Scratcher*'s pulpit was made of a modified utility pole. It was 25 feet in length and hinged to the bow, and could be cranked up like a drawbridge when the boat was in harbor. In the basket at the end of the pulpit was the "stand," a small piece of plywood, and at waist height was a padded "belly rail" for the harpooner to lean into while throwing. The harpoons were 12 feet long and an inch thick and made of aluminum (some Maine harpooners still used spruce poles). The bronze "dart" was shaped like an arrowhead and wired for an 800-volt charge. The dart was also attached to 600 feet of line and a "rig" of plastic balls, or a float, stick, and flag. In the way that an exceptionally long nose precedes a face, a harpooner in a pulpit preceded his boat by a second or two and could "get over the fish."

Brad spotted Brooksie in the sky several miles away, and before long there was a ring on the radio.

"I got fish here," Brooksie said. "Four giants." The *Scratcher* steamed toward the circling plane. A wing dipped, the pilot peering down, keeping his eye on the fish.

"Nice fish there," Brooksie said.

"Long as they're fat."

"This is Brooksie's first day out," Brad said. "Everything's gonna look good to him today."

"Head one o'clock," Brooksie said. Tuna harpooners use a clock system universal in plane and boat fishery, universal in nature—the circle of the sky or sea analogous to the face of a clock. The *Scratcher*'s bow and pulpit pointed to noon.

The *Scratcher* pushed ahead at twelve knots. "I see a stick boat," Brooksie said. Another boat was coming toward us, white water spraying off the bow. Brad said it was probably Eric Hesse, or Nick Nickerson, a fisherman from Chatham on Cape Cod, or maybe even Lexie Krause, from Monhegan Island, Maine.

"Small giants," Brooksie said. "They're swimming erratically."

"Small fish act a lot crazier," Brad said.

"One o'clock now," Brooksie said. Brad wheeled to the right. "Keep the speed up. Keep it coming. To port just a hair, port just a bit."

Sun gleamed off the plane as it turned with lowered wing.

"Six boats." Six lengths away now.

Brad cut the engine back and climbed down the tower. St. John took the wheel. He had been working for the Sampsons for five years. He'd just finished high school.

"Touch to starboard. Four boats."

Brad walked out on the pulpit, running his fingers along the guide wires. With his easy athleticism and lithe step, the polo shirt, the white-blond hair, the visor cap, Brad did look like a college student. He unfastened the harpoon, and held it out in front of the belly rail.

"Swing right," came the voice from the sky.

"Twelve o'clock. Two and a half boats. Two boats."

Brad cupped his hand over the end of the harpoon and pointed the dart into the water a few feet ahead of the pulpit. He was rising and falling with a roll of about an eight-foot pitch. St. John cut the speed to a near drift.

"Twelve o'clock. Boat and a half. Three-quarters of a boat."

Brad sighted.

"He's gone."

Brad hurriedly tied up the harpoon. He walked down the pulpit and ascended the mast into the tower.

"You see that, Brooksie? That fish changed direction on me."

"Yeah. I got another one over here. Four-hundred-pound giant."

Down went the throttle and the boat roared ahead to the circling bird.

"Four boats," Brooksie said. Brad climbed down again, and went back into the pulpit. St. John cut the engine.

"Three boats. Two and a half. Two. Touch to port and three-quarters."

We came upon a fish that was nearly showing. It was perhaps three feet below the surface. Brad coasted over it, over the gold-brown, blue-tinted body. We could see the yellow fins along the tail. The fish had been swimming away from the boat—Brooksie had brought the *Scratcher* up from the rear—but then it took a turn to the right. And then it stopped for a moment. It knew we were there. Brad flung the harpoon. With a look of annoyance and three flicks of its tail, the tuna darted down and out of sight, sounded at an angle of, well, 120 degrees.

Sounded, sound—it was the appropriate word for this movement off into the third dimension.

Brad climbed back up the tower.

"Sorry, Brooksie. He scooted away."

"Good throw. Looked like it went under."

"Fish went to starboard."

"Brooksie lined off to work another patch of water.

"That fish looked at me," Brad said. "They do that. They pause, that's what we call it. Once they pause, just a fraction of a second and they're gone. That's it. You've got to get your throw off quick."

•　　•　　•

"I'M AFRAID to stay in a place like this," Brad said, "where there's a lot of singles acting squirrelly."

We cruised, waiting for Brooksie to give the call for a charge. A red plane went by, flying well below Brooksie's altitude. Brad didn't know who the pilot was. But he talked of someone named the Hummer, who talked like a radio deejay ("Hey, this is the Hummah"), and another pilot, Trip Wheeler, who yelled into the radio when he found fish ("Holy Jesus! I got fish here!").

Brad talked of the pressure on the harpooner, with the crew watching from the boat, the pilot from above, and all the money at stake with each throw.

"Last summer I had a lot of days when I missed a lot of shots. I missed some big fish early in the day and had to settle for something smaller in the afternoon. If my father had been on the boat he would have caught a lot of fish.

"It will be a long time before I get to the point my father's at," Brad said.

Bob Sampson had almost left the Cape that morning, but then decided to hold back. "He hits fish he can't see. He knows when the school is going to turn or go down. He knows the way refraction works in the water. Actually, he doesn't know. He just does it.

"I'm competitive, though. A lot of it is ego. If you only have five fish on July 25 it hurts a lot less if everyone else has five fish, too. Ego plays a big part. Actually, my big objective this summer is to catch more fish than my dad. If I keep up with him I'm doing well, but I want to catch more than him." Brad smiled.

Brooksie found another bunch, and off we went like cavalrymen. Twenty boats—fifteen, eight, five, four at twelve o'clock. The fish went down, and then came up, two boats away, and the school settled.

A few minutes later we steamed off again. A fish went down, up, and then headed into the path of the sun. Brad got off a throw. He radioed Brooksie. "That fish was hittable, dammit."

By the amount of activity and the number of sightings, this seemed a morning show, although none of the fish had made water.

Another run: a fish went to starboard, disappeared, came up, one o'clock, four boats, twelve o'clock, three boats, and then sounded.

11

On the eighth run, just before noon, a single screwed hard to starboard. Brooksie mentioned that there was a fog bank further south. This was important news because Brooksie had to be able to see into the water to do his work. Harpooning with planes was entirely dependent on weather conditions. It was a good-weather fishery.

St. John made sandwiches for himself and Brad, from ham and cheese they'd been keeping on ice and which had seen better days. The cookies were just about gone too. They'd been moored in Portland a week. Brad said his mom would be coming in with new supplies if they stayed in Maine much longer. The *Scratcher* seemed a boys' boat now.

After lunchtime the weather changed. The temperature dropped ten degrees, and a wind came in that ruffled the water. The sky became somewhat overcast, too, and the water turned from blue to gray. Perfect weather, Brad said, rough enough so the fish couldn't see the boat coming in, and no whitecaps, "so any white water is tuna." The high tide was followed by the slack. "This is when the charge comes," Brad said.

Brad had written a paper on tuna fishing for one of his courses at Penn State, where he was studying to become a junior-high English teacher. He had defined the harpoon fishery as a cultural group, and explained terminology such as "smashing" (fish hitting prey at the surface), "lollygagging" (a fish swimming lazily along), a "show," a "charge," and a "bunch." Now Brad was writing an honors thesis on school censorship. He'd found that in Pennsylvania the most commonly banned books were American literary classics: *Of Mice and Men*, *The Catcher in the Rye*, *Huckleberry Finn*, and *The Grapes of Wrath*.

Brad would be doing his student teaching in the fall, and before long he would face a decision about whether to teach school or be a commercial tuna fisherman. Brad's mother, Penny Sampson, who had lived the life of a fisherman's wife, wanted him to teach. His father, who admired him thoroughly and loved having him in the business, hadn't done much to influence him other than making a tuna boat available in case he needed it. Brad hadn't worked for anyone but his father, and he couldn't imagine not being on the water. Until he went to college and talked to other students about what they did in the summer, Brad hadn't realized that he had lived a singular life. Some kids got to the ocean one day a year, but Brad had been on a boat every summer since the fifth grade. People remembered seeing him come into the harbor, steering the boat, when his head was just above the wheel. Brad had seen whales and dolphins and basking sharks and all the beautiful ocean scenes as a matter of course. He'd caught enough bluefin tuna to pay for his education. In certain seasons of the fishery, he could make as much money in a week as a schoolteacher made in a year.

Of course Brad remembered the hard times, too. One summer in the early 1980s they caught just one fish, and the next year they lobstered in the mornings before fishing for tuna in the afternoons. In 1985 the fish were spooking, and they got only three. Brad remembered his father working the night job and pounding nails by day, going quahogging and musseling in the dead of winter to make boat payments. But 1986 was a good year, and so were the several that followed. By 1990 the Sampsons had a second boat, the *Rush*. Brad worked on his own that year. For three years now he and his father hadn't spent a day on the same boat.

There were great memories, lots of stories: returning home along the south shore of Cape Cod on the Fourth of July and seeing fireworks in the towns all along the way; coming from Cape Cod Bay into Barnstable Harbor at the end of the day with a fish in the boat and a full cooler, and talking to the other fishermen, the best of people; working off Montauk with his father and racing two other boats for fish—one guy in a sport boat, out front in a bikini bathing suit holding a harpoon, and another guy in a Boston Whaler, a fat man with a cigar in his mouth, held by his suspenders as he leaned out from the bow, all three boats charging at the bunch; going into a cove in Maine on a foggy night, and waking up the next morning to discover a pristine coastal village. Working with his father.

Brad feared that the decision wouldn't be his to make. If the scientists with the National Marine Fisheries Service and the various conservation organizations that had gotten involved in the bluefin tuna fishery had their way, there would be a 50 percent reduction in

13

the quotas—the amount of fish that could be taken each year. That would probably mean an end to commercial bluefin tuna fishing. Brad was a conservationist. He wanted to see the stocks preserved because he wanted the fishery to survive. But they were going too far, he was certain. What those people needed to do was to get up in the planes, to see just how many fish there were out there. Some days, when the conditions were right—usually when a high-pressure weather front came through—all the fish from Nantucket Sound to the Bay of Fundy came up to the surface and showed. Fish everywhere, acres and acres of them. That's what the NMFS people needed to see.

THE FISH didn't rise to the surface this afternoon in Maine, although Brad and the *Scratcher* made repeated runs. At about three o'clock Brooksie found a school of small giants near Mistaken Ground. To get there we had to make a five-mile trip that would take about twenty minutes.

Several other stick boats, cued in by their pilots, were steaming, too. We had to cross the shipping channel into Portland just as a Navy ship was heading into port. Passing through the wake was a rough ride, the pulpit scooping low and the tower slamming back. Over the radio Brad got word that Nick Nickerson had broken a weld on his pulpit. Nickerson had an especially long pulpit on his boat, anyway, and some fishermen had nicknamed it Pinocchio. One fisherman said the Navy ship had increased speed in front of the stick boats. Would a Navy captain, looking at the awkward sight of high tower and exaggerated pulpit, get a kick out of seeing the funny-looking boats tilt and roll in his wake? The fishermen thought so.

The bunch Brooksie was on had disappeared by the time Brad got there. After a half hour we made another run, but those fish went down too. Yet another run stopped short. Between charges Brad and St. John cruised along, looking for show.

Trails of a light fog came in, and then the sun got too low for Brooksie to work the water. For a while he worked the edge of the glare, getting the sun behind him, running lines like a plowman. At

14

about five o'clock he made a low pass, and with a smile and wave headed off to Rockland.

It got cold enough for gloves. Eric Hesse called Brad on the radio. He said he had news and would be right over. Soon his boat loomed in from the edge. Eric's boat was called the *Tenacious*, after one of the qualities of a successful tuna fisherman, one of Eric's own qualities. The *Tenacious* pulled up parallel to the *Scratcher*, and the two boats, the two towers, bobbed side by side. Knees strained, stomach muscles clenched, we did the metronomic swing, though Brad, St. John, Eric, and his brother John took the to-and-fro with ease.

"These fish are acting funny!" Brad yelled.

"Water temperature's at fifty-four, fifty-five!" Eric called back. "Optimum's sixty-four!" The theory was that the cold temperatures had kept the tuna from coming north as soon as they might have, and that it had hindered the show.

"Woodsie got two fish in the bay!" Cape Cod Bay, Eric meant. Chris Woods was a member of their group, Cape Quality Bluefin, twelve Cape fishermen who had gotten together to market their catch directly with the Japanese.

Bluefin were now in Cape Cod Bay, close to home.

"And I just talked to Trip!" Trip Wheeler was Eric's spotter pilot. He had flown back to Cape Cod, and he had seen something along the way. This was the news. "Eight schools just came in! Four of them with a hundred and fifty fish!"

Now the squirrelly fish off the coast of Maine were especially poor prospects. The season, it seemed, was about to begin.

"We're going to P-town! It's eighty-five miles from here! If we leave now we can get there at three or so! We'll sleep in the boat and head out at five!" The captain of the *Tenacious* smiled broadly at the prospect of this adventure. Then his boat dropped away, and turned for the south. Brad steamed for Portland, twenty-two miles away. They'd get some dinner, and supplies, and arrange for someone to pick up Brad's car.

The sun was setting over the shore on the way in, the sky turning peach, pink, and lime, blue deepening to black. Cruising toward the illuminated sky and the silhouetted shore was one of the inherent pleasures of fishing. This ritual of heading into the fading daylight was one of the reasons fishermen could be so happy.

They were on to some different fish, some better fish. Later that night, after a few hours' sleep, Brad and St. John left for Cape Cod. Brooksie met up with them in the morning, and so did Bob Sampson. That day was one of Brad Sampson's best as a harpoon fisherman. The fish acted right that day.

SCHOOLS

I F MIGRATION is the act of moving from one spatial unit to another (this would include the daily vertical movements of herring, the inshore-offshore movements of cod, as well as the travels of the epipelagics), then a highly migratory fish like the bluefin tuna would have a highly developed sense of space, a memory finely attuned to the hydroscape. Bluefin tuna would know just when to depart from the Gulf Stream—that hot, deep river in the Atlantic—to make their way along the Great South Channel between Nantucket Shoals and Georges Bank to Cape Cod. Their inner map would correspond to the basins and bays and humps, the banks and canyons and wrecks; their senses would recognize the scent of the water and the cast of the light that mark their territories. Migrating schools would inspect or control areas of past feeding success. Oceanic paths were engraved in their memory.

In pre-Christian times along the shores of the Mediterranean Sea, *thynoscopi*, tuna watchers, looked for the schools of bluefin on their annual spawning migrations. The tuna made defined, recurring runs along the coast, eastward-moving, fat "arrival" fish coming in June and lean "spent" fish in July and August. These seasonal migrations were the basis of Aristotle's theory that bluefin tuna were an Atlantic species that passed from the ocean into the Mediterranean and Black Seas. Large nets were cast for them, and many traps were built, with long fences leading from shore. Coastal villages depended on the bluefin and celebrated them. As they hauled the nets and performed the *matanza*, or killing, Italian fishermen sang of the great fish, thanking the gods, likening the mysterious, sumptuous, silvery animals to voluptuous lovers.

The schools in the Mediterranean were often vast. One arrival school passing along the coast of Spain between Algeciras and Tarifa in June 1957, occupied 7.2 million cubic meters. Some estimates of the quantity of the school were made. If the fish were positioned twenty meters apart, the number in the school would have been 1,922. If the distance was closed to a spacing of ten meters throughout the body, their number would have been 11,163.

There are forty-eight tuna and tunalike species worldwide (albacore, yellowfin, skipjack, the bonitos, and mackerels among them). Three species are bluefin: the southern bluefin (*Thunnus maccoyyi*), the Pacific bluefin (*Thunnus thynnus orientalis*), and the Atlantic bluefin (*Thunnus thynnus thynnus*). The southern bluefin spawn in the waters between northwestern Australia and Java and migrate circumpolarly through the Pacific, Indian, and Atlantic Oceans. The Pacific bluefin spawns south of Japan and in its early years migrates to the North American coast, making feeding migrations from Baja as far north as British Columbia (where Native Americans once speared bluefin as they swam through phosphorescent plankton, a presence so numinous that the bones of the fish were laid with the bones of the hunter). After one or several seasons off North America the Pacific bluefin makes transpacific migrations to the spawning grounds, a movement that can take up to two years.

By one theory, there are two "stocks" of Atlantic bluefin. Strictly speaking, the western Atlantic stock spawns in the Gulf of Mexico and migrates to the western North Atlantic, from Cape Hatteras to Newfoundland, while the eastern Atlantic stock, after spawning in the Mediterranean, makes feeding migrations to grounds ranging from the Bay of Biscay to Norway.

Tagging programs have shown, however, that the stocks are not wholly separate, but mix to varying degrees, with pulses of transatlantic crossings, often occurring in years of strong west winds. A program begun in 1954 by Frank Mather of the Woods Hole Oceanographic Institute proved that bluefin swim from the Gulf of Mexico to the North Atlantic on feeding migrations. Nine bluefin tagged in the Florida Straits near the Bahamas were later caught off Norway. One fish tagged off the Bahamas in June 1962 was captured off Norway only fifty days later, having migrated 6,200 miles. Two other bluefin tagged near the Bahamas were recaptured in South American waters, in the habitat of the southern bluefin. One fish tagged in 1963 was captured off Brazil in 1965. Another bluefin tagged in 1969 was caught four years later off the coast of Argentina, 6,600 miles away, the farthest direct migration. The longest time between tagging and recapture in Frank Mather's program was twelve years: a fish that weighed 275 pounds when tagged in 1966 was trapped in Barbate, Spain, in 1978 at a weight of 634 pounds. The longest period of any tag and recapture was eighteen years, from 1966 to 1984.

A Norwegian tagging program conducted from 1957 to 1962 showed that bluefin often arrived in Norwegian waters at sixty-two degrees latitude. The largest fish arrived in July and migrated north, while younger fish arrived in August and September and migrated south. When the assemblage of giant bluefin disappeared, or was fished out, the mediums took over their route (bluefin virtually disappeared from Norway in 1973). While most recorded transatlantic migrations were from the western to the eastern Atlantic, in 1970 two of five small bluefin tagged in the Bay of Biscay were captured off the United States. Between 1987 and 1994 ten fish tagged off the United States were recaptured in the Bay of Biscay. Since 1986 six fish tagged in the United States have been recaptured in the Mediterranean or near Gibraltar.

Overall as of 1988, 3.2 percent of fish tagged in the west were recaptured in the east, and 4.5 percent of eastern fish were recaptured in the west. Because of the nature of fish reproduction, a 3 percent transfer rate after six years results in 20 percent of the fish having originated from the other side. Because of the nature of fish genetics, a single transmigratory fish, having spawned, significantly colors the entire gene pool.

Bluefin tuna are an oviparous fish, meaning that eggs are shed into the water and then fertilized externally by the males. The eggs hatch into larvae and are swept along by currents. It's a shotgun approach to procreation, more like pine trees shedding clouds of pollen, or queen bees laying thousands of eggs, than the intercourse of mammals.

Even among the oviparous, bluefin are highly fecund. Each year a female bluefin produces a relative mean of 128.5 eggs per gram of body weight. Thus, a 700-pound tuna could shed 40,837,300 eggs. The eggs are one millimeter in diameter (a small size for so large a fish), with a clear shell, an oil globule for nutrition, and slightly fresh water for buoyancy. They hatch two days after fertilization (nearly all eggs are fertilized, the fish are very efficient in this way), a school blooming in the wake of a spawning. The larvae grow rapidly. At a week old they are free-swimming, hunting fish, nearly a quarter-inch long. At nine days they have become feeding machines, with spiny fins, big eyes, big jaws, and sharp teeth.

The mortality rate is high. After nine days, on average only 40.8 percent of the larvae survive—of a spawn of 40 million eggs, fewer than 17 million are left swimming after nine days. Most are picked off by terns and other birds, preyed upon by other fish (an occasional baleen whale or basking shark plowing through the bloom), so that only one in a thousand is left after a year has passed—a mortality rate of 99.9 percent. But even those numbers are impressive. Of the 40 million eggs, a collective school of 40,000 fish remains after one year. A year-old bluefin has grown to about six pounds, so that school would weigh 240,000 pounds, or 120 tons. Thus, a 700-pound female would produce a mass 340 times her weight, a year after her mating. A spawning school of, say, a hundred females of the same size leaves in its wake 24 million pounds of juveniles.

The mortality continues, as is the way. At the age of ten, some biologists will say, the replacement ratio isn't even 1:1 (one fish to another) when the fishing pressure is great. If this is the case (other biologists dispute such a ratio), the mortality rate at age ten would be slightly more than 39,999,999 in 40,000,000. A surviving giant would be one fish in 40 million.

The female spawns fractionally, releasing eggs over a period of several days, pairing with a succession of males. Mating and emission usually occur when a pair of fish turn on their sides and make contact, belly to belly. Sometimes fish traveling in large schools mate simultaneously. When this happens, when the fish turn their sides to the surface, according to the work of Frank Mather, a spectacular flash of light can be seen. (With *Thunnus thynnus thynnus* this flash is seen in the Mediterranean; in the Gulf of Mexico bluefin tend to mate in deeper water.) After mating, the school leaves a milky trail of emissions behind. Mediterranean fishermen use the trail as a way to find the spawning schools.

In the western Atlantic the hatching of the larvae begins in the Gulf of Mexico and continues northward through the Florida Straits, the young fish moving along with the Gulf Stream. They migrate seven to ten miles a day and as the weeks pass converge on the nursery and feeding grounds from Cape Hatteras to Cape Cod in late June and early July. Others continue to flow with the stream north and east, perhaps into the central Atlantic. Constantly in pursuit of prey, fish spawned in the spring grow to one pound and twelve inches in August, two pounds in September, three pounds by November. During the winter the young fish move south or east. In their first year of migration, as they grow from egg to six-pound fish, they cover about 2,500 miles.

Bluefin tend to school strictly according to size. Young bluefin, or "school fish," are between one and five, from twenty to sixty inches in length, and seven to 145 pounds. From the southwest coastal waters off Virginia and New Jersey, they migrate northeasterly to southern New England. In years when the water is warm enough (young bluefin have a low-temperature tolerance of about 57 degrees F.) they move into the Gulf of Maine behind the schools of larger fish, in a kind of hierarchical succession.

Young bluefin make considerable gains in the summer—a three-year-old fish that weighs 35 pounds in June weighs over 50 pounds in November. In autumn they gather offshore at the edge of the continental shelf or migrate to the warm waters of the Sargasso Sea. Sometimes many schools merge and form great aggregations, seeming to make many tentative movements before they finally depart as one. Young fish from the western Atlantic move to the east, and eastern Atlantic fish move to the west.

Medium bluefin are six to eight years old, sixty to seventy-six inches long, and weigh 145 to 300 pounds. By the time bluefin become mediums their migratory circuit includes not only the feeding migration and the winter migration but a spawning run. Their low-temperature tolerance is about 55 degrees. The movements of mediums are much more extensive than school fish—to the Gulf of Mexico and the Sargasso Sea, perhaps for spawning; along the Gulf Stream front in the spring, into coastal waters from Cape Hatteras to the Gulf of Maine in the summer. In the fall, mediums gather in large schools in the canyons along the continental shelf off southern New England. In the winter some mediums follow the Gulf Stream to the central Atlantic where they may encounter medium bluefin from the eastern Atlantic. In the spring and summer, western Atlantic mediums may possibly spawn in the northern reaches of the Gulf Stream. They may make spawning runs into the Mediterranean.

Giant bluefin are those at least eight years old, seventy-seven inches long, and weighing 300 pounds. Since the giants, with their greater body mass, have a temperature tolerance of 45 degrees F., ten degrees lower than mediums, they can venture further north into the subpolar waters off Newfoundland, Iceland, or Norway. Their nutritional needs are also much greater. Giants must load on a hundred to two hundred pounds of fat to make it through the lean months and spawning periods. Their movements, and their abundance in various localities, thus depends on the presence of "food patches."

In addition to the spawning run, the feeding migration, and the winter period, giants sometimes make northerly prespawning runs—tentative feeding migrations, races to the picnic basket in the north. From the Gulf of Mexico and the Florida Straits, giant bluefin travel about 1,900 miles in about three weeks, swimming along the westward front of the Gulf Stream at an average speed of four miles per hour. When the Stream turns to the east off Cape Hatteras and the Chesapeake Bay, bluefin schools depart for coastal waters. They swim off the shores of New Jersey, New York, and Rhode Island, sometimes moving into the Gulf of Maine. Other schools stay with the Gulf Stream and enter the Gulf of Maine directly, through the Great South Channel near Cape Cod or through the Northeast Channel south of Nova Scotia. According to Mather, the oldest fish tend to pass through the area first, followed by younger year classes.

Other assemblages feed in eddies along the Gulf Stream, or continue to the eastern Atlantic as far as Norway, Ireland, and the Bay of Biscay, arriving in August and September, after a three-month migration.

According to the work of the biologist Luis Rivas, some schools that have migrated from the western Atlantic to Norway sometimes are "recruited" into the eastern Atlantic stock, and make the Mediterranean-to-Norway migration. Others return to the western Atlantic, migrating south from Norway to the Canary Islands off Morocco and then, perhaps after a period of feeding, to Brazil, a circuit of nearly 8,000 miles. And some schools make southerly migrations in the winter along the South American coast, to Brazil and as far south as Argentina. In March these schools may return north to the spawning grounds in the Gulf of Mexico.

The production of eggs and the act of spawning requires great energy—on the part of the females, which dispel the contents of ovaries weighing fifteen to twenty pounds, and of the males, which expel cloudbursts of sperm. There isn't much to eat during the spawning period, so fish that have left the northern feeding grounds ripe and fat end up spent and lean. The first schools to arrive in the feeding grounds are predominantly male. Feeding through the summer, preying upon schools of herring, mackerel, bluefish, hake, rosefish, whitefish, dogfish sharks, cod, upon squid, sand eels, and shrimp, the giants increase their body weight by about 7.5 percent per month. A twelve-year-old weighing 450 pounds in June grows to 600 pounds by the end of October, gaining little in length. By the end of the feeding period they have giant stomachs, enlarged, distended, valuable.

Bluefin tuna are thermotactic—they orient by temperature, following thermoclines, temperature strata, and fronts. They prefer clean water, and they prefer the warmer temperature strata, even though they migrate into cold waters to eat. At the turn of the century Don Carlos de Bragança, the king of Portugal, was perhaps the first to make a systematic study of the bluefin's response to temperature. Working aboard his yacht, the *Amelia*, observing spawning behavior, catches in traps, and the many movements of eastern Atlantic bluefin, Don Carlos concluded that all the migrations of tuna were caused by changes in water temperature.

It is generally agreed that bluefin stocks are not indigenous to particular basins or bays, but Concertina Scordia, an Italian biologist of the 1930s, maintained that a distinct stock of tuna lived in the deep waters of the southern Tyrrhenian Sea in fall and winter, occasionally surfacing near Messina in the fall to feed. She called this group the Tyrrheno–Ionian stock. In the spring when the water warmed to 64 degrees F., the fish surfaced, remaining until late June, when they returned to deeper, denser water. The largest fish sounded first, followed over the weeks by the smaller fish of the stock. The migration to the surface coincided with the spawning run. According to a contemporary theory, discrete "assemblages" of fish, one school or groups of schools, return to specific feeding areas until the prey species disappears or the assemblage is fished out.

Bluefin tuna can maintain a given direction according to the position of the sun, or perhaps of the moon and the stars. At the top of their head is the pineal window, a translucent passage that leads to the pineal organ, where photoreceptor cells assist in the processing of light. Postlarval fish, a quarter of an inch long and floating in the plankton bloom, observing the movement of the sun, must quickly develop their celestial senses. They move toward the sunset at dusk, deepward with darkness, toward the sunrise at dawn. All the while the young bluefin develop their spatial sense, their ability to communicate and move as a school.

Bluefin are polarotactic, and can read the polarized patterns of light in the water for orientation. They read temperature gradients and salinity gradients. They follow scent trails, and the lipid (or oil) profiles left by prey fish. A bluefin requires only a few lipid molecules to form a chemical search image and follow the source.

They are rheotropic, navigating by means of ocean currents. Bluefin prefer favoring currents, drifting with the stream. Since they have deposits of magnetic iron within some bones, and since ocean currents create electromagnetic fields, bluefin may also orient by electromagnetism.

As they migrate, as the environment changes, one cue gains over another, the celestial cue giving way to the visual, the visual cue to the olfactory, the olfactory to the magnetic.

In 1978 the National Marine Fisheries Service conducted an aerial survey of bluefin tuna schools in Cape Cod Bay in order to compile a stock census. Scientists at the University of Miami later analyzed the photos, and they found evidence that bluefin are cooperative hunters, like wolves or killer whales.

In Cape Cod Bay the schools were primarily two-dimensional, swimming in a single layer. There were several kinds of formations. The bluefin swam in straight lines, side by side—soldier formations, as the fishermen call them. There were echelons, or diagonal lines. There were files—one fish behind the other. And there was a parabolic school, fish swimming in a curved line—a hunter formation.

The parabolic schools usually contained only fifteen fish, probably because the fish had to be able to see one another. The parabola was sometimes 200 feet wide. Fish at the center swam side by side, but along the curve each fish was slightly ahead of the next. Outer fish were also closer to one another, so as to maintain the curve, and to see counterparts on the other side.

Such swimming requires not only great physical power, coordination, and communication, but an instinct for form, for geometry. Perhaps the widespread presence of the parabolic school (twenty-six of 141 schools photographed) in Cape Cod Bay indicates a geometric aesthetic. Perhaps the parabolic school is the ultimate development of this aesthetic, with elite fish, giants eight years and older, each of them one in 40 million by way of the mortality rate, having swum together since they were only a quarter of an inch long, pushing the straight line to a curve as they move through the water, stretching the shape, playing with the geometry.

There are disadvantages to the parabolic form, since outer fish, swimming closer together, have reduced strike zones when encoun-

25

tering prey schools. But there is compensation in cooperation, in the wrap of the school about the prey, and there are hydrodynamic benefits. Water flowing over extended pectoral fins of one fish creates a "wing tip airlift" for another, saving energy. There is also a "channeling effect," when one fish pushes off the wave of another and gains forward thrust. Such "lateral interactions" increase thrusting power from 20 percent in the center of the parabola to nearly 100 percent at the end. Outer fish ride on the effort of those at the center.

There are many other formations. Some seem random, while others seem to embody strategy. Sometimes bluefin gather into schools that are dome-shaped, a few fish, often the smallest, at the surface and the body of the school riding below. Some schools become tiered or stepped, with younger fish at the rear. Sometimes this rear guard swims at higher levels, sometimes lower. Either way, the same purpose is served—a predator approaching from the rear cannot get to the big fish without passing over the smaller ones. Sometimes the fish at the rear swim in S-curves, like scouts on a watch, so as to have a better look at what is approaching from behind. Sometimes a straight line forms with two fish on each end, hanging back. Or two straight lines, one behind the other.

Sometimes schools of bluefin swim under the curl of a wave, stacked like a flock of birds, as though trying to get a look at the upper world from an aquarium window. Sometimes, in the mating process, a file of ten or more fish will overtake another file, one fish mating with another in a kind of *thynnus* square dance, a series of paired emissions, down the line.

Bluefin also form attendant schools. They will swim below a school of yellowfin tuna, with the skittish yellowfin, by intention or not, serving as a kind of alarm system. Or they will swim behind basking sharks, a large species that feeds on plankton and lumbers along, its huge mouth swiping back and forth. Occasionally bluefin will swim with dolphins and porpoises, or with pilot whales, finbacks, and other cetaceans.

The most mysterious formation is what the fishermen call milling, or cartwheeling. When bluefin mill they swim in a circle, usually counterclockwise. The circle may be cylindrical or widespread, made up of ten fish or a pinwheel sprawl of hundreds. Going round and round, looking at each other, turning on their sides, they're certainly communicating something. Perhaps, like other fish, milling bluefin flash signals by moving their fins, or flaring their gill covers, or through changes in their color patterns. Perhaps they make sounds in the mill, manipulating their swim bladders. Maybe a milling school is resting, making a decision, reading the sun, sky, and water before making a move somewhere. Maybe milling is a function of spawning, of memory, anticipation, or broadcast. Perhaps milling is a merely social behavior, the opalescent giants going round to look at one another, to see what they're all about, to have a mirror of who they are. Though intent on themselves, a milling school is self-aware, all eyes and difficult to approach.

Schools change formation from one moment to the next. A straight line becomes a parabola, which becomes a cartwheel. Off Cape Cod one summer a school of about two hundred bluefin was milling. Then a fish broke off the edge, followed by another, and an echelon formed, a great diagonal line pulling away from the mill like thread coming off a spool.

Another time, also off Cape Cod, a spotter pilot sighted an albino bluefin in a large school. Pilots watched the white fish for several days. They called it Moby Dick. The school would mill for a while, then drop out of sight before coming to the surface in a straight line, with the fish neatly strung out side by side. The albino was always at the end of the line, in a position of prominence, perhaps, or of deference.

The spotter pilots led their boats to fish in the school, but they agreed not to put any boats on to the white fish. They liked watching it, and it provided a way to find the schools. For several days, until the school migrated away, none of the fishermen made a throw at Moby Dick.

(3)

THE FISHERMAN

❦

IT WAS a "blow day," too windy and cloudy for fishing, but Bob Sampson wanted to check an oil leak he'd been working on that morning. We cast off from the slip at Barnstable Harbor and took the *Scratcher* out into the channel. Brad Sampson had the *Rush* in at the dock. Eric Hesse was alongside, in the *Tenacious*. Ron Lein was working on the *Sandra C.*, and Chris Woods was running the *Look Out*.

They'd fished from Tuesday until Sunday, when the weather turned bad. The first schools Trip Wheeler had spotted on his way back from Maine had soon moved on, and by Sunday they'd been working on different fish, lean giants in the 500- to 600-pound range. (There had been a hundred to 150 schools all told, Bob Sampson said, with from fifteen to three hundred bluefin per school.)

Brad had harpooned five fish from the *Scratcher* the day after he left Portland, and Bob Sampson had gotten two. One weighed more than 800 pounds, another 600, and one came in just under 300 pounds. They brought from $2 to $20 a pound.

Talking to the others this morning, Brad occasionally mentioned "his five." He might have gone out to search around the Bay with two other boats out there, but just now he wasn't hungry enough.

Bob Sampson had been awake since eleven o'clock the previous night. He had worked two jobs since he was a teenager, and along with many other young men from Plymouth, he had gone to work for

28

the Commonwealth Electric Company in 1968 after the Pilgrim nuclear power plant was built. By night he was a courier, delivering company mail from Plymouth to Boston. By day he was a fisherman. In earlier years he had pulled many strings of twenty-hour workdays, sleeping from after dinnertime until about 10 P.M. Sometimes he worked almost around the clock. Now in his late forties, Bob Sampson could still pull two or three days of double duty, but when the fishing was good he'd try to get someone to go in for him at ComElectric. The bluefin tuna fishery was ideal for him, because blow days came often enough to give him time for rest.

Today was not a rest day. We motored slowly out the channel, past the commercial and charter boats in their slips and past the cluster of small boats (which often sat on mud for fifteen minutes each side of the dead low moon tides), past the two marinas on east and west sides of the harbor, past the whale watch boat and the Mattakeese Wharf. We passed the line of poles marking the channel and steamed out into the small bay sheltered by Sandy Neck and bordered by the Barnstable and Yarmouth marshes. For centuries the Great Marshes had been grazing lands, providing salt hay for cows and briny milk for the colonists and their descendants well into the twentieth century. Barnstable had been settled in 1635, Yarmouth in 1639. I knew the Yarmouth marshes well. I'd walked them as a boy, as had my grandfather and his grandfather.

Sampson steered the *Scratcher* to the east, past the defunct channel to the Yarmouth Harbor, from which packet ships once sailed to Boston. Past the weathered cottage colony on the south side of Sandy Neck and the abandoned lighthouse set amid the rolling wind-blown dunes, past the mouth of Bass Creek and Mussel Point, past the clusters of camper trucks parked at the tip of Sandy Neck, around Beach Point, the bell buoy, and out into Cape Cod Bay.

Cape Cod is young, geologically, a peninsula formed by the last of the glaciers, the sandy runoff of forty thousand years. (Nantucket and Martha's Vineyard were formed by the same sediment.) Cape Cod's ponds evolved from imbedded blocks of ice. Granite boulders, which today jut incongruously from the beach sand, were torn from upturned plates hundreds of miles to the north. Cape Cod Bay was formed by a nub in the glacier that pushed back and forth year after year for centuries, like a fist in the sand. Cape Cod, shaped like a bent arm, had lower and upper parts. The lower Cape, the biceps, running thirty miles east and west, from Bourne to Chatham, was at the terminus of the glacier. The upper Cape, the forearm, running thirty miles to the north, from Chatham to Provincetown, was at the base of a ravine, a kind of river bottom. After the retreat of the glaciers, the wind and sea eventually cut into the land along the upper Cape, pushing sand around to the north to form the dunes of Provincetown, and southward to form the barrier beaches of Orleans, Chatham, and the Monomoy Shoals, leaving the high beach cliffs along the outer shore. Sandy Neck, inside Cape Cod Bay, was made of drifting sand blown south-easterly from Sandwich and the Plymouth shores.

By the time we rounded Sandy Neck, Sampson had gone down from the tower twice to check the engine. All seemed to be well. He settled into the seat in the tower and steered a course along the shore, toward the Cape Cod Canal and Sandwich Harbor.

Bob Sampson had a reddish-blond and gray beard and a rim of red hair. When he spoke or just paused to consider things, he had a way of lifting his head and straightening his spine. He was practiced in the art of consideration, learned from solitary nights on the road and days on the water. He chose his words deliberately (except sometimes in the heat of a hunt), and with those slight elevations of his head Bob reinforced the impression that he was a most deliberate man. He was of medium height, large in the torso and short in the legs, with thick forearms, just the right build for a harpooner riding a dipping pulpit on a live sea.

Bob had put on a fisherman's sweater knitted by his grandmother years ago. Above his faded jeans and white athletic shoes, Bob wore his "Goofy hat," with long ear flaps, to "cover my Yankee ears." He wore polarized glasses with prescription lenses. Years on the water had weakened his eyes, and a gruesome accident in his charter days had nearly blinded him, making him especially dependent on the services of a spotter pilot. Pilots were his eyes, he said. If spotter planes were banned, which some fishermen wanted, he would have to get out of the business.

In the harbor that morning a group of fishermen and pilots had talked about the fishing. It was a common practice, gathering together on a bad-weather day to discuss their work. Trip Wheeler told of finding a fish for Eric Hesse. Eric harpooned it and Trip left, but later he found a message on his answering machine that the fish had "pulled a dart," freeing itself from the harpoon head. "I was mad at everyone," Trip said. "I hated everyone after that. Five thousand dollars swam away." Then, he added, almost apologetically, "I get kind of emotional."

I brought this conversation up with Bob as we moved along the edge of the Bay.

"Pilots shouldn't be emotional," he said. "It's the worst thing they can do. When a pilot becomes emotional and fired up, so does the striker. In a way, Eric and Trip are a good pair—two gung-ho, high-spirited, aggressive guys. But sometimes Eric will miss the first fish and then not be able to hit anything for the rest of the day. He loses his concentration.

"A few years ago when Eric was running a boat for me, I watched them work together. I tried to give Trip some advice, told him how Brooksie and I work together using the clock system. Eric steamed over, shouting that he had been building a relationship with Trip and I had no right to interfere. I climbed out of the tower and shouted back, told him we could have it out right there. I couldn't believe it.

"It's the duty of a pilot to inspire confidence. He should be cool, and in giving directions, keep the striker cool, never shout, never say things like 'That way! No! This way!' He should keep it on a controlled level, say, 'Come on around now, two o'clock, two boat lengths, twelve o'clock.'

"Brooksie is the best pilot. I know, because I've worked with most of them. Brooksie knows how to find fish. He knows how to anticipate them. He finds so many fish he drives the other guys crazy. He has ways of seeing fish that he won't tell anyone about. And we communicate. Sometimes I'll be thinking something, that we should go this way or do something different, and then Brooksie will come on the radio and say just what I was thinking about."

Bob had set his feet up on the panel, and was steering with a wooden knob attached to the wheel. Harpooning, he said, was an automatic skill, like throwing a baseball. "You don't think, when you're throwing a baseball, that you're gonna throw a strike. You just throw. It's unconscious."

"You have to keep your mind out of it?"

"Yeah, but sometimes that doesn't work. Sometimes you have to go up in the tower and sit down and analyze it. You've gotta sit there for a while and think about what you're doing wrong."

Bob talked about charging a bunch of fish, of how intense he felt out on the pulpit. You can see an area of only twenty feet or so, and you have to scan that patch of water for the fish. "When you do see them," he said, "you choose one and separate it from the rest, like a leopard picking an animal out of a herd.

"Your legs begin to shake. You're moving along at four knots, eight knots, chasing a bunch. The pulpit is rising with the waves, and you're twenty-five feet out there. Sometimes as you're going up you get tossed in the air and you have to grab on coming down. I've gone over. I haven't gone in the water yet, but I've come up hanging by one hand.

"When it comes time to throw, you have to lean against the belly rail and use both hands on the harpoon. It's best to throw the harpoon when the pulpit's going down, because then you can use the movement of the boat. But that's not always possible. Sometimes you have to throw when the pulpit is rising and you're moving away from the fish. You're over choppy water and aiming at a swimming fish that might be twenty feet down. You've got an ear out for the pilot's voice, and you're adjusting your aim for the refraction of the light under the water. You have to consider all those things. And it's hard knowing everyone is watching you and depending on you. It may look easy, but it isn't. It's amazing we can even do it.

"Each year I come out here my eyes are weaker and I'm a year older. But I can't think about that either."

We tossed along in the tower to the beat of waves about three feet high, pushed up by the wind. The water was steel gray, reflecting the hardened sky. Cape Cod Bay, Bob said, was like a "nursing home for giant bluefin tuna. The biggest, oldest fish come in here." Maybe the shallow water, the weaker tides, or a food source, the schools of bluefish, drew them into the Bay. Huge schools of giant bluefin tuna used to gather off Sandy Neck in the fall, before their migration south. The school was once estimated at ten thousand fish, but over the years the seiners had cleaned a lot of them out, destroying their memory, some said.

Some fishermen worked only the Bay. The show was usually a short one, an hour or two on the slack tide, and you could wait days for the show to come. You needed patience to fish there. Certain fishermen had it, that ability to go for days without seeing a fish and then stay calm during the show.

"Not me," Bob said. "I've got to go, got to get outside. I can't hang around in the Bay."

B O B   W E N T down to check the engine again. When he came back into the tower he talked about the time he'd fished for mussels.

In the late 1970s Bob needed extra money. Although he was working at ComElectric, he was loaded down with two mortgages, a boat payment, and a car payment. It was winter, the most difficult time for fishing, and so Bob went to a buyer in Hyannis and asked for advice. The buyer told him to try musseling. There were mussel beds in the North River in Marshfield, he said, above Plymouth and Duxbury. Bob said he didn't know anything about musseling. You either raked them or you dragged for them, the buyer said. Bob had dragged for scallops, and he owned scallop dragging gear. He called a friend and they drove to the North River, with a scallop dredge and a lapstrake wooden boat Bob called the *Fog Off*.

Bob hadn't listened for a weather report, and it started to snow before they reached the North River. But they put the boat in anyway and made a few test tows. All they found were old shells. The snow was coming down hard, and visibility was down to 200 feet, but Bob noticed a smaller river that fed into the one they'd been dragging. They headed over that way, made a tow, and the dredge came up full. After two hours they had forty bushels of mussels. Since the price was $2.25 a bushel, Bob and his friend started to get excited. They could see the possibilities.

With the forty bushels of mussels on the *Fog Off* they headed back upriver, but by the time they got to the boat ramp there was a foot of snow on the ground. They didn't have any shovels, so they kicked at the snow and pushed it away as best they could. After an hour and a half Bob backed the truck and trailer down to the boat, but they couldn't tow it back up the ramp. Bob noticed a dock on the other side of the river. They tied the boat to the dock, left the trailer on the shore, and returned to Barnstable with the mussels, celebrating all the way.

The next day they went back to the North River with snow shovels and more equipment for dragging. Bob had been thinking overnight and was sure he could get rich on mussels. When they arrived at the dock they saw that their boat was filled with water. Fortunately the engine was hanging from the stern of a dragger and had not gone under. The heavy scallop dredge had sprung a seam in the *Fog Off*, and when the boat had begun to sink the dragger captain had been kind enough to hoist the engine, a new 50-horsepower outboard, up out of the water. They spent that day making repairs, but Bob returned to the North River and eventually, by hauling 400 to 600 bushels of mussels a week, made some money. Within two years he had a 31-foot boat fitted with hydraulic winches for hoisting the mussels. He'd rigged his truck with winches too, so they wouldn't have to carry the bushel bags up the ramp.

After they fished out the North River Bob moved his operation down to Barnstable and musseled inside Sandy Neck and around the islands in the Great Marshes. He worked year round, musseling during the winter and hiring a crew in the summer, when he went out charter fishing. One winter when Barnstable Harbor froze over and the other boats couldn't get out, Bob ran the *Scratcher* down from Sandwich every day. Because of the freeze, the price of mussels went up, and Bob had the mussel beds mostly to himself. One day the weather was especially bad, with southeast winds of eighty-five miles per hour. A fishing boat went down that day, off Georges Bank, and a 90-foot scalloper had come into Cape Cod Bay and anchored a mile off Sandy Neck to wait out the storm. Bob was able to run along the beach in the lee of the dunes. There was still a lot of wind, but little sea. It was actually rougher outside Barnstable Harbor than it was in the Bay that day. Rain began to come down as they worked, a freezing rain.

Bolstered by the knowledge that they were the only ones working, Bob and his mate dredged up a hundred bushels of mussels. They stacked the bags on deck, on the engine box, in the wheelhouse, and in the forward cabin. Bob even sat on bags of mussels while he steered the boat.

On the trip back to Sandwich Harbor the bilge pump was running more than usual. Bob didn't know at the time that an inspection well leaked whenever the boat was overloaded, and on this day the wet bags of mussels were especially heavy. Bob sent his mate down below to get some docking lines. He climbed into the forward cabin, and when he came back on deck he told Bob there was quite a lot of water down below. Bob thought, well, what's quite a lot of water? He stayed at the wheel, running along the Sandwich shore.

By the time they got to the Cape Cod Canal the tide was coming in strong, a full-moon tide. But Bob figured that once they unloaded the mussels everything would be all right. They tied up to the pier outside the harbor, and Bob went down to look in the cabin. The water was already a foot over the floorboards. When he climbed back on deck the flood tide was running so hard that it was pulling the stern of the boat down, nearly underwater.

Bob didn't want his boat to sink in the canal, where it would be an obstruction to traffic. So he decided to run for the harbor and try to beach the boat on the ramp. He told his mate to go call the Coast Guard, to tell them to bring as many pumps as they could. Then he tried to untie the stern line, but there was too much strain on it from the pull of the tide. He took his knife out and cut the line, and the stern went down underwater. Bob ran to the wheel, pushed the throttle, and started chugging ahead. The boat was listing hard to the side.

Bob had been in bad situations before. He hadn't been scared often, but he was scared now. When he reached the entrance and turned toward the ramp, the boat began to roll. Standing in water up to his knees, he pushed the throttle forward all the way. Behind him the boat was underwater, but he was moving fast enough that water was spilling out over the stern. He skidded the boat up the ramp, and he shut off the engine just before water went into the intake. He'd gotten far enough up the ramp that water could run out the scupper holes on deck. It was still raining. Gale winds were raging, and the moon tide was roaring.

They tossed the mussels onto the ramp, where they could retrieve them later. The water department brought a pump, and the Coast Guard supplied another, but the two weren't enough against the rising tide. The water started to rise over the engine. People came, and people went. A newspaper photographer came to record the event. Bob unfastened his electronic equipment, all but the radar on the wheelhouse roof, and that was about to get wet. (Bob didn't realize until later that his boat was uninsured.)

Then a dragger captain arrived, and backed his boat up to Bob's. After three tries they fastened a bridle under the *Scratcher*'s stern and up to the dragger's net winder, and managed to get the rails above water. The pumps still weren't clearing the water fast enough, though, so Bob got a five-gallon bucket, and standing in the frigid water, he bailed as fast as he could. He figured that he could bail a lot of water in a minute with a five-gallon bucket.

And he did. The water level lowered, but by the time Bob finished bailing, his legs had gone numb. He could feel pressure, but otherwise they had gone to stubs. When he tried to take a step he fell over. Once again, the dragger captain came to the rescue, hitching Bob up to the winch and lifting him onto his boat. He helped Bob into the wheelhouse, and they shared some brandy. Gradually feeling returned to his legs. Once he could stand again, they retrieved the mussels and hauled them off to the buyer in Hyannis.

"Musseling was the most enjoyable fishery I've been in, besides tuna fishing," Bob said. We could see the Sagamore Bridge ahead.

"What would ever possess you to go out there in the middle of the winter like that?"

"Money," Bob Sampson said. "And when you're a fisherman and catching fish, everything is right. Nothing bothers you. That's what it means to be a fisherman."

(4)

SCRATCHER

❦

IN 1945, shortly before Bob Sampson was born, his father, Robert Sampson, Sr., was flying a B-24 on a bombing mission over Germany. On the return trip over the English Channel the plane began to lose altitude, and the crew prepared to jump. Sampson, the pilot and last to abandon ship, was too close to the ground for his parachute to fully open, and so the landing broke both his ankles. A telegram about the accident arrived just as his wife, Cynthia Drew, was going into labor with Bob Jr., but they waited until after she had delivered to give her the news.

As Bob would put it, "When I came into this world there was already adversity."

He grew up in Plymouth, and under the influence of his uncle Heinz Oehme, Bob Sampson took an interest in hunting and fishing. Uncle Heinz was a renowned duck hunter and fisherman, and Bob loved to be there with him. He didn't always get invited, though, and sometimes during the duck season Bob would sneak down behind the blind and hide in the grass—just to be part of the game. Uncle Heinz would hear him rustling around and come out and say, "All right, Jughead, what are you doing out here?" Heinz let him come into the blind, and he was allowed to watch, and they let him row out to get the decoys. He was known as a boy eager to learn, and accident prone.

Heinz owned a Shiverick boat, the *Snark*, which an old Yankee sold to him for a dollar because Heinz was sure to take proper care of it. A common sight around Plymouth Harbor was Heinz at the tiller of the *Snark* heading out through the anchorage. Often he'd stop near Buoy Number One off the Gurnet to jig for mackerel, which he'd use as bait for striped bass. Heinz could read the sea, the sky, and the birds, and he knew how the tides would influence the feeding habits of the fish. Though he tended to fish alone, Heinz had a rapport with his nephew, and Bob spent many hours aboard the *Snark*, learning what would become his trade. Bob's parents were members of the Plymouth Yacht Club, and Heinz later became its steward, but Bob didn't join. He preferred to be off alone, fishing and hunting.

Heinz kept a flat-sterned canoe in Plymouth Harbor, and Bob would sneak down in the night to take it out fishing. One calm and star-filled summer night when Bob was twelve, he got up at midnight and rode his bicycle to the harbor, carrying his grandfather's bamboo pole, a few of Heinz's hooks, and some seaworms he'd dug. The tide was coming in. Bob was way up inside the harbor by Eel River, stars reflected in the water, when he heard a tremendous explosion— striped bass, feeding. It was an adventure for a twelve-year-old to be out on the water alone at that time of night, but this sound was especially arousing. Bob had heard that striped bass fed at night, but he'd never caught one. He baited a hook, and a fish immediately snapped the line. The second hook broke off at the strike, and so did the third. Bob paddled to shore, raced back to his uncle's barn, found more hooks, went back to the harbor, and paddled out again, but by this time the tide had turned and the stripers were gone. He would always remember that sound, and he would seek it again. But even a whale breaching next to his boat wouldn't excite him as much as the bass in Plymouth Harbor did that night.

After Bob's father built a sixteen-foot skiff and outfitted it with a small engine, Bob through his teenage years fished regularly in Plymouth Harbor. One day he noticed a flock of terns diving into the water. He had fished for mackerel before, so he put a mackerel spinner on the line and trolled by the birds. There was a strike, and he caught his first striped bass, a seven-pound fish. A big fish. He caught three more. Though he'd forget the reception he got at home that day, Bob

Sampson would remember the attention he attracted carrying those big stripers on his bicycle along Water Street by Plymouth Rock on his way home.

THERE IS a long line of Sampsons in Plymouth and in neighboring towns. Henry Sampson (Henery Samson), a "small cousin," came to Plymouth on the *Mayflower* with his uncle Edward Tilley. Abraham Sampson—Henry's brother, it is assumed—emigrated in 1629 or 1630 and settled in Duxbury, a town north of Plymouth founded by Miles Standish and John Alden. Abraham Sampson had four sons. The third son, Abraham, married Miles Standish's granddaughter. They named one of their sons Miles.

The Sampsons took up the common occupations of the time, becoming farmers and landowners, shipbuilders, merchants, and mariners. They prospered, and they multiplied—after four generations about 575 Sampsons had been born. Many of them became soldiers, and it could be said that the lineage flourished during the Revolutionary War. Among them, Private Anthony Sampson (b. 1728) marched to Rhode Island in December 1776. Zabdiel Sampson (b. 1727) fought in the French and Indian War and was killed in the battle of Haarlem in September 1776. George Sampson (b. 1759) marched in the expedition to Rhode Island. Enoch Sampson (b. 1759) served under Captain Simeon Sampson on the *Hazard*. Abel Sampson (b. 1750) served under Captain Sampson on the *Independence* and in 1777 died in prison in Halifax, Nova Scotia, after the ship was captured by the British.

Simeon Sampson went to sea as a boy, made many voyages, and in his twenties became a shipmaster. In 1762, during the French and Indian War, he was the captain of a Plymouth merchant ship captured by the French. The vessel was released but Sampson was held as a hostage for a ransom. Dressing as a woman, he escaped back to Plymouth.

At the outset of the Revolutionary War the Massachusetts Congress appointed Simeon Sampson their first naval captain. He took command of the brig *Independence*, a ship built under his direction in

Kingston, north of Plymouth. He captured five British ships in 1776, but early in 1777 he was defeated by a British cruiser. Sampson fought so fiercely that he astounded even his enemies. During a crucial part of the battle, two of his men abandoned their cannons, and Captain Sampson ran them through with his sword. He was held prisoner in Halifax until August 1777, and after his release took command of the brig *Hazard*, capturing several more British ships. In 1779 he commanded the packet ship *Mercury*, built at Plymouth to carry dispatches to the U.S. ministers in France. In 1780 he took command of the ship *Mars*, and in 1781 from the *Warren* captured the British flagship *Trial*.

Simeon Sampson retired soon after the capture of the *Trial*. Short of funds, he sold his house in Plymouth and bought a farm in Plympton. In 1789 he died of apoplexy. He and his wife Deborah had eleven children, six of whom survived childbirth. A daughter, Martha Washington Sampson, born in 1779, lived only three weeks, but a son, George Washington Sampson, born in 1781, survived his father, inheriting his sea chest, clothes, instruments of war, charts, books, and maps.

Of the hundred men raised to defend the fort on the Gurnet, a bluff at the end of Duxbury Beach, guarding the channel into Plymouth Harbor, seven were Sampsons: Isaiah Sampson (b. 1758), Colson Sampson (b. 1758), William Sampson (b. 175[?]), Beriah Sampson (b. 1728), Elijah Sampson (b. 1757), Robert Sampson (b. 1753), and the commander of the company, Captain Andrew Sampson (b. 1749).

The family's most renowned soldier was Deborah Sampson, the only woman to have fought in the Revolutionary War. She was born in 1760, the daughter of Jonathan Sampson and Deborah Bradford (a daughter of Elisha Bradford and great-granddaughter of William Bradford, governor of Plymouth Colony). Her grandfather died after investing in a merchant ship and losing everything in a shipwreck. Her father, Jonathan Sampson, lost his inheritance after giving it to his brother-in-law to invest. He left home, went to sea, was not heard from for years, and ultimately died in a shipwreck.

When he left, Deborah had just been born, and his wife, unable to support her children, eventually gave them away. At age five Deborah was sent to live with a Miss Fuller and then a Mrs. Thacher, and at ten she moved in with the family of Deacon Jeremiah Thomas in Middleborough. The deacon disapproved of her love of books, and Deborah was forced to read in secret. At seventeen she began teaching at a school in Middleborough. At twenty she dressed as a man and joined the Army.

She'd been thinking about it for some time. She wanted more than feeding livestock and teaching school. She'd heard the sound of the cannon announcing the Battle of Bunker Hill, and she had strong feelings of patriotism. She hired a tailor to make a suit with cloth she'd woven at home, telling him it was for a man who was about to join the Army. In 1781 she left the deacon's home in the night and walked through Taunton and Rochester. In New Bedford she almost joined the crew of a privateer but changed her mind after someone told her how the captain mistreated the crew. Instead, Deborah Sampson enlisted in the militia of the town of Uxbridge, using the name Robert Shurtliffe.

Twenty-one years old, five foot seven, with blue eyes, fair and delicate, she was called the "smock-faced boy." She would be known as a soldier who showed alertness, courage, and valor. She was also known as the fastest runner in her outfit. In June 1781, on a reconnaissance to Haarlem and White Plains, Deborah Sampson's company skirmished with a party of Tories. The man next to her was killed by the second discharge, but her company pushed the enemy back. In July, most of her company was transferred to Henry Jackson's regiment and joined by a detachment of the French army from Newport. In August, with the entire allied army under the command of George Washington, they marched through the streets of Philadelphia and boarded barges for Chesapeake Bay to join in the siege of Yorktown. She labored in the trenches, and felt the wind of a cannonball that killed four men behind her. For a week, day and night, the air was filled with shells. On October 15, two fronts of British soldiers advanced, and Deborah fought in a bayonet charge commanded by the Marquis de La Fayette. On October 19, 1781, she witnessed the surrender of Cornwallis.

Deborah's company set up winter quarters on the banks of the

Hudson River, and in June 1782 she volunteered for an expedition against a band of Tories that had been attacking farms east of the Hudson. She received two wounds, one in the left temple and another from a pistol ball to the thigh near the groin. She was treated for the head wound, but concealed the other, extracting the ball herself.

Before her company was disbanded she came down with a fever and was taken to a hospital. While she was sleeping, a pair of orderlies, thinking she was about to die, began to argue over her boots. Deborah awoke and scared the orderlies away, but after she fell asleep again a surgeon came by to examine her. When he reached under her shirt and the compress she wore, to feel for her heartbeat, he found the true gender of Robert Shurtliffe.

Deborah was moved to the doctor's home, and before her discharge he wrote a letter to General Paterson, who was especially astonished. He had known Deborah as a brave soldier. She had served as his aide-de-camp, and had lived with his family. The general offered Deborah female clothing, but she declined, preferring to wear her uniform.

Deborah received an honorable discharge and left for Massachusetts. At first, arriving among her family, she kept her identity a secret. A few months later, however, she married Benjamin Gannett, a farmer from the town of Sharon. They had three children.

Deborah Sampson wore her uniform again when, to satisfy public curiosity, she went through the manual exercise on a stage at Boston Common. She could, they said, make the gun talk. In 1792, after petitioning the Massachusetts legislature, Deborah Sampson received a military pension (". . . said Deborah exhibited an extraordinary instance of female heroism, by discharging the duties of a faithful, gallant soldier, and at the same time preserved the virtue and chastity of her sex, unsuspected and unblemished . . ."). She died at her home in Sharon in 1827 at the age of sixty-six. In 1832 Representative John Quincy Adams brought a petition on behalf of Mr. Gannett, so he could receive the benefits of a widower of a soldier of the Revolutionary War.

One line of Sampsons went: Abraham Sampson (b. 16[??]), Abraham Sampson (b. 1658), Miles Sampson (b. 1690), Miles Sampson

(b. 1731), Miles Sampson (b. 1766), Eden Sampson (b. 1794), Isaac Sampson (b. 1833), George Sampson (b. 1866), Warren Sampson (b. 1892), Robert Sampson (b. 1919), Robert Sampson (b. 1945), Bradford Sampson (b. 1970).

BOB SAMPSON married Penny Clark, and in 1966 they moved to Barnstable. Bob fished off the beach for stripers and, for the first time, sold his catch. When the bass moved offshore in late summer he trolled for them in the boat his father had built, but he could see he'd need something bigger if he was going to fish commercially.

Bob Sampson hadn't been living on Cape Cod for very long when he began to feel the romance of wresting his living from the sea. And there was also the adversity of the weather. When Bob went fishing during rough weather he came back with a different outlook on life—especially if he had been the only one on the water that day. He came back stronger. The Indians, he thought, would have said that the sea gave you power, and that seemed to be true. When Bob fought the weather and produced, he came back a better person, a victor—not over the sea, of course, but over the day. Bob thought that if he came back a victor enough times he would learn things and progress. He would be able to handle more.

Bob hired the Plymouth boatbuilder Alden Vaughn to make him a 20-foot skiff, and in the summer of 1968 he began to work Pleasant Bay in Chatham. Pleasant Bay is an extraordinary place, an estuary of thousands of acres of marshes, islands, and tidal flats on the elbow of the Cape. On the west side are the towns of Chatham and Orleans, shielded from the sea not only by the shallow bay but by the long and narrow Nauset barrier beach, which trails for miles to the south and forms the eastern boundary of Pleasant Bay. A funnel-shaped entrance runs between Nauset Peninsula and the Monomoy Shoals, where the *Mayflower* was nearly wrecked in 1620. Great flocks of seabirds stop there, and deer swim from island to island. The flats teem with shellfish, and schools of stripers come in to feed—though they are hard to catch in the warm estuarine waters.

Pleasant Bay, with its beauty, remoteness, and intricacy, has a mystique that draws fishermen from New Jersey and Long Island, and from north of Boston. Bob became part of a group of friends who exchanged ideas and developed techniques. Bob thought it was important to have friends on the water, even if you fished by yourself, and he was generous with his knowledge. When Bob found menhaden in Nantucket Sound and used them to catch five stripers in the middle of the Pleasant Bay fleet, he let his friends know.

A number of commercial fishermen emerged from the group at Pleasant Bay—cod fishermen, tuna fishermen, shellfishermen—and among them Bob experienced his greatest increase in knowledge. They nicknamed Bob the "Scratcher," because he scratched out his living, working around the edges, picking a fish here, a fish there. The name had further meaning for Bob, and in it was the origin of his philosophy for fishing. A scratcher is someone who doesn't try to catch other people's fish in other people's ways. A scratcher goes off on his own and develops his own resources, away from the others (even as he helps and relies upon them). A scratcher is independent, though he may also be richly connected. Bob would name several of his boats *Scratcher*, and in the 1990s, twenty-five years later, some fishermen from Pleasant Bay would still greet Bob Sampson with "Hey, Scratch . . ."

In Pleasant Bay, Bob caught a striped bass that nearly broke the world record. Running late one day in a falling tide, coming from Saquatucket Harbor in Harwich and wanting to avoid the long southerly route around Monomoy, he tried to skim over the sand flats and ran aground. He got out and pulled the boat through the shallow water, but at the edge of a deep spot the surface exploded—with the sound he'd first heard in the night in Plymouth Harbor. Down in the hole, he realized, were some big fish. It was the first hole just off the flats, and the big stripers were sitting there waiting for smaller fish to pass over. His splashing alerted the fish and Bob knew he wouldn't get any that day, but he took bearings.

The next day he returned to the spot with his father. They eased into the north side of the hole, slipped their anchor overboard, and trailed some live menhaden in on their lines on the tidal stream. The big fish weren't interested. Bob cut some bait and put it on hooks, but the fish still weren't interested. Then he tried chumming—dropping free bait to get the fish into a feeding mode, then following with a baited hook. Bob drifted a few pieces in, and the surface churned. He baited the lines, and caught five giant striped bass.

Bob had caught so many big stripers that summer that he lost the ability to estimate their size. Most of the fish had weighed about 20 pounds, so he figured the big stripers were 30, maybe 35 pounds. Bob's father thought they weighed much more than that.

For some time Bob had been snagging menhaden, but menhaden didn't bring anything at the market. Striped bass were worth 30 to 50 cents a pound, so the young Scratcher developed a technique of stuffing his leftover menhaden into the bellies of his striped bass, thus getting 30 to 50 cents a pound for menhaden. It was a way of working the edges.

Bob and his father went off to the fish buyer in Hyannis. They put the smallest fish on the scale first, and it weighed in at 45 pounds. Bob was worried as he threw the biggest fish on the scale. It had a grotesquely swollen belly, a girth of about three feet. The weight was 72 pounds—a new world record for striped bass, Bob was told. Robert Sampson, Jr., fisherman and scratcher, looked at Robert Sampson, Sr., bomber pilot and bank president, and saw concern. The owner of the market was off in the restaurant, and Bob didn't want him to see this fish, not stuffed. The owner would have been upset and their relationship would have been in trouble. So Bob reached down into the striper and started pulling out menhaden. It hurt, because striped bass have a stiff and abrasive muscle in their throats, used to crush prey, and it scraped the skin from Bob's arm, but he rolled up his sleeve and kept at it. The final weight was 61 pounds. Bob wanted to sell the fish, but the buyer told him to wait, just in case it remained the biggest fish he caught that year. Eventually this fish would hang over Bob's mantelpiece.

Bass fishing is a summer pursuit, and Bob tried other fisheries in other seasons. The winter after he had the boat built in Plymouth he tried scalloping. He had heard of a bumper crop in Osterville, on the south side of Barnstable. He set up a stand with a davit, and bought a large steel dredge.

Pulling the big bag along or hauling it by hand was a precarious business. Bob figured that older scallopers must have been laughing at him, but he got his limit the first day out. He knew he had to make some adjustments in his gear and learn more, but during those weeks scalloping Bob began to feel more confident about his future in commercial fishing. There was money to be made, and though the work was difficult, it was enjoyable.

By March, only two boats were working in Osterville. Bob was there, and an older fisherman with a crippled arm. He was a very good fisherman, but a hard man, and he didn't like Bob very much. Bob figured it was because of his youth.

Bob was alone on the *Scratcher* and the older fisherman was running ahead, with his girlfriend at the culling board. It was cold and icy, and they probably shouldn't have been out fishing. When Bob reached for some water to wash off his scallops, he slipped and fell overboard. He grabbed at the dragline, caught it, and eventually pulled himself back into the boat. It wasn't easy. He had his rain gear on, and everything was wet underneath, and cold.

For lunch every day Bob brought two peanut butter sandwiches and one beer, and he took a nip of Southern Comfort for warmth. Back in the boat, shocked with cold, he drank the Southern Comfort. It warmed him up, and it gave him some courage. Bob looked up ahead at the other boat, and he realized that the older fisherman hadn't paused in his work, even though his girlfriend must have seen Bob fall in. Bob wondered if the man would have come back to get him, and figured probably not. The older fisherman didn't look back until Bob was fishing again, and he didn't acknowledge the accident until much later, when they became friends. The telling of the story even helped the friendship along.

Bob scalloped in other winters, and continued to fish in Pleasant Bay. In the fall he followed the stripers and bluefin to Nantucket Shoals. He took the exam for a charter captain's license and for a few years took parties to the most productive waters around Cape Cod, wherever the fishing was best. Bob would wonder whether chartering had been the right way to go, and what might have happened if he'd stayed commercial, but he had some good experiences. He did find

it difficult to work with the high-strung people who approached recreational fishing the way they approached business, becoming disappointed and melancholy if they didn't catch more fish on the second
trip than on the first. Or the weekenders who were more interested
in getting drunk than fishing.

Some winters Bob jigged for cod, catching from 1,000 to 1,700
pounds a day. After building a larger *Scratcher* he dragged for black
bass, scup, and flounders in Nantucket Sound. He potted, or trapped,
black bass, conchs, and lobsters. He dragged hundreds of tons of
mussels in the marshes from Marshfield to Barnstable. He harpooned
swordfish and bluefin tuna.

Bob chose day fisheries, to fit into his work schedule. Though his
friends at ComElectric advanced to higher positions, Bob stayed at
the bottom of the ladder so he would have more time to fish and more
freedom to think about it. Except for weekends, he slept only three
or four hours a night. At the halfway point on his route in Cambridge,
he usually grabbed an hour of sleep. He drank a lot of coffee. Sometimes he fell asleep at the wheel, waking with a start when his head
nodded. He once drove all the way from Falmouth to Hyannis in his
sleep, touching along the edge of the road.

Bob could have taken the days off and rested, but that would have
cut into his fishing. He was afraid someone else would catch all the
fish. He didn't have to outfish other people, but he didn't want to be
outfished. He wanted to be out there when there was a chance to
catch them. In most fisheries, and especially in the bluefin tuna harpoon fishery, most of the money is made in just a few days. You have
to be out there when the fish show. Though Bob stayed in on the worst
days, he refused to call a day a no-fish day until he'd been down to
the harbor and, if possible, gone out a little ways in the boat. Once
out there, he might go a little farther.

Bob joined the Coast Guard Reserve, as did many other young men
on the Cape during the 1960s. The reservists went to sea on summer
maneuvers, and one summer Bob planned to take his fishing pole
along. Penny drove him to the dock in New Bedford, but when Bob
saw the 311-foot cutter, he changed his mind and left the pole in the
car. At sea, however, he found some fishing poles in the ship's rec-

reation room and began dragging baits off the stern. A line of reservists soon crowded the stern, even though the cutter was steaming ahead, and not running back and forth the way most trolling boats would. When Bob got a strike he yelled for someone to run up to the bridge and tell the captain to slow down so he could haul the fish in, but they laughed at him. Then the captain himself came by. He ordered the engines to full stop, and the Scratcher landed a barracuda.

Some of his first efforts as a tuna fisherman were as a mate on sport boats during tuna tournaments. These were busy, spirited local events in New England and on the East Coast, where strings of the unsalable fish were hung up as giant trophies. Then the bluefin were sunk, or hauled off to a dump. Bob usually did well in the tournaments, often winning, almost always placing.

In the 1970s, however, when the price for bluefin went to five cents a pound, then ten cents a pound, and, with the entry of Japanese buyers, to as much as a dollar a pound, tuna tournaments altered in their purpose and then gradually faded, as there was serious money to be made.

Bob outfitted the *Scratcher* with a pulpit and tower and spent several years chasing big schools of bluefin off Martha's Vineyard. In 1982, though only twelve, Brad steered the boat and put the stand over the fish while Bob developed his harpooning technique. They caught bluefin and swordfish, and in 1983 had another good year. That was the year Bob and Brad saw fireworks all along the south shore of the Cape as they rode in the tower with six giant tuna on deck.

In 1983 Bob had what he thought was his best day fishing, when they found a school that stretched across the horizon, and they picked along the edges, harpooning twelve and bringing in six. That was also the year of Bob's worst day ever, when Brad fell overboard. They were heading up Buzzards Bay toward the southern end of the Cape Cod Canal, and Bob was at the wheel. Brad went below and stood at the stern. Bob had a rule that anyone who went to the stern had to let him know—he'd heard that 75 percent of drowned fishermen were found with their flies down—but Brad forgot. Bob didn't see him go over, but Bob's other son, Tucker, who was along that day, happened to look back just as Brad fell in. When Bob pulled Brad back on board the first thing Brad said was "Dad, that's where I ran the Falmouth road race." Bob had nightmares for weeks.

The next year, 1984, was a poor one. In 1985 they lobstered in the morning and fished for bluefin in the afternoon (the traditional daily routine of a Maine harpoon fisherman), but got only three fish, at $2.25 a pound. A few of the spotter pilots who had been working in the swordfish fishery on Georges Bank had begun working for bluefin harpooners, and the next year Bob used several pilots and harpooned fifty fish. It was the time when pilots and captains communicated with CB radios, and they considered it a good day if the plane found the boat.

Bob and his pilot, Cary Fitch, would seek bluefin as they chased bluefish on the outer banks of the Cape off Truro. On a hot day in July thermal waves were rising off the beach, and Fitch was getting tossed around in them. For several hours he made passes while the *Scratcher* waited offshore. Finally he called Bob to say that he was exhausted and was going to make one last pass before heading for the airport.

Just off the beach he made a circle and told Bob to hurry. Bob steamed toward Fitch, but before he got there he came upon a line of bluefin swimming in water so shallow they were making sand clouds with their tail fins. He went out on the pulpit and harpooned a fish in about twenty feet of water. It shot off for the beach, then doubled back straight for the boat. As it passed under, the rope got caught in the propeller. By the time Bob cleared the line, the fish had pulled a dart. Fitch called and said he had another bunch, even closer to the beach. When Bob finished rigging another harpoon, he looked up to see about ten boats, most of the Cape Cod harpoon fleet, bearing down on Fitch's circle. The *Scratcher* charged ahead, and Bob harpooned another fish. This time he yelled at his mate to go in reverse, but Fitch came on the radio and said to wait, that there was a surfer behind the boat. They let the surfer paddle by, brought the fish aboard, then charged at another bunch. Bob got three fish that day.

In 1987 Fred Brooks began to fly for Bob Sampson, and they

formed one of the most competitive teams in the harpoon fishery. The pairing of pilot and fisherman was well suited to Bob's nature. He loved the camaraderie, the joint effort, the communicating, but he was still the Scratcher who got out and away from the pack. Pilots drew the fishermen offshore, moving the fishery to the 100-fathom line and beyond. Bob and Brooksie shared an affinity for the ocean, and they became close friends.

Brooksie's abilities were confirmed late one summer when they were working the edges of a fog bank off Nantucket. Brooksie had found a pod of dolphins and, although bluefin tuna are usually shy around dolphins, a few were moving under the pod. In the fog Brooksie got over the dolphins, followed the shadow of a single tuna, and led the *Scratcher* in for a strike. Fog closed over the boat, but Brooksie, who liked to come down low for a look at the catch, punched through and flew just a hundred feet above the boat. Bob was both amazed and upset, and though he warned Brooksie about taking such chances he praised him for his flying.

With the use of spotter pilots the ocean became smaller, and the network of communication became more widespread. Though some boats started using the best military technology available to scramble or mask their signals, word of their discoveries spread quickly from the Islands to the Gulf of Maine. Cape Cod fishermen went up to Maine more often, and Maine fishermen roamed down to Cape waters when the schools moved away from their shores. Though Bob Sampson was hesitant to travel so far—a nomadic approach didn't fit well with his job at ComElectric—he did range to other waters and stay in other ports. Sometimes Bob would have Brooksie fly him home so he could go to work. With the accurate destinations that spotters provided, and the faster boats tuna fishermen were building, it also became less daunting to leave Cape Cod in the morning, steam to the waters off New Hampshire for the afternoon, and come back the same night.

The electrification of harpoons—the zappers—spread throughout the fishery in the late 1980s. The technology had been developing since the 1950s, when German fishermen first experimented with it. In the 1970s, a Massachusetts eye doctor who was an avid swordfisherman worked for several years on an electric harpoon, but he found that the electricity tended to jell the meat of swordfish close to the bone. This didn't happen with bluefin tuna, though a fish could be ruined if too much current was used. In Chatham, an aeronautical engineer who was a friend of Norman St. Pierre, a fisherman and spotter pilot, developed a zapper after watching them use harpoons attached to ropes, balls, and flags. St. Pierre then built a line of zappers and leased them out.

It seemed a gruesome way of fishing, electrocuting an animal, but as one fisherman said, zapping was the most humane death. In the days before zappers ("B.Z.") the water sometimes looked like a golf course, with flags and buoys spread out, and fishermen hunted around for hours, finding about half of their kills. Zapping was a quick death: "If I was going to kill you, would you rather have me stick a hook in your mouth and drag you around the parking lot for an hour, or press a button and get it over with?" He had a point, but most of the harpooners were quiet about their tools. They suspected few people would endorse zapping, even if it was a more humane and efficient way to harvest the big fish.

In 1988 the prices took a leap, and in 1989 Bob Sampson had his first big-money year. A new population of medium bluefin had appeared in the Gulf of Maine, and though a fisherman couldn't legally target them, he could keep three mediums and a giant. In 1989 large numbers of finback and humpback whales were feeding on sand eels off the Wellfleet shore, and giant bluefin were feeding among them. Bob Sampson planned his days accordingly. In the morning he and his crew searched among the whales for a giant. In the afternoon they went up to Stellwagen Bank north of Provincetown and caught as many as three mediums. These were 150- to 300-pound fish, six to nine years old. Bluefin that size hadn't been seen off Cape Cod for many years. Suddenly there were large schools of them.

The liberal rule was intended for rod-and-reel fishermen, who could not choose their fish, but harpooners reasoned that they should be allowed to catch mediums too, especially if there were no giants around. Harpooning, after all, was an old New England fishery, with historic claims as valid as those of rod-and-reelers. Bob caught his limit, a giant and three mediums (one per crew member), nearly every fish day. When he filled out his government reports, he always noted that he'd harpooned the mediums, and he urged others to do the same.

There were complaints, and Bob eventually met with an enforcement officer from the National Marine Fisheries Service. He explained his position: harpooning was a historical fishery, and mediums were everywhere, all the way from Cape Cod to Georges Bank. They were worth too much for fishermen to pass up. The prices they were getting were extraordinary, so why not catch them? Bob was told to wait for a decision. He did so for three days, and then called the NMFS officer from his boat. There were calls back and forth, from Stellwagen Bank to Gloucester. Finally Bob was told he could fish the mediums, and the matter would be reexamined during the coming winter.

After the 1989 season Bob Sampson invested $93,000 and built a second boat, the *Rush*. He named it for the feeling he got when he caught a bluefin tuna—a mental rush. Everything was a rush when you were out on the pulpit. Bob didn't know it, but the root of the word "tuna" in Greek (*thuno*) means to rush, after the speed of the fish.

In 1989 there was a breakthrough in prices returned to the fishermen. That July, Bob caught a giant that brought $28.46 a pound, on consignment, a system by which a fisherman sent a fish to Japan and gambled on the auction price, with the buyer taking a percentage. Bob had been told by his buyer that mediums weren't worth anything in Japan, but after receiving only $3.50 and $4 a pound at the dock, $800 to $1,000 for a single fish—a long way from stripers in Pleasant Bay, but also a long way from $28 a pound—Bob decided to gamble. He told the buyer to send all mediums to Japan on consignment from then on. The first consigned medium brought $43 a pound. When the season was over, a group of Cape Cod harpoon fishermen got together and formed Cape Quality Bluefin, negotiating their own deals in Japan. A century after the clipper ships, Cape Cod captains were again trading with the Orient.

One night that winter Bob went home to see his wife walk into the living room in a new mink coat. As far as he knew, Penny hadn't even wanted a mink, but she'd bought one to celebrate the year. She had been through the hard years, and there had been more hard years than good ones. When Bob was scalloping and she was pregnant with Brad, she had spent many afternoons shucking scallops over the kitchen sink. In those days they couldn't afford to eat any of the profits. Not many wives could have put up with his hours, Bob thought, and Penny had spent a lot of time alone while he worked twenty-hour days (Penny sometimes thought the long hours had helped to keep their marriage afloat). She had made the bad days seem not all that bad, and she was someone he could enjoy the good days with. There weren't many people you could enjoy the good days with.

As the man called Scratcher would put it, in 1989 they had the world by the cazongas. And those medium bluefin that were out there in 1989, three years later they were showing up as giants.

(5)

A RICH MAN

❧

THE TUNA fishery had picked up in the Gulf of Maine. On the morning of July 22 Bob Sampson had received a call from a chummer who told him the bite was on and the fishermen were catching fifty bluefin a day along Jeffreys Ledge off southern Maine. At that rate, they figured, the general quota would be filled in late August.

Fishermen in the Gulf of Maine fished primarily within two permit categories—the general category and the harpoon category. (There were five categories in all, with another for purse seiners, an "incidental" category for longline trawlers, and an angling category for the recreational and charter-boat fisheries.) The entire western Atlantic quota, allowing for a total harvest of 2,660 metric tons of bluefin per year (from 1983 to 1991), was shared by the United States, Canada, and Japan, set by international agreement, and administered in the United States by the National Marine Fisheries Service.

The general and harpoon categories were a little nebulous, because harpooners worked in both. General-category fishermen could use handlines, rods and reels, or harpoons. Harpoon-category fishermen could use harpoons only. The general was by far the larger of the two categories, with a quota in 1992 of 531 metric tons—approximately 3,000 giant bluefin. There were approximately 10,000 general-category permit holders, covering ports along the East Coast. The daily limit in the general category as of July 1992, when new regulations were issued, was one giant bluefin, at least 70 inches long, per boat.

The harpoon category was much smaller, with a quota of 53 tons, about 300 fish. Approximately two hundred boats were registered (nearly all of them in New England), and about thirty of those boats actually caught fish, working primarily from Cape Cod to Maine. Because the harpoon category was small, and involved such a high level of skill, few fishermen would register their boats in it. But the distinction, advantage, and temptation of the harpoon category was that there was no daily limit. A boat could land one or ten fish in a day, and a skilled fisherman working the right place at the right time could make a year's income in a few days. Only the best harpooners had boats in this category. Some had a boat in each category. Bob Sampson, for example, with the *Scratcher* in the harpoon and the *Rush* in the general. Or Sonny McIntire, from Ogunquit, Maine. The Sullivan family from the Cape, with the father running one boat, the mother another, and two sons in the pulpits (with the former javelin thrower on the harpoon boat).

All the Cape harpooners, and some from Maine, hoped for a fall like 1991's, when, after the general category had reached its quota and closed for the year, a dozen harpoon boats had a productive ground east of Chatham all to themselves. The fish, then in their last stages of the feeding cycle, were loaded with fat, and brought the highest prices of the season. One day Eric Hesse, running the *Scratcher* while Bob was hunting elk in Colorado, caught two fish worth $18,000 each.

Now, in late July 1992, the quality of the fish had improved somewhat but prices were down at about $9 a pound for the best fish, because Japanese purse seiners were catching tons of bluefin—5,000 pieces at one auction.

THIS WAS a questionable fish day. At sunrise a fifteen-mile-per-hour easterly wind had come up. The scrub oaks behind Bob's house were rustling—a sure sign that things were rough on the water. Fish didn't usually show during easterly winds, which pushed colder water inshore. Cape harpooners tended to stay inside during easterlies, but there was a chance the wind would "lay down," so Bob decided to head offshore to give it a try. He was the only one who did, and he came back a victor.

We planned to get under way from Sandwich Harbor at 8 a.m., but there was a delay. Bob's crew included Wade Behlman, first mate, and a summer helper, Matt Bunnell, a junior at Barnstable High. I was along for the ride. We left the slip and went to the fuel dock. There were two tanks in the *Scratcher*, filled through screw caps flush to the deck. Bob filled one tank with diesel fuel, closed it off, opened the other, and told Matt to finish. Matt hadn't fueled up before, and he'd never handled the high-pressure hose. As he bent over the tank his pants rode down, and when he stood to hitch them up the nozzle burst into the air. Matt took a blast to the chest and in the face, and when the hose skittered around I took a stream from the waist down. I tried to jump over the engine box to get out of the way, but hit a storage box headfirst and rebounded into a puddle of fuel.

It was potentially a hazardous situation, not so much because of the fuel, which wasn't very flammable, but because two Coast Guard boats were moored nearby. The Coast Guard frowned upon the slightest of spills. Bob and Wade poured laundry detergent on the oil slick spreading out from the boat. Matt left to wash his face. I took the keys to Bob's truck ("We don't wear good clothes on the boat," he told me) and with eyes glued to the road, pants drenched with diesel, I drove off to shower and change. Matt didn't get that opportunity. An hour later he was still blinking as he scrubbed the deck. The *Scratcher* finally left the harbor at 9:30 and cut across Cape Cod Bay toward Race Point at the tip of Provincetown.

The ride across the Bay seemed to bring stories out of Bob, and in the early part of a trip he liked to talk. Some buyers, Bob said, had gotten rich while the fishermen were kept in the dark about the prices bluefin were bringing.

"Years ago I had an experience with the Moonies," he said. The Unification Church of Reverend Moon had been involved in the bluefin tuna fishery for several years. "I don't agree with their beliefs, but

I sure did like the way they made all the other dealers honest by offering honest prices for the fish.

"I caught a giant on the northwest corner of Stellwagen. I was chumming then. So I steamed over to the Moonie buy boat instead of going in. The price on the dock was about three to four dollars. Well, the Moonies offered me seven dollars, with the next load of chum bait free. They said they'd pay cash, but not that day because they didn't have enough money on the boat.

"I came back a few days later for my chum bait and my cash. When I steamed up I saw the man I'd done business with, a Southerner. He was smiling. Most of the other guys on the boat were Koreans, and they were smiling from ear to ear. When I saw that, I knew I'd done well in the market. The buyer said he was going to give me cash, and pay me a dollar-fifty extra, because the fish had done so well. In all my years of fishing, I had never been paid more than the buyer said he would originally pay, never. I went off with my chum and my money, happy as could be.

"The buyer I'd been dealing with came up three dollars a pound the next day. But he got me back later on. I had caught six giants off Nantucket. It was the Fourth of July. I called him from a phone booth at the dock, and left a message. I kept calling back, and his wife kept telling me he wasn't there, but he'd be getting in touch with me soon as he got in. I stayed in that phone booth all night long. I literally slept in the phone booth, waiting for him to call. The next morning I sold the fish to Canal Marine for a dollar twenty-five a pound.

"I would call all the buyers, looking for the best price. To them, we were whores, but to us, they were thieves. It wasn't too long before one of them had two Mercedes and had put hundreds of thousands of dollars into his freezer plant. They didn't get that by selling bait to lobster fishermen."

On it went, stories of the lobster pot festival at Monhegan Island in Maine, of a trip to Tsukiji market, of how bluefin would trail along behind the draggers picking at the trailings, of how they'd bang against the bottom of the boats hauling cod off Chatham.

When we crossed Provincetown the waves got larger. The clouds were gray and black. There had been thunderstorms the day before, and Brad, fishing in Cape Cod Bay, had found it necessary to shut off the engine and go below. A stick boat was the tallest tree in the forest. There were times when there was so much electricity in the air that arcs crossed the struts in the tower.

This morning Brooksie was flying thirty-five miles northeast of Provincetown. He was coaxing Bob on, telling him to come out and join him.

Bob wasn't so sure. "I'm gonna be upset, you bring me all the way out here for clouds."

"Well, it's a gamble like every other day," Brooksie said. "You're the captain."

"I talked to Kevin," Bob said. "They're pounding them on Jeffreys."

At noon patches of blue opened up. The seas were strong, but workable. When the *Scratcher* reached Brooksie, more sunlight came through. They cruised the area, plane and boat, and at 2:15 Brooksie found a school of a hundred giants. Wade Behlman took the wheel and they steamed toward Brooksie's circle. The fish were in a loose pack, their fins above water.

Bob went out on the stand. The waves were still rough, and he was riding up and down about ten feet with each dip of the pulpit. Coming on the bunch, he tried to take aim with the harpoon, but it got caught on the line; then the wire connecting the zapper came undone. Flustered, he threw anyway and missed. By the time he'd reconnected the wires and gone back to the pulpit, Bob was not in the best frame of mind.

Brooksie was off to find other fish. "You excited and ready?" he asked.

"Well, I'm not excited," Bob answered, "but I guess I'm ready."

BROOKSIE HAD flown for Bob Sampson for six years now. He had started spotting fish in 1982 when he was twenty-one and a student in a flight management program in Florida. He had grown up in Thomaston, Maine. From the time he was nine he worked as a clam digger, except for a year in high school when the clamming shut down and he went into the woods to work as a logger. He came out appreciating the old-timers he met there. Brooksie's parents, thinking their son needed some direction, gave him flying lessons for his birthday.

His first spotting job was for a swordfisherman out of Owls Head, Maine. He made long trips, flying 200 miles to the far side of Georges Bank, working the plateau that formed one of the richest fishing grounds in the world. He flew over the canyons and ledges of the continental shelf. On his first day out, his boat got twenty swordfish. The plane got $100 per fish, which the pilot split with the owner.

Brooksie loved being a swordfish spotter, and the flights to the Southeast Part, the Northeast Peak, and Browns Bank south of Nova Scotia. Because they were so far out from shore, their lives on the line, the swordfish pilots tended to look out for one another. To Brooksie it seemed like a social event, with all the talk and stories. Sometimes, if he didn't have a job, he would fly out to the dumps south of Nantucket in the morning, get on the radio, and ask around until he found a boat. He worked primarily for American boats, but when they got fogged in he'd call the Canadian boats and fly over the Hague Line to work for them.

When Brooksie finished school he interviewed with Continental Airlines and by chance was hired to fly for Plymouth and Brockton Airlines, out of Provincetown and Hyannis. For some this would have been an outpost job, but for Brooksie it meant he was two hours away from Georges Bank. During the summer he signed up for the early morning flights. When he saw a high-pressure area coming in, which meant clear flying weather, he'd pay another pilot to take his shift and he'd go off spotting.

As Brooksie took on more responsibilities with PBA, it became more difficult for him to make the trips to the swordfish grounds. A pilot from Nantucket said there was money in spotting tuna and gave him Bob Sampson's number. Brooksie didn't like tuna then. There had been many days when he found a swordfish only to have a big school of tuna come charging through, driving the swordfish to the bottom. Tuna were skittish and difficult to harpoon, unlike swordfish, the kings of the sea, which usually didn't back off from anything. Brooksie didn't like bluefin tuna, but he liked spotting.

He called Bob Sampson, and asked Bob to pay expenses for the plane and $50 per fish. Bob told him he'd be better off taking 25 percent. Brooksie discussed it with his wife. A Canadian swordfisherman had sent $3,000 for Brooksie down to New Bedford in a lobster truck. He'd use that money to pay expenses, he told her, and when it was gone he'd be finished with tuna fishing.

On his first day flying off Martha's Vineyard he didn't see anything. He didn't see anything on the second and third days, and he began to doubt himself. He had been productive. He didn't take his eyes off the water, not even to eat lunch.

On the fourth day, there were tuna everywhere. Bob harpooned ten, and brought in five. Brooksie's career as a tuna spotter took off.

Brooksie made good money spotting tuna. After that first season he bought a new Camaro Z-28. He bought his own plane. He built a house in Maine with tuna money.

WHILE BROOKSIE was off looking elsewhere, Bob and Wade Behlman discovered a school near the boat, and Bob went out on the stand. His right hand up on the butt of the pole, his left hand steadying the middle, Bob waved and pointed, raised up and threw. The pole entered the water, stopped and bowed. But the dart had pushed through, the fish had been "buttoned," so they were unable to zap it fully. Wade hauled the line in, and when the tail fin touched the boat the fish came alive, flapped wildly, and shot off to the bottom with the line. They put a rig out, two orange balls and a flag, and would return later to haul it in. Brooksie had found two bunches, small giants.

Again Bob went out on the stand, raised up, took aim, and threw the harpoon. It hit. He howled, while brown fish darted away like a flock of birds. Wade hit the button to the zapper, which worked this time.

It was a hard thing to see, the fish straightening out with the surge of the current, flashing a silver side as if lit up by the juice. None of it was quite as hard as that, not the bleeding of the fish, the cutting of the subcutaneous arteries under the lateral line, the dark blood clouding the water; not the evisceration, or the snapping back of the gill plate, not Wade with his thumb in the fish's eye, holding it like a codfish about to be gutted, not even the sawing off of the head, or the sight of Matt shoulder-deep in the body cavity.

Matt was happy, moving with sureness. "Something happens to me," he said. "I don't know what it is. Something clicks, soon as that fish comes aboard."

What a beautiful creature the fish was. And what an odd way to see its beauty. Perhaps this was the only way for us to see it, to truly know it, through this harvest.

There was something both awkward and almost sacred about two fishermen with blood up to their elbows.

Brown, like horses in the water. A blue line along the side. Tail-let fins lemon yellow in the sunlight. Iridescent blue patches along the top of the back, the dorsal area. Gold along the crown. The beak of it, the narrowing head, the large eyes. Head and gills up front, and muscle all the way down. Fish of show, splendor, and speed.

Once I'd asked Bob what the killing felt like. He took a look at me and said, "I love the prey." Indians, he said, believed that when they killed a deer the spirit of the deer came to them. It was something like that. He was a hunter. Hunting put you in touch with something deep. Up until a few generations ago man had hunted, and that instinct hadn't been bred out of all of us yet. It had merely been subverted into other things. When Bob killed his first pheasant, at twelve, he broke down crying and was sick. But he went back the next day.

There was dignity in this death, Bob thought. There wasn't much dignity in the way the purse seiners caught fish, surrounding them with a net, cinching it in, all those bluefin, the embodiment of all that was wild in the sea, wriggling on top of each other, tearing each other up. But chasing them with a harpoon boat at least gave the fish a fighting chance. That was a dignified way to go. If Bob had to die, if he had a choice, he'd want to go out there on the water, chasing tuna.

Hunting was a matter of shared experience with a prey, accumulated over a period of years. It was like a marriage, in which things understood are not communicated. Bob was a deer hunter, too, and while the deer on the wall of his living room was not one he had shot himself, it reminded him of the countless hours he had spent in the woods hunting. Taking an animal's life brought you close to that animal, as close as you could come. Because of the responsibility for that life, you had to do it right.

And they were commercial fishermen. That meant catching fish for a living.

And there was Matt, who had screwed up royally that day. Bloody to the throat, happy to be doing what he did well, he held the fish's head up and gave a victorious, affirmative, almost reverential nod. This could have been a kind of ritual, this young man face to face with the head of the fish he'd just gutted, before he let go and the head went splashing away in the wake. With a block and tackle they lifted the carcass into a tank of brine and ice, to keep it as fresh as possible.

The sky cleared, the day became calmer. Bob sent Brooksie to find the rig they had left behind, and when Brooksie flew a loop over it they headed that way. Wade and Matt pulled the fish aboard and cleaned it. Brooksie found another bunch and they steamed toward them, but the fish went down. We were getting farther offshore, and Bob didn't like that, since he had to go into work that night. He had been working about seventeen hours now, with a good part of the day to go. And there would be another full day tomorrow, if the weather was favorable.

They ran a bunch and caught a third fish and, after two misses, a fourth. Bob was four for eight now. It was after five o'clock, and he wanted to head back to the canal. The trip in would take three hours.

"Bob, I'm seeing fish everywhere out here," Brooksie said. "They're just coming up."

"I've gotta go to work, Brooksie," Bob said.

Brooksie protested, but only a little. He made a low pass over the boat and then flew off for Maine. "Nothing like it," he said, "fishing the New England coast."

Bob turned the *Scratcher* for the Cape. He hit the way points for Race Point on the loran set. Wade and Matt worked below, cleaning and hosing off the deck. Wade had been working as Bob's mate off and on for fifteen years. They had dragged together, musseled, and fished for tuna. He worked quickly, effortlessly.

"You don't have to tell Wade anything," Bob said. "Matt's getting an education today."

After the cleaning was done, Wade climbed into the tower and took the wheel. Bob went below and tried to get some sleep, but he lasted only an hour. He'd never been able to sleep well on his own boat. A half hour from Provincetown he called the manager of Cape Quality Bluefin and told him to meet the boat at Sandwich Harbor at nine o'clock.

We steamed across Cape Cod Bay, 190 feet deep at Race Point, 160 feet to the west of Truro, the slope rising all the way to Sandwich, eighty, sixty, forty feet of water. Then to the canal, which was lit up along the edges and over the span of the bridge connecting the Cape to the mainland. They went into Sandwich Harbor to the pier where they'd gotten fuel that morning. Bob lowered a chain hoist. Wade tied on a tail rope, and they lifted each fish onto the back of Bob's flatbed truck.

The manager of CQB was on his way. A renegade company, CQB could not take fish directly from a boat at the Sandwich pier. Instead, the members had to load their fish onto their own trucks, drive to a parking lot, and make the transfer.

The fish lay side by side on Bob's truck, lit by a streetlamp. The vividness of their colors had faded, and from a few feet away they looked black and silver, but the variegated and complex patterns were still there.

A fisherman, a weekend warrior, Bob called him, was looking for information but wasn't getting much. Bob didn't stop to talk, but he did say he hadn't seen any kind of fish until after 3:30. This fisherman had recently tried to follow the *Scratcher* out, but Bob had run the boat in a circle to ward him off.

"There's a whole lot of water between all those fish," Bob said to the warrior.

Under the streetlight, from different angles, the skin of the fish was crystalline. Blue and salmon, silver and green, blue and salmon, silver and green, but infinitely more.

Four of them, lying side by side on the flatbed, while the fisherman asked: where are you finding them, how much are you getting, where are you selling them? There was a whole lot of water between those fish, and riddled into those skins.

What a strange way to approach this bluefin. What a strange way to love this prey.

It had been a ten-thousand-dollar day.

Bob walked by, smiling about the weekend warrior trailing hesitantly behind.

"You're a rich man," I said.

"I'm not a rich man," Bob replied. "I just have little debt. I'm rich because I have two good sons."

Up came the truck, and off they went to make the transfer.

(6)

A H I G H - V E L O C I T Y
L I F E S T Y L E

❦

B LUEFIN TUNA have evolved into high-mass, transoceanic, high-speed organisms. Though they weigh from 300 to more than 1,000 pounds and move through a medium eight hundred times denser than air, bluefin can swim in bursts of up to fifty miles per hour. Though they are six feet to ten feet in length, robust and muscular, they can beat their tail fins at frequencies of thirty cycles per second, an indistinguishable rate, a blur to the human eye.

Bluefin have the ideal streamlined shape—a fusiform body that tapers at both ends, thickest at a point one-third of the way from nose to lunate (crescent-moon-shaped) tail fin. The head is triangularly pyramidal—flat on the top, oblique on the sides. At the point of greatest depth are the first dorsal fin, the ventral fins, and the pectoral fins. The first dorsal fin folds back into a groove, to decrease drag. The pectorals can lie back into hollows on the side of the body. Like wings, they are used for gliding and turning, and to provide lift. A line drawn vertically from the dorsal to the ventral fins and horizontally from the tip of the nose through the eye to the fork of the tail fin would cross at the pivot point of the pectorals, at the center of gravity—one-third of the way along the fusiform body.

A bluefin's muscular power is concentrated upon the tail fin, which sweeps from side to side, providing 90 percent of the locomotive power—the thunniform mode of swimming. Most fish swim in the subcarangiform mode, flexing their bodies back and forth, creating

65

waves that produce acceleration. But the bluefin body is rigid, with a robust midsection tapering elegantly to a tail—a caudal peduncle—that is round and narrow. Rather than undulate, the thunniform swimmer oscillates, moving its sickle-shaped tail fin like a bird beating its wings, progressing like a boat with a propeller. The tail fin is rigid, unlike the brushy fins of other fish; prehistoric fishermen in Japan used the fin rays of the bluefin for spearheads.

The musculature of most fish is arranged in a geodesic interplay of rows and bundles and opposing cones that contract to create waves of increasing amplitude—a lateral orientation for a flip-flop movement. Bluefin muscle is also highly geodesic. The vast musculature, though, focuses its power not laterally but to the rear, upon an elaborate bundle of tendons passing through the caudal peduncle like a high-power cable, attaching to the base of the tail fin.

The caudal peduncle is also machined with pulleys and levers. Though the spine is rigid, the tail is double-jointed. Thus the lunate fin can vary its angle of attack for optimum efficiency, turning slightly inward, say, after the tail sweeps outward. There are also two caudal keels—bones which look like small lateral fins and which function as pulleys, increasing the leverage of the lateral tendons upon the tail fin. The keels converge at the fork of the tail fin, directing a high-pressure jet across the middle of the fin. This reduces turbulence at the top of the fin and improves lift. The lifting force of a lunate tail fin is a product of its "aspect ratio," the relationship of span of fin to its total area—the tall, triangular sail. A bluefin has the highest aspect ratio among the thunniform swimmers.

The pyramidal head consists of elongated cells that form a hard surface or "corselet." The eyes have adipose, fatty lids that also reduce turbulence. Their nearly spherical lenses can focus on objects both near and far. The brain, large as a man's thumb, tightly enclosed in a bony box, warmer than the surrounding water, is remarkable for the enormously developed optical lobe.

The bluefin has a large heart designed to work as a high-pressure pump. Tuna have large blood volumes, with the highest proportion of oxygen known among fishes, and a concentration of hemoglobin as high as that of humans. The gill surface area of the tuna is the highest, per unit, among fishes, a respiratory area that also approaches that of humans. Since fast swimming requires substantial energy, it follows that the metabolic rates of tuna are also the highest known among fish.

Bluefin are passive or "ram" ventilators—a mode of respiration for the perpetually moving. Even at basal or resting phase, tuna are moving at from one to two body lengths per second. As they swim with open mouths, a rush of water passes through the gills and then streams along the sides. Grooves along the tongue direct the flow of water, and when the tuna are moving at speed, with pectorals folded at the hollows, these grooves help to provide lift. The stream of water along their sides also reduces turbulence, increasing the streamline effect. And the ram of water through the gills serves the high-oxygen, high-metabolism needs of the bluefin's high-velocity lifestyle.

Fish have two kinds of muscle, distinct from each other. Dark muscle is highly vascularized and tends to work aerobically, processing food by oxidation. Light muscle is less vascularized and metabolizes anaerobically, altering glucose by means of fermentation. In tuna, dark muscle operates continuously, contracting to propel the fish during its steady-state, cruising phase of swimming. Light muscle comes into play during high-speed, or burst, swimming. While dark muscle tends to function like a slow-burning flame, light muscle tends to explode, and to exhaust quickly.

In most fish, the dark muscle runs along the side, just underneath the skin. It's an arrangement well suited for the subcarangiform swimmer, making its switching undulations back and forth. Tuna, however, in developing the thunniform mode of swimming, internalized the dark muscle. Rather than a strip of muscle under the surface, the tuna has a larger mass of dark muscle situated in a broad band between the backbone and the skin, running along the midplane of the body. This dark muscle, directed at the tail fin, provides the continuous contractions that propel the tuna at one or two body lengths per second, at four to five miles per hour.

The vast majority of fish are ectothermic, with bodies at the temperature of the water around them. Bluefin tuna, however, are endothermic, or warm-blooded, able to maintain body temperatures between 77 and 86 degrees Fahrenheit while inhabiting waters between 45 and 86 degrees, from the Gulf of Mexico to Norway. They do this by means of a system of cross-current heat exchangers which capture and retain the heat produced by the dark muscle. These heat exchangers are called the *rete mirabile*, which means "wonderful net."

Water is a difficult medium from which to satisfy the demands of the highly oxygenated. It contains thirty times less oxygen than air, yet it has three thousand times the capacity to absorb heat. When blood moves through the dark muscles of the fish it rises in temperature by about one or two degrees. The blood flows into the gills through thin and elongated cells. Coming in near contact with the water in order to absorb oxygen, all the heat is lost.

In most fish the blood flows below the spine and radiates outward to the muscles, returning along the same central pathway. Tuna reverse the system. Their blood flows just under the skin, and then branches into the muscles. Tuna have four pairs of subcutaneous arteries, a pair above and below the dark muscle bands, on each side.

Fine networks of vessels, each a tenth of a millimeter thick, branch off to form the *rete mirabile*. In a rete, cold blood coming from the surface flows next to warm blood coming from the muscles. There are many surfaces of contact along hundreds of thousands of vessels, thin enough for diffusion of heat but thick enough to prevent the diffusion of oxygen. The system is so efficient that nearly 98 percent of the muscular heat is shunted back into the system.

Warm blood allowed for niche expansion (the bluefin tuna, a tropical fish in essence, ranges into cold waters to feed on underexploited food sources). Warm blood also allows for faster swimming, since a muscle ten degrees warmer can contract three times as fast. Thus, a fish like the bluefin can pursue faster prey such as squid, mackerel, and herring. Bluefin also have retes to warm their stomachs, and so digestion is faster, another advantage for a fish that feeds seasonally and opportunistically.

Dark muscle operates continuously for sustained swimming. Light muscle, forming two-thirds of body weight, comes into play during burst swimming. Then the fish approaches velocities of twenty body lengths per second.

Light muscle in tuna creates unusually high activity—the most intense anaerobic glycolysis known in nature. One enzyme (lactate dehydrogenase) appears in the highest presence known—an average of 5,500 units per tenth of gram of muscle, while dolphin muscle, at the same temperature, contains only 600 units of LDH. Such high levels of activity would seem so explosive that the fish could cook itself, but tuna somehow are able to shunt off the heat.

Another enzyme that appears in tuna light muscle converts energy at levels similar to the flight muscles of hummingbirds and bumblebees, also creatures with high-velocity lifestyles, oscillating their locomotive organs—lunate tail, diaphanous wings—at rates that blur recognition.

7

BUSINESS
RELATIONSHIPS

JAPANESE FISHERMEN have caught bluefin in their coastal
waters for centuries. As Japanese fishing fleets ranged throughout
the world's oceans, they discovered that Mediterranean and Gulf of
Maine bluefin had a higher fat content than Pacific bluefin. Japanese
fishermen pursued these fish, and as taste for exotic raw fish caught
on and the postwar economy grew, demand for these tuna increased.

In the two or three days from the time a bluefin is landed in New
England and sold on the floor of a Japanese auction house it is repeatedly appraised. Prospective buyers look long and hard at the fish.
They contemplate its condition, discuss its color, shape, and quality.
They touch, press, and poke the skin, they run their hands along the
side and down the tail. They hold cuts of meat up to the light. They
rub, bend, and squeeze to assess the oil within.

In Japan it can take up to twelve years to become a fish grader, or
technician. Japanese fish companies often send their technicians to
the United States to work on the docks with the American companies
they trade with. The technicians arrive in midseason and stay until
the quota is filled.

In 1992 TriCoastal Seafood Cooperative in Newburyport, at the
head of the Merrimack River north of Boston, was selling its bluefin
tuna to Tsukiji Toichi Uoichiba, the fourth-largest seafood trading
company in Japan. Toichi, with 310 employees, bought seafood from
fishermen and 4,000 trade houses throughout the world and resold it

to 1,600 wholesalers and dealers in Japan. In 1989 it had a gross income of 150 billion yen, and a net profit of 961 million yen. During the 1992 season, Toichi sent its head auctioneer, Ryozo Moriwaka, to Newburyport.

Bob Campbell, the operations manager at TriCoastal, didn't know why the head auctioneer had come to work with him, but he was pleased about it. Campbell saw Moriwaka's stay as an opportunity to learn how to grade fish, to learn how to think like the Japanese. Halfway through the 1992 season, he thought he was coming closer. He had been told that Ryozo Moriwaka was a famous grader in Japan, and after Moriwaka arrived in Newburyport TriCoastal kept his presence a secret, so as not to offend other companies also dealing with Toichi. But then one afternoon some Japanese technicians dropped by the dock, and his cover was blown. Moriwaka, in turn, said that TriCoastal was a famous company in Japan.

TriCoastal was formed in 1973 by a group of tuna fishermen who wanted to ship their bluefin to Japan. The board of directors consisted of several dozen fishermen. In its first decade TriCoastal was open only during the summer, but in 1983 the company bought a space on Newburyport Harbor and began to operate year round, selling striped bass, cod, flounder, and shrimp. TriCoastal sold bluefin and monkfish livers to the Japanese, and bait and ice to fishermen.

One morning in early August a crew was at work on the dock at TriCoastal. Sparky Jahnren, the dock manager, was running a forklift, and four others helped him pack bluefin into coffins. Nine fish had come in the day before, ranging from 275 to 650 pounds. When Jahnren drove up to the big brine tank, a helper reached into the icy water, lifted a fish, and put the canvas strap over the tines of the forklift. Once the fish was in the air, one of the crew took its temperature, and if it had come with an elevated temperature, from a long struggle, they took a core sample of the meat with a tube called a *sashibo*. Sometimes during the fight the meat burned and changed color close to the backbone. "Ya-ke," the Japanese called this condition.

The crew made a tail cut. They set the fish into the coffin, and packed the visceral cavity with ice. They pressed rice paper onto the

71

skin to preserve color—the better the color, the more valuable the fish—shoveled ice over the paper, wrapped plastic sheets around the fish, and tied them off at the ends. They set down an insulating cover and the coffin lid. Then they sealed the entire package with plastic straps, and loaded it on a truck bound for Logan Airport in Boston.

The tail cuts, a row of crescent-shaped steaks, were set out on a table in the sun. Notebooks in hand, Ryozo Moriwaka and Bob Campbell leaned over the table, studying them. This was the second grading. The first had come the day before when they gave the fisherman a price. A third grading would come when the fish arrived at Toichi in Tokyo, and a fourth before the auction at Tsukiji market.

Sparky Jahnren came up, sliced off a piece of the tuna, and ate it raw—he, too, was trying to learn the Japanese way. Ryozo told him he hadn't paid for his meal, and laughed. Flies darted around. A mound of flies had been caught in a big screen trap a few feet away, near the entrance to a walk-in cooler.

Ryozo would hold a cut at arm's length, move it through the air, and then pull it up tight for a close look. He would pinch the meat, or bend it, then look to see how it responded. He ran a finger over a cut, traced a line on a piece of cardboard and then studied the line for oil. He looked from steak to steak, down the row, with fixed concentration. He turned the cuts over and looked some more. He did not taste them. He flipped the pages of his notebook and made marks. Bob Campbell, working beside him, kept notes too, but he was more laid back about it. Bob was an affable man, bearded, white-blond, and round—as a tuna should be, he said. Later, when the grading was done, he would compare their marks.

They gave out four marks per fish: for freshness, color, fat, and shape. A typical line of grades might be: B+, B, B−, B−. Rarely did a fish get an A grade.

Freshness was determined by sight and by touch. This first grade was based on the whole fish. The technician looked at the skin, to see how the colors had lasted. He touched the skin to feel for its resilience, the quality of fat underneath, and the condition of muscle. The ability to judge freshness came from the experience of looking at hundreds of fish, Ryozo said.

Preserving freshness was the work of the fisherman, Bob said. Those who had brine tanks filled with water and ice reached port with the freshest fish and got the best prices. Those who didn't have tanks but who bled and gutted the fish, and packed it with ice and kept it cool in a tuna-keeper bag, got the next best. Some boats processed the fish, covered it with a wet blanket, and hosed it down. Some covered the fish and kept it out of the sun. Others didn't process the fish at all, and left it in the sun. They got next to nothing.

The second grade was for color. A light shade of red was preferable, one that was translucent rather than cloudy. When Ryozo held the meat to the light, he was looking for clarity. When he pinched the meat he was testing durability of color. Early in the season, before a fish accumulated fat, it had water in the meat, and this water could be pressed out. Water in the meat meant that the color would change in a day or two, probably before auction time, and the technician had to anticipate this change in the grade and bid.

Defining the preferred shade of red was an elusive matter. It was very, very difficult to say, Ryozo said. He later solved the problem by pointing to a Japanese calendar in the office. One row of lettering was a bright shade of red, and this was good. Another row was a red with a bit of brown in it, and this was not good.

"White plate," Ryozo said.

"What?"

"It goes on a white plate."

When Japanese people eat, Ryozo said, the first thing they do is look. The Japanese, he said, eat with their eyes. And in Japan red-and-white is an auspicious color combination. This contributed to the mystique of bluefin tuna, and *maguro*—red tuna meat.

Fat was the third grade, though fat actually played through all four categories. Fat determined the texture of the meat—coarse or smooth—which affected appearance. The presence of fat played into the lucidity of the color, and its stability—if a meat was well supplied with fat the color lasted. Fat determined taste (a worker who had sampled both lean and fat bluefin said the difference was like that between hamburger and steak). Fat accumulated first under the skin, and then built inward. When technicians examined a cut for fat they looked for marbling, the striated lines of white built up between the bands and whorls of red muscle. A meat that was marbled all the way through received the highest grades.

As with humans, the presence of fat determined the shape—the fourth grade. A bluefin tended to become round in the middle and then to fill out along the tail. A fish caught early in the season had a flat tail. A well-fed bluefin had a round tail, and a fish that was round all the way down brought the highest prices.

Grades, in combination with market conditions, determined price. It was always a gamble, Ryozo said.

He had been grading fish for twenty-three years. It took a long time to become a technician in Japan, but he was teaching Bob in two years. Ryozo said he was teaching experience. He wanted Mister Bob of TriCoastal to have the benefit of his long experience in the business.

"I like Mister Bob," Ryozo said.

Mister Bob was indeed likable. He had a solidity about him, a kind of gravity that set one at ease. After college he had gotten a job as a mate on a tuna boat. He had then worked on draggers and gillnetters, fishing for tuna in the summers, to break the monotony of working with nets. After eight years on a gillnetter his hands gave out, so Bob looked around for other work. He felt lucky to have found something in the fishing industry. At TriCoastal he was a kind of middleman, a negotiator between the fishermen he had worked with and the Japanese businessmen he was getting to know.

Both men talked of relationships. Bob Campbell said that he always preferred doing business face-to-face. He had discovered that this was especially important to the Japanese. Bob believed that by working with Ryozo Moriwaka he was learning more than the grading of fish—he was learning about relationships. Several times that day Ryozo mentioned that the tuna business was built on relationships between the Japanese customer and the American supplier. "All business is personal relationships, don't you think?" he said, after the grading was done and the wait began for boats to come in.

• • •

IN MIDAFTERNOON a fish arrived on a boat called *I Don't Know*. It was a chum fish, taken by a boat that had been on Jeffreys Ledge, a string of hills twenty-five miles offshore running from Newburyport to Kennebunkport. The Jeffreys Ledge fleet was perhaps the most productive tuna fleet in the Gulf of Maine, but it was one of many tuna fleets, and the *I Don't Know* was one of many hundreds of boats tossing up to 200 pounds of cut herring or mackerel overboard each day—an offering of tons of fish food that, some fishermen claimed, had trained the bluefin to show up like goldfish at feeding time.

Ryozo put on some boots and jumped on deck. His method was to look at the fish for at least a minute, to gather impressions. ("First tuna looking is feeling only," Ryozo said.) Thumbs at his belt, Ryozo watched while others watched him, curious about his approach or anticipating the grade his assessment would bring. Then Ryozo crouched and examined the fish more closely, touching the skin, running his hand along the tail. He took out a knife and made a cut just above the caudal keel. The fishermen looked over the tail cut, and then Ryozo climbed up to the dock and joined Bob Campbell. They turned the cut from hand to hand, held it up, squeezed it, set it on the table, looked some more, and made their marks.

Ryozo gave freshness a B+, because the fish had been packed with ice and kept covered. Color was a bit watery, and he gave it a B−. He gave fat a B−, and shape as well, because of the flat tail. The fish was a big giant, more than 700 pounds, and it was too early in the season for it to have accumulated much fat.

Bob had been more generous about the fish's color and given it a B, but his other grades were identical to Ryozo's. Off they went to the office to make a conference call to New York. The man on the other end was a "Japanese gentleman," whom Bob addressed only as "Sir." Bob spoke in English, Ryozo in Japanese. They told of the boat, and of the size, the shape, the color, and freshness of the fish, and eventually arrived at a price of $9 a pound. The fish was too lean, and too big, and the market in Tokyo was too active to merit more. Bob went out and told the captain of the *I Don't Know*, who got aboard his boat and left to get other bids from buyers further up the harbor.

A second fish came in on a TriCoastal truck. It had been caught on a boat called *Stormy Weather*, and picked up at a port in New Hampshire. The *Stormy Weather* showed up with a fish nearly every day, Bob said. The grades for this one were B+, B−, B−, B−: good freshness, watery color, low fat, and flat tail. Another conference call followed, and even though the fish was lean they gave a price of $9.50 because it was small, 314 pounds, and so would be easier to sell to a restaurant in Japan—and because the boat had been so productive.

The captain of the *I Don't Know* then returned to take the $9 price. Campbell lifted the fish from the boat with a chain hoist, and for a while it hung over the dock for a viewing. The fish was about nine feet tall. Suddenly fifteen people arrived, and soon there were thirty. Some had cameras, including the captain, a shirtless, bearded, tattooed, very happy, nut-brown man. His family showed up. They took photos of the fish, of the captain, of the captain and mate.

The fish was lowered to a hand truck and Ryozo and the crew went to work, using an electric saw to cut off the head, the tail, and the pectoral fins. Gore flew through the air. They picked away at the inside of the visceral cavity and hosed it out. They laid the fish on a scale, and it weighed in at 641 pounds. The captain, for his day's work, would get a check for $5,769.

They carried the fish to the brine tank, and by the time they had lowered it into the icy water the crowd had drifted away.

A lull followed. The crew cleaned the dock. Fishermen stopped into the office. One said the tuna were now milling, which was bad for chummers and harpooners but good for seiners, once they got started. An idle spotter pilot said the harpooners hadn't been able to get out, but when they did they'd clean up. Another fisherman said the bluefin were feeding on butterfish, jumping right up through them. Bob Campbell said that, judging by the size and condition of the fish on the *I Don't Know*, a new school of bluefin had shown up at Jeffreys Ledge.

Ryozo kept busy, in and out of the office, on the dock. He was perpetually busy, and he smoked Winstons halfway down. He appeared to be shy, so much so that when I first approached him he had darted away into the office. Our relationship, the one we'd developed, was a kind of hit-and-run affair—I'd say something and he'd answer and run off. But later I saw that the shyness was also caution. Ryozo felt relaxed around the fishermen. He called to them and joked with them. When the owner of the *Stormy Weather* arrived, Ryozo greeted him cheerfully and with a full swing of his arm slapped him on the rear, saying with a laugh, "You're getting too fat!" This stopped the fisherman in his tracks, and he stood slackjawed while Ryozo disappeared into the cooler.

Sparky Jahnren arrived from Maine with a medium bluefin, dressed weight 190 pounds. B, B−, C+, B−.

A dragger called the *Paulie Girl* arrived with another big fish. Ryozo and Bob studied it, took a temperature (20 degrees Centigrade), made a tail cut. The fish had been bled, iced, and kept covered, but it was another very large and lean fish with a flat tail. They gave it grades of B, B−, C+, C+, and went off to the office.

"Very skinny belly," Ryozo said.

Meanwhile, a fax had arrived from Tokyo with the information that Japanese purse seine boats had unloaded 500 pieces of Pacific bluefin. After a conversation with the Japanese gentleman, Bob Campbell came out of his office with a price of $6 per pound. The captain left to try his luck elsewhere.

"To tell the truth," Bob said as the boat pulled away, "if he gets a better price, that's okay. If he comes back, then there'll be some money going through my company, a break-even price, but that's about all.

"Was that a good fish, Mister Zo?" Bob asked, with a smile.

"No-o-o-o," Ryozo growled.

"It just takes so much feeding to get fat going through a fish that size."

Other buyers were even less willing to take a risk on the big lean fish, so the *Paulie Girl* returned to TriCoastal. The crew lowered the hoist, fastened a tail rope, and raised the tuna above the dock.

"It's a shame to let it go at that price," the captain said. Bob said he knew.

The captain walked about anxiously. The fish had dressed out at 652 pounds, and he had made $3,912, but there was the mate's share, and taxes, perhaps a boat payment, and fuel, and dock fees, and bait, and food, and on it went—and how many days had passed before he caught this one? Certainly, on the way in, the dragger captain had not been thinking $4,000, but $10,000. All the fishermen knew the stories about the big-money fish—the fish, for instance, that had recently gone to the auction on just the right day and brought $41.50 a pound.

The bluefin hung by its tail over the dock, and the setting sun cast a red glow on its silver body. Suspended by a chain, reflecting the light, the ovoid fish looked like a great jewel.

It seemed odd that all this narrowed down to a white plate.

Bob Campbell knew the captain had been disappointed. That was the hard part of the business, though he'd gotten better at it. He gave out information, explained as much as he could, passed on what he learned. He was in the middle, but he was there for the fisherman.

This had been a good year so far, Bob Campbell said. TriCoastal had bought 160 bluefin so far. Of those, a hundred had been good enough to ship off to Japan.

8

THE SEINERS AND
THE MARKETS

THE EARLIEST fishing for bluefin tuna may have been with harpoons along shores with deep dropoffs. Four thousand years ago in the Mediterranean the Phoenicians set traps made of palm branches stuck into the sandy bottom, and fish herded into small spaces were then harpooned. Haul seines, or dragnets, were pulled by hand or held between a crew and a small boat offshore. Purse seines—nets set in circles and then cinched at the bottom—were developed centuries ago for small fish. In the nineteenth century, schooners functioned as offshore purse seiners, and the crews used rowboats to set the nets around schools—mackerel purse seiners replaced the traditional handline mackerel fishery off of Cape Cod and on the Grand Banks. In the twentieth century the technique became motorized, quicker in the wrap of the prey, and the boats became bigger, able to set on as many as 50 tons of fish at a time, and planes were used to locate the schools. The first known purse seine fishery for bluefin tuna was in Yugoslavia in 1929.

The fisherman Salvatore Ingrande emigrated from Sicily to the United States in 1917, and made his home in the tightly knit Italian fishing community of San Diego. His son Leonard worked around the docks as a boy, unloading boats in exchange for fish, and then, during the summer of 1943, at the age of thirteen, worked as a crewman on a purse seiner, fishing for tuna and mackerel off the coast of California. After fishing trips, which would end just before the full moon when fish didn't come to the surface, the captain would sit at a table and divide the money from the catch—two days before and two days after the full moon the crew would mend the nets and set them in tubs to cure. In 1948 Leonard had a good year, making $8,000, and so at age eighteen he bought a thirty-year-old boat and went into partnership with his father. They worked together, seining, through the 1950s.

Leonard's future partner, Roger Hillhouse, was in the Navy during the Korean War, stationed at a base in Santa Barbara. Roger had been a lookout on a purse seiner, standing in the mast, scanning the water for fish—like harpooning, seining is a surface fishery and schools must be sighted before they're set upon. Roger knew what it was like to watch the water all day long. Working in Navy communications, he often switched the radio over to a channel used by two spotter pilots working out of Santa Barbara. They were, as far as Roger knew, the first spotter pilots in California. Listening to them lead the boats, describe the schools, and assist with the sets, Roger thought, that's the way to do it. He decided that he would become a spotter pilot.

Spotting fish with planes had been practiced at least as early as 1947 in the menhaden fishery in the Gulf of Mexico. The sardine fishery in California used a plane to locate schools, but the pilot didn't lead the boats, merely reported to them. The swordfish harpoon fishery of New England used spotter planes, and some of those pilots later moved over to the bluefin tuna harpoon fishery. In California in the 1950s there were ready pairings between the tuna purse seiners, pursuing fast-moving schools of skipjack, albacore, and yellowfin, and the fleet of thirty to forty pilots that worked for them. Roger Hillhouse formed a group with seven other pilots, the Flying Fishermen, and they worked on a freelance basis for a number of boats, including the one owned by Leonard and Salvatore Ingrande.

When Salvatore Ingrande died in 1960 Leonard and Roger Hillhouse became partners. Roger, the lookout by nature, was always searching for new grounds. He read a Bureau of Commercial Fisheries bulletin which stated that the Atlantic coast had a readily available and underexploited population of bluefin tuna. A government fisheries vessel had made impressive sets in the Great South Channel off Nantucket. Since 1958 in Cape Cod Bay a small seiner called the *Silver Mink*, captained by Manny Phillips, had been netting 500 to 600 tons of school bluefin per season. Phillips was filling his boat with single sets of the net. He was coming upon schools too big to set on. He was giving fish away. He was selling school bluefin for five cents a pound to a cannery in Maine. Roger and Leonard both knew that only a puddle of the population came that close to shore, and that there must be huge schools further out. Roger flew across the Gulf of Mexico and up the East Coast to have a look. He liked what he saw. Leonard Ingrande moved his family to New Bedford, and in 1962 took his boat, the *North Queen*, through the Panama Canal to Massachusetts.

Ingrande and the *North Queen* caught 400 tons of bluefin tuna that year, and 100 tons of skipjack tuna. Another fisherman, Frank Cyganowski, in his first year as a seiner captain, making his first set off Martha's Vineyard, hauled in sixteen tons of sixty-pound bluefin. The fish were sold to Cape Cod Tuna, the cannery in Eastport, Maine, for five cents a pound, and so Frank Cyganowski's first set was worth $1,600. Since the canneries wanted only young bluefin tuna, with its lighter meat, giant and even medium bluefin were worthless on the market—except for the occasional giant sold to Italian or Portuguese buyers.

By 1963 word had spread. Much larger seiners, after finishing their season in the Pacific, unloaded their catches at canneries in Puerto Rico and headed up the East Coast. A superseiner arrived from the West African coast. Four Canadian seiners with capacities of 1,000 tons each began to work the stocks. From 1962 to 1970, a fleet of two dozen seiners made yearly catches of from 6,000 to 10,000 metric tons of tuna. Into the 1970s the landings continued at between 4,000 and 6,000 metric tons yearly.

A thousand metric tons of eighty-pound bluefin is 27,500 fish. Gradually, as the schools thinned out, the larger seiners left. Leonard Ingrande, Frank Cyganowski, and Roger Hillhouse continued to work, though the price of fish fell so low, down to a penny a pound, that Leonard ran a boatyard and rebuilt boats to supplement his income. When Cape Cod Tuna went bankrupt in 1968, the three men bought the cannery's three boats, and then sold two, which gave them the ownership of one, the *AA Ferrante*, free and clear. That left the partners with two boats, though in time they'd add a third. It took three boats to support a plane, Leonard figured. In 1968, unable to find enough school bluefin to support the crew, they agreed to catch two loads of giant bluefin to sell in Italy. They caught 100 tons of giants on each boat—six hundred fish—and gave everything after expenses to the crew.

The three partners worked with Frank Mather in his tagging studies, and Mather tagged hundreds of fish on the purse seine boats. In 1970 they caught two of five school bluefin that had been tagged in the Bay of Biscay, one released in 1968 and the other in 1969. The fishing improved for the three partners in 1969, and they caught 240 tons of school bluefin in the two boats. The tag retrievals and the improved fishing seemed sure evidence that there had been a major transatlantic migration of the fish they were working.

It did appear that the seiners working off New England in the 1960s and 1970s had made reductions in the bluefin stock that were felt throughout the North Atlantic Ocean. After 1966, medium bluefin disappeared from the Gulf of Maine. They disappeared from fisheries in Europe, as well, until Italian fishermen began taking them again in 1975.

The catch of a recreational bluefin fishery off Newfoundland declined from 635 fish yearly to fewer than a hundred fish after 1972. A sport fishery off Prince Edward Island declined from 1,048 fish in 1974 to 343 fish the next year. An international tournament that had been held in Nova Scotia since the 1930s ceased after 1975.

Off the coast of France, a live-bait fishery in the Bay of Biscay dropped from 2,500 tons a year to 100 tons yearly throughout the 1960s and 1970s.

A Norwegian purse seine fishery that had averaged 10,000 tons per year in the 1950s landed only 100 tons in 1972 and 1973.

A German and Danish handline fishery in the North Sea that landed 2,400 tons in 1952 dropped to 200 tons in 1962, and only one fish was caught in 1963 and 1964.

The central Mediterranean trap fisheries in Italy, Tunisia, and Libya took only a few hundred fish after 1972 and 1973. It was thought that the fisheries had become commercially extinct, and that the fish itself might soon become extinct, until the traps began producing again in the 1980s.

Portuguese traps caught one fish in 1971. The two Moroccan traps left in operation caught twelve fish in 1973. The trap in Barbate, Spain, which averaged 20,000 fish per year between 1946 and 1961, took only 388 fish in 1972. In 1975, however, the catch in the Barbate trap increased to 1,842 fish, a trend that would continue into the 1980s.

Fisheries other than the American purse seiners contributed to the decline. Purse seining for bluefin of all sizes—including sardine-size fish—was practiced throughout the Mediterranean. In 1972 a fleet of modern Italian seiners began fishing the spawning and post-spawning giants, and the young of the year. Though laws had once prohibited the capture of young bluefin in Italian waters, catches had increased steadily since the 1920s.

IN 1956 Japanese longline trawlers began to fish in the Atlantic Ocean, first in equatorial waters, later expanding into tropical and temperate waters in both hemispheres. Japanese longliners typically set lines fifty miles long with two thousand hooks per line. By the peak year of 1965 a fleet of several hundred boats was setting 100 million hooks. At first they targeted yellowfin and albacore tuna, and the catches were landed at ports in the Atlantic. But in the 1970s, with increased demand for tuna, target species changed to northern and southern bluefin and to bigeye tuna, which inhabit colder waters. Japanese longliners entered the Mediterranean Sea in 1972, though after 1974 they stopped fishing there during the spawning season.

In 1974, because of the alarming decline in catch rates, the National Marine Fisheries Service was preparing to declare the bluefin tuna a threatened species. The state of Massachusetts began to regulate the bluefin tuna fishery, but its regulations were supplanted in

1975 by those established by ICCAT—the International Commission for the Conservation of Atlantic Tunas.

The previous year, unannounced, uninvited, Roger Hillhouse and Leonard Ingrande showed up at the annual ICCAT meeting in Madrid. They told the delegates that it was time to place a quota on the seiners—on themselves. They also proposed a minimum size of 15 to 20 pounds. The ICCAT delegates were surprised, but ignored them until Frank Mather stepped in. Together they established a 1,100-ton voluntary quota; for the rest of the decade, Ingrande, Hillhouse, and Cyganowski stopped fishing when they'd reached their limit.

The purse seine quota was lowered to 1,000 tons, then 800, and in 1982, after a contentious ICCAT meeting, to 150 tons. The seiners and other fishermen formed the East Coast Tuna Association to fight for higher quotas. The next year, after a political battle that would continue into the 1990s, the seiner quota was set at 382 tons.

B Y   T H E N the bluefin tuna fishery in New England had undergone remarkable changes, and Leonard Ingrande, Roger Hillhouse, and Frank Cyganowski had all played central roles.

After Cape Cod Tuna went bankrupt in 1968 there was no longer a cannery in Eastport, Maine, so the seiners sold their fish to Bumblebee Tuna in Cambridge, Maryland. At that time some of the Japanese longliners were also selling albacore tuna to Bumble Bee, and one day a representative from Nichoro Fishing Company saw a load of school bluefin that Frank Cyganowski had caught. The man wanted to know if Cyganowski could catch giant bluefin.

Bumble Bee then arranged a meeting between Leonard Ingrande and Roger Hillhouse and a group from Nichoro. After dinner, Ingrande and Hillhouse and the Japanese men went to a motel room, where they cut up a school bluefin for a sashimi tasting. They arranged that a Japanese longliner would leave the Canary Islands and go to New Bedford to clear customs. The boat, *Kuroshio Maru 37*, had a capacity of 300 tons and was capable of freezing 10 tons of fish per day to minus 45 degrees Centigrade. In August 1971,

Frank Cyganowski led *Kuroshio Maru 37* through the Cape Cod Canal and into Cape Cod Bay, where it anchored.

The air turned red that day, Frank thought. Listening in to channel 15 on the radio, he heard what sounded like a revolution going on among the fishermen in Cape Cod Bay.

Frank got on the radio. He said he wasn't leaving, and the longliner wasn't either. The air turned redder. Then Frank said he would pay ten cents a pound, guaranteed, for giant bluefin tuna.

The air turned a little less red. Without knowing it, Frank Cyganowski had blurred forever the distinction between sportfishing and commercial fishing for bluefin tuna. Until that point, after you'd caught a bluefin and hung it up for everyone to see, the big problem had been how to get rid of it. You might get a few cents a pound—the fish were used for cat food—if you could sell them. Now Cape Cod Bay fishermen could get ten cents a pound for each bluefin delivered to *Kuroshio Maru 37*. Unknown to them, Frank Cyganowski—perhaps the first American bluefin middleman—was getting twenty-one cents a pound for those fish, and he didn't even have to handle them. It was the beginning of a somewhat cooperative and sometimes friendly relationship between the seiners and the new commercial bluefin tuna fishery in Cape Cod Bay and other waters. Sometimes, for example, if Roger Hillhouse found a school of fish and the seiner couldn't get to them, he'd let others know where the fish were.

Kuroshio Maru 37 left Cape Cod Bay in October and arrived in Japan with its load of frozen bluefin at the end of the year. The next summer Nichoro sent *Kuroshio Maru 32*, which could freeze 15 tons a day. The price that year was forty cents a pound. In 1973 Nichoro's price was as much as $1 per pound, and a fish that had brought $40 two years earlier could now bring $1,000. In 1973 other freezer ships anchored up in New England—the *Tat Sumi Maru 25*, in Portland, paid twenty cents to $1 per pound. Leonard Ingrande, now working on the *Sea Rover*, came into Cape Cod Bay in September to fish with Frank Cyganowski.

In 1974, two sportfishermen on Cape Cod shipped a single bluefin, fresh, to Tokyo by airfreight, and a new era in the bluefin tuna fishery began. Atlantic Coast Fisheries in Sandwich began shipping bluefin by air. The owner of Fresh Water Seafood in Boston flew to Japan and hired a bellhop to be his interpreter in negotiations with Japanese buyers. Fishermen in Newburyport formed TriCoastal Seafood Co-op. Companies, and buyers, proliferated.

In 1982 in New England the going price for bluefin tuna was between $2 and $3 a pound. Over the next four years it rose slightly. Then, in 1988, the price shot up to $12 to $14 per pound. The National Marine Fisheries Service issued 23,000 permits that year.

There were two causes for the increase: the exchange rate between the yen and the dollar, and developments in the Japanese tuna market.

I N 1971, as *Kuroshio Maru 37* arrived in Japan with a load of Cape Cod bluefin, leaders of the major non-Communist countries met secretly in Washington to establish a new system of currency exchange rates. President Nixon called the new system "the most significant monetary agreement in the history of the world."

It was a response to the collapse of the gold standard, in which dollars could be exchanged for gold. That system, established during World War II, had pegged international exchange rates to the dollar. Dollars, backed by $25 billion in gold reserves, were the basis of the free world's international monetary network. By 1971 foreign governments were holding $30 billion in U.S. dollars, but U.S. gold stocks stood at only $10 billion. With the balance of trade and balance of payments rapidly shifting, President Nixon ended gold redemptions and established a 10 percent import surcharge—bringing on a monetary crisis that went unresolved until the December 1971 agreement.

By 1971 the values of currencies—in relation to the dollar—had become misaligned. The dollar was the pivotal point in the system, and other nations tended to devalue their currency in relation to it. This made American products more expensive. Gradually the dollar became overvalued, and American products became less and less competitive. Due to inflation after 1965, huge deficits followed. While other countries could change the values of their currencies to stimulate their economies, the United States could not, because the dollar was the pivot point of the system, and the whole structure moved with it.

President Nixon changed all that.

On December 19, 1971, after the agreement, the price of gold was raised from $35 to $38 an ounce. Thus, the dollar was devalued by 8.75 percent. The 10 percent import surcharge was dropped.

Government officials predicted that 500,000 jobs would be created. The reasoning was that for every percentage point of devaluation an $800 million erasure of payments would result, due to the revaluation of currencies. Every billion dollars gained, they predicted, would bring 60,000 to 80,000 jobs. Therefore, the 8.75 percent revaluation would result in a total of approximately 500,000 new jobs, for an economic turnaround of 11 percent. This seemed an incredible manipulation, and was widely praised.

The currencies of the other countries taking part in the agreement correspondingly increased in value. No increase was greater than that of the yen of Japan, whose gross national product had grown fivefold during the 1960s. On December 19, 1971, Japanese money markets closed, and the Japanese cabinet approved a 16.88 percent upward revaluation of the yen. The exchange rate rose from 360 yen to the dollar to 308 yen to the dollar. It was the first readjustment of the yen since 1949, and the greatest economic shock Japan had suffered since World War II.

The idea was that the realignment of currencies would make Japanese products more expensive in the United States, and thus slow Japanese imports and the resulting imbalance of payments. Conversely, American products would become less expensive, and therefore more attractive in Japan, if trade barriers could be relaxed. That was the two-pronged approach to the problem of Japanese industry and competition—realign the currencies and break down trade barriers.

There was an advantage for the Japanese in this realignment, in that imported raw materials such as petroleum and food would become less costly. A 500-pound bluefin tuna priced at twenty-one cents a pound, for example, cost 37,800 yen on December 18, and 32,340 yen on the 19th. Carrying these currency realignments to Cape Cod Bay, a fisherman would have received $105 for that 500-pound bluefin before December 18, 1971, and $123 the day after.

This was just as President Nixon had intended.

During the next fourteen years, from 1971 to 1985, the relationship between the yen and the dollar changed only slightly. The imbalance of trade continued to grow, however, and more dollars than yen flowed overseas. In the fall of 1985, officials of the monetary world gathered again, this time at the Plaza Hotel in New York, and reached the Plaza Accord, which proposed a rapid strengthening of the yen as the best way to restore American competitiveness in the markets. Soon the value of the yen shot up to 200 yen per dollar. By mid-1987 the yen was at 150 per dollar. After the stock market crash of that October, the yen rose a bit more, and by the summer of 1988 the exchange rate stood at 125 yen per dollar.

The changes brought political peace for the Japanese in Washington. Japanese products again became more expensive while American products became less expensive in Japan, though trade barriers were still a problem. On the other hand, the rapid appreciation of the yen made it easier for Japanese companies to buy American companies, and to purchase technology and real estate. Japan quickly became the dominant economic power in Asia, and the largest donor of foreign aid in the world. Due to the strengthening of the yen, Japanese manufacturers, now investing great sums in new factories, were forced to become more efficient.

Japan also became the world's largest importer of tuna. By 1990 Japanese were consuming 800,000 tons of tuna a year—30 percent of world landings. The Japanese tuna fleet, fishing worldwide, was able to supply 690,000 tons per year between 1985 and 1990, a lot of fish but only 74 percent of demand. Consequently, imports swelled to $1 billion worth of tuna, bought from fisheries in sixty-one countries.

Japan is the only major market for raw fish—400,000 tons are consumed yearly. Thirty-five percent of the supply is imported, and the raw market is the only niche for U.S. fisheries. Bluefin tuna has the highest status on the raw market. Through the 1980s, with a growing preference for fresh gourmet food ("the fresh food rush"), increased levels of disposable income, and a desire for *maguro*, demand for bluefin tuna increased markedly.

Japanese landings of bluefin tuna had been quartered between 1981 and 1990, primarily because of declining catches in the northwest Pacific. Imports of fresh bluefin increased sixfold, to 3,000 tons during the same period. The United States was the leading supplier, shipping up to 600 tons of fresh bluefin per year from 1983 to 1986, and up to 900 tons per year from 1987 to 1990.

Meanwhile, average wholesale prices for bluefin had more than doubled, from 2,200 to 4,937 yen per kilogram. Because of exchange rates, these increases had amplified effects for the American bluefin tuna fishermen, especially those catching jumbo bluefin in New England. In 1983 a price of 2,200 yen per kilogram meant $4 per pound. By 1990, the price of bluefin had doubled, and the exchange rate had been halved. As a result, the price had more than quadrupled, to $18 per pound.

This too was just as the leaders at the Plaza Accord had intended. It could be said that the bluefin tuna fisherman in New England was the best example of improved trade and perhaps the most fortunate beneficiary of the economic manipulations and currency realignments that took place from 1971 to 1991.

IN 1992, the stock assessment for bluefin tuna in the western Atlantic Ocean looked particularly gloomy. Fisheries scientists working for the National Marine Fisheries Service at the Southeast Fisheries Center in Miami had calculated that the population of giant bluefin had dwindled to from 20,000 to 22,000 spawning-age fish, a drop of 90 percent over twenty years. The stock was in danger, both economically and genetically. The Southeast Center urged ICCAT to cut the bluefin quota in half.

The fishermen responded with disbelief. They were sitting on a golden egg, and their views were biased accordingly. But they claimed that there were a great many more than 22,000 giant bluefin left. It was possible to see that many fish on a single day in the Gulf of Maine. They'd seen them, and so had their spotter pilots.

From 1983 through 1991 the western Atlantic quota, shared by Canadian, Japanese, and American fishermen, had been 2,660 tons, but in 1992 there was a 10 percent reduction, to 2,404 tons, after calls for stricter limits by conservation organizations.

In 1992 the European fishery for bluefin had recovered, especially in the Mediterranean. Operating without quotas, fishing for bluefin of all sizes and in all stages, Mediterranean fishermen were harvesting more than 27,000 metric tons of bluefin per year without apparent harm. Fishermen in the western Atlantic, looking at their counterparts to the east, had begun to question their own role in the conservation of the Atlantic stocks.

In 1992, after the 10 percent reduction, the quota for purse seiners fishing for bluefin tuna was at 301 metric tons. The seiners had given up fishing on school bluefin a decade earlier (though they'd been replaced by a recreational fishery on the Middle Atlantic coast). A limited-entry system had been established, and only five purse seine boats could take bluefin tuna in the western Atlantic. Leonard Ingrande and Roger Hillhouse owned three of them.

There were many who thought Leonard Ingrande and the seiners should be eliminated, especially with the declining stocks. Some didn't even use the conservation argument, and just said that one person shouldn't be making that much money, which Leonard Ingrande figured was the real reason people were attacking him. He hadn't heard these things, he said, when the fish were twenty cents a pound.

In May 1992, he flew out to San Diego. It was hard to see the waterfront, to see the canneries gone, the heart of the fishing community changed so. Leonard took his mother to church, and there he noticed someone he'd known as a boy. Leonard went up to him.

"Do you remember me?" Leonard asked. The man looked, but couldn't remember.

"Leonard Ingrande." Oh, I heard you went East, the man said, heard you did good things. Leonard said he went East in 1962. He'd been out there thirty years.

He'd come a long way from the time, in the 1950s, when his wife had given him $7 pocket money for the month. Going back to the summer of 1943, Leonard Ingrande had been at it almost fifty years.

(9)

A   MILLING   FISH

❦

THE SAMPSONS hadn't been able to get out for eight days. There had been rain for twenty-one of the past fifty days, and much wind. With ten days left in August the general category was half full, at 262 tons. If catch rates held steady and predictions held true, it would close sometime in late September. Fishermen in the harpoon category, held back by the bad weather, had caught 113 fish so far—20.2 tons, 38 percent of their quota. It seemed that the harpoon category would stay open after the general closed, that the harpooners might get a fall fishery.

The weather was warm and clear on August 21, though early in the morning the winds were at 25 knots. Bob and his crew left Sandwich Harbor on the *Scratcher* at 7:30. Brad Sampson left from Barnstable Harbor on the *Rush*. They crossed Cape Cod Bay, rounded Provincetown, and headed thirty miles out to the southeast. The trip took three hours and the ride was rough, and for the rest of the morning the boats cruised around, riding the waves and waiting for the wind to lay down. Brooksie arrived at eleven, made a few passes and then flew into Hyannis for fuel, stopping off at the Tiki Port for lunch.

At noon, as if on cue, the winds and the water calmed. Brad was off in the distance, out of sight. Bob had come upon a pod of whales feeding at the surface, and decided to sit near them for a while. Some tuna might be feeding around the whales. They were pilot whales, also called blackfish, because of their color, or potheads, because of their bulbous foreheads. Pilot whales, which grew up to twenty feet long and weighed up to 6,000 pounds, were the species that sometimes beached themselves on Cape Cod and other places. Here they were feeding by running along the surface in quick bursts, charging into the prey school, spraying water with their heads.

But then they stopped. We had noticed them, but they had also noticed us, and soon the pod came swimming toward the boat. Some of them bobbed up to get a look at the boat, at us, while others swam on their backs and rolled to their sides. They seemed interested in the propeller. They were a mixed group, actually. A school of dolphins, gray with white sides, was traveling with the whales. They were also curious, but more timid, and stayed on the outside, catching looks as they surfaced for air. Some of the young, three feet long and fifty pounds, perhaps, skimmed along the surface playfully. When Brooksie's voice came over the loudspeaker they dove quickly, leaving rings on the water, but soon they came up again—they seemed to be curious about this sound too. The entire mixed pod made a couple of passes and then, curiosity satisfied, diversion done with, they went off and resumed feeding.

Activity had picked up all around. Fish were beginning to show, and Brooksie was already working with Brad. There were from four to eight planes in the air. Within the circle of sight over the water were about a dozen harpoon boats and several troll boats, and Leonard Ingrande's boat, the *Connie Jean*. The purse seining season had started six days earlier on August 15, but this was the seiners' first day out. They'd been held up by the weather, too.

Bob got his first call from Brooksie just after two o'clock, and went charging off toward him. Along the way he passed the *Connie Jean*. Two planes were above it. Roger Hillhouse was in one, and Jonathan Mayhew, a spotter pilot from Martha's Vineyard, was in the other. Mayhew sometimes flew for Bob Sampson, who had introduced him to Leonard Ingrande. When a troll boat ran toward the area underneath the two planes, Mayhew flew off and made a false circle, acting as a decoy to throw off the troller.

"Eleven, eleven-thirty," came Brooksie's voice. "Ten boats to go. Starboard a little, eleven o'clock. Good, just like that." Bob went out on the pulpit.

The school was swimming erratically, Brooksie said, changing directions. By the time the *Scratcher* got close to Brooksie's circle the fish had turned toward the boat. It would be a head-on shot, the most difficult throw to make.

"Six and a half, seven boats now. Just like that. Eleven-thirty, eleven o'clock, if you want a head-on. I think you guys might have this. Stay just like that. Two boats."

Bob lifted the harpoon high and looked for a target.

"Eleven o'clock. Stay just like that a boat and a half."

He leaned into the belly rail and raised himself up.

"Twelve o'clock and half a boat."

He waved the dart.

"Take your time, Bob," Brooksie said.

The school ran by, off to the left of the pulpit, and Bob made an awkward throw. The harpoon splashed sideward into the water. A mighty captain's voice rose up.

"What! A head-on shot! Take your time!"

Bob grabbed the line, and while he hauled in the harpoon he yelled to Wade Behlman. "Tell Brooksie no more trips to the Tiki Port! Too much MSG!" Wade got on the radio.

Brooksie went off to find another bunch. The *Scratcher* cruised, and the crew watched the water. Two other seiners had arrived, with their planes. The set boat on the *Connie Jean* had pushed off with the net and begun to make a wrap—the first set for the seiners that season.

As the *Scratcher* cruised, waiting for its plane, Bob watched the seiner at work. But he didn't get too close.

IN THE YEARS after the seiners arrived in New England and began taking their great scoops out of the stocks of bluefin tuna, they did their best to promote good public relations among other fishermen. Only seiners had planes then, and it was sometimes difficult for a harpooner or troller to see a plane come out of nowhere like a mad bee, followed by a purse seiner that might then take up a hundred giants at one time. This was especially hard to accept if that fisherman had been seeing and running bunches in the very same area. There were arguments, but the seiners knew of the imbalance, and they wanted to make friends. Thus, up into the 1980s, Leonard Ingrande and Frank Cyganowski and some of the other seiner captains didn't mind if a harpoon boat or troll boat worked in the area around the nets.

Bob Sampson did his share of this. He was the Scratcher, after all. He worked the edges. And if there were fish swimming near the net, why shouldn't he get them, why shouldn't anyone take a free-swimming fish? In the process, over the years, he became friends with Ingrande and Cyganowski.

Early in his career, when he worked the tuna tournaments, Bob hired on as mate of a boat called the *High Roller*. It was a well-appointed boat, equipped with a "throwing iron." Frank Cyganowski had made a set in Cape Cod Bay, and Bob worked the perimeter. The net had been pursed in and the school was packed tight. Bob noticed two men in wet suits walking on the fish. He didn't know why, though he'd soon find out they were tagging fish for Frank Mather's program. What Bob then noticed was a big bluefin go over the corkline and then come up to the surface, swimming on its side. He ran out on the stand, lofted the throwing iron in a long arc, and hit. The crewmen of the seiner cheered—they had grown tired of seeing the scientists poke and prod the fish. One scientist, however, seeing Bob Sampson harpoon the fish he'd just released, was furious, and screamed at him. Frank Cyganowski told Bob he could get $5 for returning the tag, and Bob, not to be outdone, backed up the boat, handed over the tag and asked for his $5—after all, it was a free-swimming fish.

The story made the newspapers, and the captain of the *High Roller* was accused of being a poor sportsman. A rule was passed prohibiting a boat from coming within a hundred yards of a working purse seiner, but harpooners often ignored it, and the seiner captains continued to let the boats patrol outside the nets to take stray fish.

A few years later, after Bob had a poor season off Martha's Vineyard, he went into the Bay in late August. One day he had seen bunches and was waiting for them to show when Frank Cyganowski steamed up in the *AA Ferrante* and made a set.

Though Bob didn't like this, he accepted it and cruised around the perimeter. Well into the haul, he passed close to the seiner and said hello. Then a wind came up from the north and blew the *AA Ferrante* over the net while it was still pocketing the fish. Something on the boat tore a hole in the net, and the more they pulled the bigger the hole got. Fish started to get out.

Bob worked the edges. He saw a fish on its side, and, "an opportunist at heart," he harpooned it. He harpooned a second, and then a third.

Bob was in a gray area—it was illegal to take a seined fish by then. When the *Scratcher* arrived in Barnstable Harbor a buyer and a Japanese technician looked at Bob's fish. "Purse seine fish," the technician said—it was bruised from beating around in the net. Bob could see it was going to be difficult to sell his catch.

Barnstable Harbor is a busy place, with many highly competitive fishermen, and "other interested parties" called the enforcement officer for the National Marine Fisheries Service. A conference followed, with Bob, the officer, and also Leonard Ingrande, who helped to explain what had happened. Nevertheless, it was going to be difficult to sell the fish. But Leonard Ingrande helped with this, too. He arranged for his buyer to take one, and for Pasquale's restaurant in New Bedford to take the other two. Bob said he'd take $4 a pound, and he agreed to deliver them. He hoisted the tuna on his flatbed and headed off to New Bedford with his mate.

Pasquale's was a Portuguese restaurant located on the fish pier, and it shared a parking lot with Louie's, the ritziest restaurant in New Bedford. Bob drove around to the back of Pasquale's, but there was no service entrance, so he parked in the only space he could find, right next to the front door. There was a Lincoln on one side and a Cadillac on the other. Still dressed in the clothes he'd worn on his boat, Bob walked through the restaurant to talk to Pasquale.

"I've got two tuna fish for you," Bob said.

"Bring 'em in."

"These are giant tuna fish," Bob said. "Five hundred pounds. Seven feet long." Bob's mate was big, but the two of them together couldn't carry one of the giant tuna, and they would have to carry them through the dining room. Pasquale gave Bob a hand cart, but it wasn't big enough, and he gave him a door to set on the cart, but that wouldn't work either. Bob considered his options. He wanted to get paid, and he'd driven all the way to New Bedford. He told Pasquale he'd steak out the fish in exchange for a free meal. Bob loved Portuguese-style fish, cooked with tomatoes and onions and spices. Pasquale gave Bob a knife, and when Bob asked about the parking lot, about cleaning the fish in view of Louie's, Pasquale said he could do what he wanted out there.

He went out and climbed up on the bed of the truck. Wearing sneakers, standing in ice, Bob began to work. A crowd gathered. Bob had filleted a lot of fish in his life, but he'd never filleted a 500-pound fish before. It took about an hour. It was nine o'clock when Bob and his mate loaded the fish steaks onto the door and wheeled them through the dining room and into the kitchen. This sort of thing wouldn't have been done at Louie's next door, but most of the customers at Pasquale's were Portuguese, and many were fishermen, and they weren't offended.

Flecked and spotted, Bob and his mate sat down to large platters of Portuguese-style codfish. They had several beers, and they left in a better frame of mind than they'd arrived in. Bob thought it had to be the first and last time a giant bluefin tuna had been filleted in the parking lot of a posh restaurant—with witnesses. Everyone who came out of Pasquale's or Louie's had to walk by Bob's truck, and they had lots of questions about the big fish. There had to be a moral to the story, but Bob wasn't sure what it was. Stay away from the seiners, maybe.

Another time, working close to the nets, Bob harpooned a fish and then it went flying back inside the seine. Roger Hillhouse called from the plane, wanting to know what was going on, why someone had harpooned a fish inside the net, but Bob pulled it out and smoothed things over.

The last time Bob worked up close to a seiner—the last time anyone did—was near the end of the 1985 season. Leonard Ingrande was working in Cape Cod Bay, and he needed one more set to fill the seiner quota. He made a set, but it had more fish than he was allowed to take, so he invited fishermen working nearby—Bob Sampson was one of them—to take from the surplus. That was the kind of thing Leonard did that made him a nice guy. Certainly he didn't have to do that. Bob went right in and harpooned a fish.

Word traveled quickly, and soon boats from all over the Bay were steaming in. There were tuna boats, lobster boats, draggers, party boats, all lining up for the free fish, the $1,000 bills Leonard Ingrande was giving away.

One boat got a fish and pulled away, and another boat backed into the net. That fisherman harpooned two tuna, tied the ropes down, and dragged them out. Suddenly there was so much going on. Bob had stayed around to watch, and he thought Leonard was getting nervous. One man ran from stern to stern along a line of boats with a harpoon in his hand. There was a rope tied to it, and the rope led back to a dragger. He harpooned a fish, then used the net winder to reel the fish in. Then he ran across the boats again and harpooned another, since there was a two-fish limit at that time.

It ended when a man in the cockpit of one boat, aiming for the twenty-foot circle inside the net, threw a harpoon over three other boats and stuck it in the side of the *AA Ferrante*. Leonard Ingrande told everybody to leave then. He loosened the purse strings and let the rest of the fish go to the bottom.

"That was the one that did it with the three-hundred-foot rule," Bob said.

BROOKSIE WAS off working with Brad when Bob and Wade spotted a school of milling fish, a round patch of roiling water. Bob ran out on the pulpit and Wade took the wheel in the tower. Off ahead were fins, the suggestion of the circle.

Bob reached up, leaned forward, aimed the dart, and hit. When he yelled Matt held the button on the zapper for two seconds, but when he let go the fish raced off. Maybe the transformer was weakening.

They put a rig on, and the fish took out 600 feet of line. The poly-ball bobbed along, then suddenly stopped. Maybe they'd lost it, Bob said. But when Matt hauled in the line, up came a giant. It was shaped like a football. It had a green stain on one side, and must have rubbed against the ocean bottom, 500 feet down, before it died. Bob leaned over the rail and cut the arteries, and bled it, and then they hauled the fish in through the transom door. On the deck, the oval body tottered with the rocking of the boat.

What an especially brilliant fish it was. You could see why they milled; one reason must have been to watch their own bristle and beam as they rolled in the sun, as they turned in the afternoon's slanted rays. Did a bluefin become more brilliant as it became rounder, as it completed its feeding migration, its seasonal fulfill-ment? Taken in the mill, was the fish in its most resplendent guise?

This fish was bluish-black on the top. Over the mouth and above the eyes, the colors of precious metals—iridescent gold, then copper, then silver. A cobalt blue stripe running down the back. Along the sides, mottled areas of pinks and peach, and many shades of blue—opal, azure, turquoise. Strokes of gold-green, patches of yellow and red, brilliant yet subdued, almost hidden.

This fish would bring $19.50 per pound. Bob climbed the ladder to the tower and shook my hand.

Going straight at the sun, Bob missed his next shot. But Brooksie immediately found another bunch, and this time Bob hit. The fish froze when Matt hit the zapper, but again it raced away after he let off the button. They put a rig on, and the poly-ball stopped bobbing, but this time the line came up empty—the fish had pulled the dart. There definitely were problems with the zapper, Bob said. He did not like losing a fish, once he'd hit it.

On the *Rush*, Brad had missed all his throws. One was a "barn door shot." The other was "the second easiest shot" he'd ever had. Brad was in a slump, and hadn't caught a fish since the day he'd harpooned five early in the season. He was an unhappy camper, Bob said, and in fact he was thinking about camping out, staying on the water through the night.

Bob was worried about how Brad felt. Brooksie had joked about the misses, but Bob had told him to keep his disappointment to himself. "When you miss a shot you want to quit, it hurts so bad. You want to quit and not fish again."

Just before six o'clock Brooksie found another bunch, and both boats raced toward the plane, but then Bob backed off. Brad ran in, got a throw off, and missed.

The sun was getting low, but Brooksie kept looking about. Brad came over to the *Scratcher*, and stern to stern, father and son talked. It had been a hard day, but Brad was smiling. He wanted to stay out. Matt decided to stay out, too, and he jumped aboard the *Rush*. They bobbed off as the *Scratcher* turned and headed for Provincetown, twenty-seven miles away. Bob wouldn't get in until ten o'clock. He'd been to work the night before, and that meant he'd have worked twenty-three hours by the time they reached Sandwich. Unless Penny found someone to fill in for him, he'd have to go straight in to ComElectric. "No sleep tonight," he said.

Other boats were heading to shore. Now and then a plane would swoop down by a boat and make a departing pass, like a goodbye kiss.

On the way in, Bob talked to Brad on the radio. He told him to make a sea anchor, to cast it overboard—a rope with buckets, anything heavy, to cut down on drift. Maybe he should tie up to the seiners for the night, and try to get some food from them. He didn't want Brad to stay, didn't think it was a good idea, but he didn't protest. And Eric Hesse would be out there—when Eric heard that Brad was staying overnight, he decided to stay, too.

"An easterly at fifteen knots will pick up tonight," Bob said to me, "and they won't sleep. The boat will rock, and it will be cold." He smiled. "You can only tell, you can't teach."

The *Scratcher* rounded Race Point and headed across Cape Cod Bay. Bob and Wade stayed in the tower, running in the dark, all the way.

They moored at the loading dock. The manager of CQB was already there, waiting in a parking lot fifty feet away. They hoisted the fish, and the manager put an NMFS tag on it and filled out the forms.

100

Penny arrived with pizzas. She had found someone to take Bob's place at work, so he would sleep that night.

On the bed of the truck the bluefin glittered softly, like light on the water after the sun has gone down.

(1 0)

THE MARINER

❧

BILLY MCINTIRE yelled for someone to hit the switch that
raised the little wooden drawbridge over the entrance to Perkins
Cove at Ogunquit Harbor. The perplexed vacationing couple who
were about to cross the bridge looked back at the fisherman, and
the *A. Maria* drifting their way, but they did as asked, and up went
the bridge, and out went the boat, this foggy August afternoon on the
Maine coast.

Billy's father, Sonny McIntire, was at the wheel. I'd heard Sonny's
name from nearly everyone who talked about the history of the bluefin
tuna fishery, and I'd been told that I should meet Sonny because he
best represented the Maine point of view, which was antiplane. I'd
also heard some wild and odd stories about him. His father, Carl
McIntire, talked about the time, in the fifties on Cape Cod Bay, when
a boat crossed the bow as Sonny was taking aim, and of how Sonny
had not for a moment wavered in his aim. I'd heard from a fisherman
that Sonny, in a nomadic stretch of the season, had been soaped up
and showering in the rain on the deck of his boat when the storm
suddenly stopped, and that he'd expressed his displeasure over the
radio in a Maine drawl that the Cape Cod fishermen found exotic and
humorous. And I'd heard from Sonny's mother, Priscilla McIntire,
that when Sonny was a young man he was crazy about tuna fish, so
crazy that he said he was never going to get married and would chase
tuna around the world. This turned out not to be his destiny. His

three sons were all in the fishery, had deep respect for their father, and enjoyed his company.

There was a breadth to Sonny—not just in his experience, but in his appearance. His body was a fit fisherman's body, but his face suggested broadness, in the forehead, the wide-set eyes, the mouth, the gapped teeth. His was a face for looking, for watching. And though he was one of the best and most experienced harpooners, a fisherman and thus a true predator, there was also a peace, a quietness to Sonny, in his manner and in his voice.

On the way out of the channel Sonny handed me a bluefish plug, and said that it had come out of the stomach of a bluefin tuna that had taken a hooked bluefish, line and all. Just then another boat came up, headed into the harbor, and both boats cut back their engines. It was Joe Jancewicz, of Newburyport, and his mate, Keith Hudson. They had a fish on deck. Joe bent over it and lifted the tarp. They'd been in Ogunquit since leaving the chum fleet on Jeffreys Ledge four weeks ago, and they'd been doing well.

Joe had been trolling, and he'd been able to work in the fog, and there were chummers offshore, too, but the other harpooners at Perkins Cove, except for Sonny, had stayed in. Sonny liked working in a moderate fog, and he was known for his ability to harpoon fish during marginal weather. Earlier, in the harbor, several fishermen had been talking before Sonny arrived, and one said he had never seen Sonny McIntire so happy as he'd been the day before, when he caught a fish in the fog, without a plane.

One of those fishermen in the harbor had told how on certain occasions bluefin tuna from Cape Cod to Maine came up to the surface all at the same time.

Sonny didn't know whether they acted together in that way. "I do know that they come up at certain times, though," he said. "There was one spot we fished out near one of the islands where they came up every day for a while at four o'clock, every day right at four.

"Sometimes they come up at daybreak. In the old days when they were out at the islands, when we weren't going so far out, you'd see them at daybreak. Then they'd swim in the direction of the sun, soon as it came up. They would turn and look back.

"Years ago, we left before daybreak, and were out there when it was dark, just before the sun came up. We saw some, and got five fish out of a bunch just before daybreak. Then they went into the sun and we lost them.

"We got the five fish on the boat. It was nine-thirty and we were sleeping on the cabin roof and my father came up.

" 'Seen anything?' my father said.

" 'Not lately,' I told him.

" 'Where did you get them?' my father asked me, and I told him we got them before daybreak." Sonny smiled, and laughed softly. "Seen anything, not lately," he said.

Sonny's father, Carl, was born in 1910 and started harpooning tuna in 1926. For many years he got three cents a pound, although he might get a bit more for the first one or two fish he caught each year. In his best year he harpooned 136 bluefin. Carl worked along the Maine coast and as far south as Cape Cod, marketing his fish at any port where he could sell them. One time he brought five bluefin into Boston and stopped traffic on Atlantic Avenue. Carl fished in the period when whiting were so thick in Casco Bay that the draggers could tow for only fifteen minutes, when bluefin got fat very early in the season, when the bluefin schools were so thick he sometimes rode through them, when in order to find fish in the fog he sometimes shut off the engine and listened for the sounds of their wakes. When the National Marine Fisheries Service was establishing categories and quotas, officials went to Carl McIntire's house in Small Point to study his records, for proof that the harpoon fishery was in fact a historical fishery. At Carl's retirement party he was given a silver harpoon head by other Maine fishermen.

Sonny's uncle, Earl Wallace, started harpooning bluefin at about the same time as Carl McIntire, in the 1920s. Uncle Earl had started his career as a cabin boy on a swordfish boat, and he was said to have had the best eyes in the bluefin fishery. He caught more than three thousand bluefin in his time, with a high year of 212 fish. Every one of them was a thrill. It didn't matter that he got one to three cents a pound. Earl thought $30 for a single fish was a great price. He once told a buyer that all the man had to do was pay Earl to deliver them and he would catch them.

Sonny McIntire's grandfather, Orlando Wallace, was one of the first, perhaps the first, to harpoon bluefin tuna commercially. Orlando sold his first tuna in 1910, to oilers, who boiled the fish out to produce lamp oil. Most people didn't eat horse mackerel then. They were thought to be poisonous.

Sonny "ironed" his first fish in 1952, at the age of twelve. He worked on his father's boat through his teenage years, and eventually on other boats, lobstering, dragging, trawling, and seining for herring. In 1964 he bought a boat of his own. That year he caught eighteen fish in two days, got $1,100 for them, and thought he was rich. Generally he figured that if he got $50 a fish, and got six fish, that was $300, good money in those days.

Sonny would sometimes say this: "My father told me they're gonna stop us from doing this. It's too much fun."

Planes, Sonny said, had taken the fun out of the fishery. You used to go out and look. Now, you look some, and the plane calls, and you steam hard for six miles, one boat going this way, another boat making white water the other way.

The planes, Sonny said, were the reason he had caught only five fish this year. Most years, he would have had fifteen or twenty at this point. Two years ago, he had caught sixty. With all the planes on the fish, chasing them so hard, you couldn't get near them. You had to go out forty or fifty miles now.

At first, only two or three fishermen used planes, and they were at an advantage. Now the whole fishery was at a disadvantage because there were too many planes out there, twenty or thirty, maybe more.

Sonny used a plane because he had to, in order to keep up with the competition, but he wanted to stop. His sons, just getting into the fishery, didn't have enough experience to hold a pilot. There were a lot of people in that position. Sonny was afraid that, with the way he was fishing this year, he wouldn't be able to keep a pilot. It would get so only the rich would have planes.

There was something else that Sonny liked to say: "It used to be that we didn't see many fish and got a lot. Now we're seeing a lot and getting a few."

WE WERE headed out to work the fifty-fathom line, ten miles offshore. Now and then a chummer drifted in and out of the fog. Then, ten miles out, they used a loop of rope to connect the wheel in the cabin to the one in the tower. Billy climbed to the tower to steer and to watch. Sonny put on a fisherman's hat with a long black brim, and some polarized glasses with side shields made of electrician's tape, and he went out to stand on the cabin roof. He was wearing a T-shirt, even though it was foggy and cool.

Then he watched the water, through the afternoon. He moved his head back and forth, looking east to west in a slow rhythm, like a guard on a watch.

A simple thing, watching the water. Watching Sonny, I thought of something my grandfather used to say about his grandfather, a sea captain. "Those boys," he would tell me, "went around the world with only a compass and a sextant and by dead reckoning." My grandfather didn't know what dead reckoning was, and neither did I, but the term had an intuitive ring, a connotation of great mental powers, as if the captains had found their way about the world by a homing instinct acquired from the time they were cabin boys. We would dwell on this mysterious phrase, dead reckoning, in consideration of the long-lost powers of the ancestors.

I thought I could see those old mariners in Sonny, the seamen who'd come to work these shores, Cape Cod to Newfoundland, four centuries ago. This was an old mental process at work, and there was a peace in this looking, a sense of rightness and connection, a lineage—the narrow one that ran from Orlando Wallace through Sonny McIntire and his sons and to many other fishermen in the Gulf of Maine, and the much broader lineage that radiated from the oldest of cultural traditions—the fisherman, the seaman, the mariner, working the waters on these shores.

Sonny watched the water as we had for thousands of years, as he had since the earliest days of his childhood. In this seeing, this dead reckoning, was an affinity with water and sky, sun and stars, and through these things, to the milling fish, in their orbits and considerations. In this looking, standing on the bow, was Sonny McIntire's experience. His displeasure with planes was partly about money, and access, but only partly. He disliked planes because they negated his experience, the meaning of looking. Planes took away his eyes.

He watched the water, but there were no tuna to be seen that day.

(1 1)

THE LAST DAY
OF SUMMER

❧

THE SAMPSONS had moved up to Maine, and were working out of a marina in Portland. It was the Thursday before Labor Day weekend, a clear summer day, warm on the land, cool at sea, and Brad's last day on the water before he went off to school for a semester of student teaching.

After Bob Sampson caught the milling fish the weather had turned foggy and windy again. They had gotten a fish the day after that catch, though. Wade and Bob had ridden across the Bay as far as Province-town, and then turned back toward Barnstable, when they saw a plane spiral down to 200 feet. The pilot worked for the seiners, and he was just out looking. He told Bob he could take the fish he'd seen, and so they moved up on a line of seven giants and harpooned one. It weighed 650 pounds dressed, and brought $10,000.

The reports were that the fishing was better in Maine. Schools that had been on the chum bite had moved to the north and east, and so the Sampsons went after them. Along the way they found schools to the south of the fleet of forty harpoon boats and five seiners working east of Portland, and ran those for a while before joining the fleet. Brooksie had been shuttling Bob between the Cape and Maine so he could get to his job at ComElectric.

As of September 1 the catch in the general category stood at 362 metric tons, or 68 percent of quota. By some predictions, the general category would now close in mid-September. The harpoon catch was

25.75 tons, 49 percent of quota. Harpoon-category fishermen now figured to be operating into October.

There had been two accidents in the New England bluefin fishery. A fisherman on Jeffreys Ledge got caught in a line, was pulled overboard, and drowned. Another fisherman lost a finger and thumb when his hand got caught in a line pulled by a hooked fish.

Brad was in "a major league slump," as Bob called it. He hadn't harpooned a fish the night he stayed out on the water, and he hadn't caught one since. He'd arrive late, and he'd miss shots. When you were on a streak, Bob said, you thought positively, but in a slump you doubted yourself and made bad decisions. It was better to sit back, think things over, and come back with a fresh attitude rather than to keep trying and trying. Brad didn't have time to sit back, though. He wanted to end the season successfully. He made an early start, and by midmorning was thirty miles offshore (seventy-three miles north of Race Point, ninety-three miles north of Barnstable), working with Brooksie.

The *Scratcher*, though, was still in the harbor. Someone had left a switch on, and now the boat's battery was dead. Bob spent the morning locating a charger, and it was two o'clock before he was ready to go. Bob wasn't sure he wanted to go at all. He wanted to make it into work that night, but he followed his policy of not making a decision from the harbor, of at least taking a ride a little way out. That way he could get Brad's car keys from him, so he could drive one of the cars back from Portland.

Brooksie was coaxing him along too. The water was cold, 60 degrees, but Brooksie talked of a "color change" he'd seen—a body of cold, nutrient-rich blue water lined up against a body of warmer, green water. Such a thermocline acted as a fence, and marine life tended to pile up against it. Bob looked for these color changes on the way out, and thought he saw blue water once, but then decided it was just "optical confusion."

Bob was cruising slowly, and wanted to stay close to shore, to work inside. Then the *Rush* came in from the east. Brad got on deck, tossed his car keys to his father, climbed back into the tower, and headed away again. The *Scratcher* cruised a while longer, and then they turned the engine off and checked the oil. Still there was a leak. Bob topped the oil off and swabbed up the excess from the bilge with cotton pads.

At four o'clock Brooksie came on the radio and said he had found bunches to the southeast, sixteen miles away. By now the *Scratcher* was twenty miles offshore. Bob had to make a decision, and though he wanted to stay inside he steamed south, saying he was out there to make money. Twenty minutes later, accustomed to the new plan, he called Penny and asked her to find someone to go into work for him.

Now they were thirty miles out, above the north corner of Platts Bank, where off in the distance a chum fleet was anchored up. Two seiners were in this area, the *Connie Jean* and the *White Dove* (one would make a set and take eighty-three fish). There were half a dozen planes in the air.

Word came over the radio that Eric Hesse had gotten a fish. Eric was from Barnstable, and had gotten his early education in the fishery in Captain Joe Eldredge's mosquito fleet, a group of twenty-foot skiffs with outboard engines, pulpits, and towers run by teenagers who worked on shares. Eric harpooned three fish that summer. He had worked for Bill Steros and Faith Idlehart on the *Esperanto*, and for Chris VanDuzer on the *Sea Baby*. In 1988, after the price for bluefin jumped from $4 to $12 a pound, Eric took a year off from college and used his earnings to travel around the world. He had spent a winter ferrying scientists in Antarctica, and then returned to the Cape to run the *Sandra C.* for Bob Sampson, grossing $60,000 in 1989 and $97,000 in 1990. In 1991, while in graduate school, studying environmental engineering at the University of Massachusetts, he built the *Tenacious*. Eric figured that while he didn't yet have the skills of harpooners like Bob Sampson or Billy Chraptes or Sonny McIntire, he would make up for it by putting in the most hours. He was known as the first one out and the last to leave.

Brooksie said he'd seen a bunch go deep. Another fisherman went out on the stand. Racing along, Bob didn't like his position as latecomer, and expressed it by pastoral metaphor: "Nothing like sucking hind tit, huh?"

Ron Lein called from the *Sandra C.* to find out what Bob was doing. Ron and Bob owned the *Sandra C.* in partnership, and they sometimes worked near each other. Ron had been a tuna fisherman since 1981, when he and his wife, Merilyn, went chumming. When they caught a bluefin that weighed 804 pounds and got $1.25 a pound, Ron told her he could make a living doing this. He was building post-and-beam houses at the time. That winter he built a boat, the *Merilyn J.* Ron moored in Barnstable Harbor, and for seven years he fished only in Cape Cod Bay—trolling and harpooning, averaging about fifteen fish per year, most of them 750 pounds or more. But then the traffic increased, and he began to use a plane, and pilots didn't like working in the Bay, so Ron began to move offshore. As he had told Merilyn, he was able to make a living harpooning bluefin. In the off season Ron had moved over from housebuilding to boatbuilding, working in a shop in New Hampshire.

Bob picked up the microphone. "Steaming into it big time," he said to Ron.

"Don't run over any bunches."

Off to the east, Nick Nickerson went out on the stand of the boat they called *Pinocchio.* Billy Chaprales, on the *Easy Does It*, went out too.

Bob saw the silver side of a smashing giant, 200 yards away, but then Brooksie came on the radio and said he had found a bunch of forty to fifty giants, nine miles away, and they were "up to stay."

Brad was steaming southward too, east of the *Scratcher.* "I'm gonna catch a tuna fish," he said. "See you in a half hour." Slowly he pulled ahead. The sun was warm, but the air off the water was cool.

At 5:30 Brad went into a bunch, halfway between the *Scratcher* and a pair of breaching humpback whales. He threw, and hit. A flag went up and a rig went out.

Just as this was happening the *Scratcher*'s engine stalled. "Oh no," Bob said. He and Wade quickly climbed down from the tower, opened the engine box and checked the oil. No mark registered on the dipstick. They added oil. Still no mark. Bob started the engine, and it clacked away badly. This didn't look good at all, not the prospect of being stranded on the water—help was everywhere—but the possibility that the Sampsons no longer had a boat in the harpoon category for the fall fishery.

Maybe the engine needed an overhaul, Bob said. He had run it for eight years. They would have to take the boat out of the water, remove the tower, pull the engine. The mood on board the *Scratcher* was somber. Words of disappointment came down from the air.

Bob was on his knees peering down into the engine box, his nose smeared with oil, when a gillnetter from Cape Porpoise, Maine, floated up. Two men, working in a shelter, were pulling fish from nets, gutting them, and throwing entrails down a ramp into the water, where seagulls leaped at them. It must have been warm in the shelter, because they were shirtless, wearing oilskins with suspenders, while Bob and Wade had on sweatshirts. I had on a jacket and gloves.

The captain of this boat leaned out of the wheelhouse. He was also shirtless, with long hair, and wearing mirrored sunglasses. He shouted, "How long can you keep a tuna fish on ice?" Then he grinned.

"Indefinitely," Bob said. "You catch a tuna?"

"Got two," the captain said.

"You can only get one, you're only supposed to get one."

"I know," the captain said, still grinning. A school of bluefin had come up into the gurry and started feeding wildly. In the midst of the smashing the fisherman had put out two handlines and immediately gotten two fish.

"How big are they?" Bob asked.

"One's about a hundred pounds and the other's about two-fifty."

"Let the small one go," Bob said. "Throw it back. You can only take one to sell. It's not worth getting arrested for."

"You missed a show," the captain said. "About a half hour ago. They were everywhere. You missed some show. What's the size limits?"

Bob told him—70 inches total length, from fork of tail to tip of nose, or 52 inches from fork to pectoral fin. The captain asked what Bob was doing, and he told him about the engine seizing.

"You got enough oil?"

"We got some, but we need more," Bob said. "If you could spare some that would be helpful."

"I think I got some below. About half a five-gallon can." The boat drifted away, then returned a few minutes later. The captain backed its stern up to the *Scratcher*'s, and the two crewmen lifted the oil can over to Bob and Wade, who swung it onto the deck.

One of the crewmen smiled, a friendly gesture, in response to the fate of the day. His arms were sinewy, and he had a tattoo on his shoulder. His skin was flecked with glittering fish scales. His long brown hair was parted in the middle and came to his shoulders. He was missing a front tooth. What was it about a friendly smile from a man missing a front tooth, why was it touching, and genuine? On land you'd have a different impression, but out here, despite the batteries and the oil and the planes and the lorans, here it could be said, as someone had once told me, that fishing was the last medieval occupation.

"Aren't they something?" Bob said as the gillnetters drifted away, and the captain called out, "What hump you on? We'll call you anytime."

THEY POURED the oil and started the engine, but the clacking was just as bad, so they shut it right off. The *Scratcher* wasn't going anywhere under its own power. Bob decided they'd tow it to Cape Cod, ninety miles away.

Brad came over in the *Rush*, and rigged up a towline. Ron Lein had come over, and he contributed some rope and helped take up the anchor lines. Already, acceptance had set in. There was no panic, no frantic emotion, and even the somberness had gone. Over the years they'd had to adapt quickly to many dangerous situations, and in this crisis they'd been calm. It was the psychological benefit of working the last medieval occupation. Bob was a little concerned, however, when Brad walked along the rails to the stern. "Don't fall in now," Bob said, a reference to the time Brad had fallen off the back of the boat a decade ago.

"Dad, did you know there's oil in your bilge?"

"Not this boat. No oil in this bilge."

They put a grill and hot dogs and beer on the *Rush*. Bob and Wade got aboard, and the two boats headed south in tandem.

The *Sandra C.* left for Portland, two hours away. Ron Lein was in the tower. Brad was on the deck, and his mate today, Kip Lewis, and Ron Lein's mate, Matt Comeau.

Brad had lost the fish he'd harpooned. The hit had not been solid, and Kip hadn't gotten to the zapper in time, so the fish had pulled the dart. Though Brad had accepted this, and the season's end, the miss had left Kip nervous. Kip was afraid of Bob Sampson, and he worried that Bob would get angry with him. Whenever Bob was around, Kip jumped about the boat. Privately, he called Bob "Miles."

Platts Bank receded behind us, and with it the chumming boats, aglow in the setting sun. The sky turned orange above the boats, and orange over the land, and then the color deepened and gave way. A quarter moon lit up in the southwest, and cast a path across the water. The light of the moon was not enough to dim the stars, though, and the Milky Way emerged from the blue and formed a dusty belt across the sky. Then there were shooting stars.

And the water itself responded to the night. There was "fire in the water," as the fishermen called it—phosphorescent plankton that formed embers in the wake. The water sparkled about the boat. Ron Lein was going at full speed, about twenty knots, and as the boat hit the waves, water sprayed over the cabin roof and the stern. There were phosphorescent embers in this water, too, and as they flew by they looked like shooting stars.

We stood on the deck, with this water flying over our heads. Brad had wanted to get a fish on the last day of the season, but now the season was over. It was hard not to get one, day after day, when you were sure you would.

He talked of one missed chance. They'd just arrived in Maine.

"Brooksie had called us, and we were steaming toward a bunch. But as I was going along I saw, two miles off, a boat with someone waving a white flag. I backed off and turned and went over to them.

"It was eleven in the morning, and they had been drifting since

114

nine o'clock the night before. They had gone twenty miles out, turned in, stalled four miles from shore, then drifted forty miles back out. It was the first day in their new boat. They had no radio, and no water. The owner of the boat didn't even try to fix the engine. They just waved a flag, and a lot of boats had passed them by. Three of the guys were up and about, but one of them was sitting on the transom and he didn't look too good.

"I called the Coast Guard, and I gave them all the food I had on the boat, a six-pack of soda and some cookies. Then I left and steamed off to where my dad was. He'd already gotten on the bunch and stuck two fish, and by the time I got there they were gone."

Brad Sampson stood under the lit sky, trails of lit water flying overhead, the lit houses of Portland coming closer. At the restaurant at the marina in Portland, the waitresses called Brad "fisherboy," because he looked so young. Here he stood, riding in, on his last day of summer, this fisherboy, this grandson of Miles Standish and Abraham Sampson.

"Ten thousand dollars was over there waiting for me. But I couldn't go by them. You just don't do that."

The *Rush* and *Scratcher* would travel ten hours through the night (Bob and Wade were unable to light the grill, since they couldn't find matches), and get into Sandwich Harbor just before six. A day later the *Scratcher* was taken out of the water and lifted onto mounts for repairs.

(1 2)

THE CHATHAM FISHERY

T HE BITE increased, and by September 8 there were reports
that the general category might close as early as midnight of the
12th. In fact, it lasted through Tuesday night, September 15. This
was two weeks earlier than in 1991, and many fishermen were disappointed or angry at the quick closing. Some continued to work,
however, since NMFS officials had reallocated 20 metric tons for the
area east of Chatham. A number of fisherman moved from the Gulf
of Maine to the Cape and remained there until this secondary quota
closed eight days later.

The harpoon category was still behind the pace at that time. While
347 landings were reported in the general category during the week
ending September 17, only eight fish were landed in the harpoon
category. The next week, twenty-seven landings were reported, and
the harpoon quota stood at 65 percent of the allocated 53 metric tons.

After Labor Day weekend the seiners moved into Cape Cod Bay.
During 1991 the seiner season had been disrupted by a hurricane in
late August and then by a nuisance lawsuit, and the seiners had fished
into November without filling their quota. This year they were taking
no chances on higher fall prices. On September 8 Jonathan Mayhew
put one of Leonard Ingrande's boats onto a set of twenty-seven fish,
then put another boat onto a set of 123. By September 18 the five
seiners had filled their quota of 301 tons.

The engine in the *Scratcher* couldn't be rebuilt, so Bob Sampson decided to buy a new one, a Volvo diesel with 380 horsepower, up from 300. Bob and Wade installed it, but at first the bigger engine didn't fit into the old space, and when they did get it in they had trouble lining it up. Through September they worked on the *Scratcher* on the blow days and fished the *Rush* on the good days.

On the last day of the general category Bob and Wade caught a fish. The next morning Bob was flying to Wyoming to hunt for antelope with his son Tucker. The trip had been nine months in the planning, but because of the problems with the *Scratcher* Bob hadn't had time to prepare. Most of the fun of hunting was in preparation, and Bob didn't even get to clean his guns before he left. He got in late to Osterville Harbor that night with the fish, and was at the airport for a 6 a.m. flight. He also left with a pinched nerve and numbness in his left arm, from a fall on the boat. He needed the rest, and it was important to see Tucker (who now lived in Florida) and hunt with him again, but the fishermen and pilots who worked with Bob couldn't understand why he'd go off hunting at this time of the year, or why he'd leave the *Scratcher* before the engine was functioning.

While Bob was in Wyoming there was a big day in the harpoon fishery off Chatham. Brooksie and Trip Wheeler teamed up with Ron Lein and Eric Hesse to work as a group of four. Ron Lein got nine fish that day, and his mate, Matt Comeau, working without gloves, hauled lines until his hands were bleeding. A disgruntled fisherman didn't believe Ron had caught all nine fish, and accused him of taking "passed fish" from other general-category boats, which could take only one. This fisherman made a complaint to the director of East Coast Tuna. There was a reporter from a Cape Cod newspaper in Trip Wheeler's plane that day, and he witnessed the catch, but the disgruntled fisherman didn't know that, and neither did Bob Sampson when he heard about the complaint in Wyoming. Bob didn't sleep well after that. Though he enjoyed his time with Tucker, and shot an antelope, he returned to the Cape distracted and frustrated, and there was still that harpoon boat sitting in a parking lot.

Bob hired a Volvo mechanic upon his return, and fished another day on the *Rush* in the extended quota. He and Wade got a fish that day, and Eric Hesse got one, as did Sonny McIntire (now moored in

Saquatucket Harbor), and Billy Chaprales. Ron Lein got five—in two days, he had a season. After a summer of feeding, the fish were in prime condition, and because this small zone off Chatham was the only active area in New England, prices soared. Bob's fish, 270 pounds dressed, brought $6,300. Eric Hesse got $42 a pound for a 285-pound fish. Ron Lein got almost $40 per pound.

By the last week of September the temperature had dropped into the 35- to 50-degree range. One afternoon while Bob and Wade worked on the *Scratcher* there were snow squalls, but they hoped to get the boat in the water by Tuesday, September 29. Working on the boat by day and at ComElectric by night, Bob was getting the same four to five hours of sleep he had gotten for twenty years, but with the engine problem and the complaint about cheating and the tingling arm, he felt like he'd aged a year in the last three weeks. At least it was his left arm, not his throwing arm. But he was not going to miss a day of the Chatham fishery if he could help it. He would wait until the harpoon quota was filled to get his arm checked out.

Ron Lein and Trip Wheeler went off Chatham on Tuesday, September 29, the day the *Scratcher* went back into the water. Ron and Trip didn't get anything, though. The fish were out there, but they weren't staying up, and they kept running into the path of the sun. The water was rough, Ron said, like a washing machine. The tides were incredibly strong—a good thing, since bluefin fed in strong tides. The planets must have been aligned in a funny way, Ron thought. (The full moon was coming on, and Saturn was in the southern sky.)

Friday, October 2, looked like a possible fish day, though there was the chance of a small-craft advisory, with winds projected at 20 to 25 knots, and seas at three to six feet. There would be a frost that Thursday night, but the sky would be clear, and the water might be workable.

IT WAS calm at Saquatucket Harbor in Harwich that Friday morning. There was just a slight wind, and the sun's heat was glancing off the docks and the boats. Bob had little hope of a pleasant trip, though.

"They say of this time of year," he said, "that what you see is what you get. Well, it's not true. What you get is what you get. A lot of people are gonna be taking a thrashing coming in today if that southwest wind comes up. It's an ugly ride. We'll be coming right into it."

Many of the boats had left Saquatucket, which had the look of a harpooners' convention site this week. *Hungry Eyes* and *Risky Business* and the *A. Maria* were docked there, and *Easy Does It*, and *Tenacious*, and *Intense*, and *Panda Power*, and many others. Bob and Wade and Kip Lewis got everything aboard, and the *Scratcher* got under way, heading out the channel into Nantucket Sound, and then ten miles south to the point of Monomoy. .

Monomoy was partly the reason this was called the Chatham fishery. A landform made from sand moved southward down the outer side of the Cape, Monomoy had once been a peninsula, and there had been a fishing town on it, but now it was an island, a wildlife sanctuary. Historically, the waters and the shifting sands off Monomoy were the most treacherous on the Atlantic shore. There had been hundreds of wrecks over the past three centuries, more than half of all the wrecks on the Atlantic and Gulf coasts. There had once been three lighthouses and four lifesaving stations along the shore of Monomoy and the Nauset Peninsula, and when boats ran aground Coast Guard lifesaving crews rowed out to help them. In the past century, one Cape Cod captain had made a business of blowing up wrecked boats to get them out of the way. There had once been a cemetery for sailors whose bodies washed ashore, but it too washed away in a storm. Among sailors there once was a saying about being on a ship driven toward Monomoy—"sand in your ears before morning." Sonny McIntire had said that the best advice he got about rounding Monomoy was to shut the depth gauges off. The fluctuating numbers worried you too much.

Bob Sampson had many years' experience navigating Monomoy, of "getting around the corner." Now he ran a winding path around the point and headed to the southeast toward the Great South Channel.

Kip Lewis and I stood in the wheelhouse on the way out. Kip had gone to Cape Cod Community College and then to the University of Maine, where he'd planned to major in wildlife management until he was told there were no jobs in that field. He then transferred to Texas A&M, where he played on the golf team as a walk-on, but it proved too expensive, so he returned to the Cape. He worked as an assistant golf pro until he got carpal tunnel syndrome and had to quit. Now he was picking up odd jobs, including an occasional day as second mate on the *Scratcher*. Kip wasn't sure what he was going to do. He was the kind of person the fisheries had always made use of—in transition, headed somewhere, willing to work long, hard days.

Just before ten o'clock Ron Lein came up from the east. Ron didn't like the looks of the day, with the winds coming on, and he wanted to head in. Bob wasn't willing to make that decision yet, though, and he slowly continued out. Ron turned and came along, off to the side. Jonathan Mayhew flew by, on his way to the zone. After the seiner quota closed, Mayhew had begun to work for the harpooners—now he was teaming with Trip Wheeler and spotting for Lein and Eric Hesse. Trip was already out there, looking along the South Channel. Eric Hesse was there, too. "Captain Courageous," Bob said, with a little smile. Bob had located a harpoon boat for Eric to lease, an old wooden boat called the *Kembe*. Eric had been stripping the boat down to lighten it, and had gotten the *Kembe* to go 14 knots. When a piece of wood floated by Bob pointed to it and said, "Eric's bow board. He's been down below with a crowbar."

Pushed by the wind, we ran along easily in 90 feet of water, by the Great Round Shoal channel buoy and over the northern part of Nantucket Shoals. We passed near scallop boats, draggers, tub trawlers, and cod skiffs. Once, "waiting in anticipation," as he put it, Bob swung the *Scratcher* around and headed into the southwest wind, the one we'd be riding into later. It was a strong, cold wind.

"This is insane," he said.

Trip Wheeler called on the radio. The water was murky, but workable. You could see down into it. "I've seen some whales and some basking sharks," Trip said. "Should be a few fish." The water temperature had dropped off though. It had been 64 a few days ago, and now it was high fifties, maybe low sixties. Trip got nervous when it hit 57.

Bob increased his speed to 16 knots. It seemed a bit calmer now. We moved from green to blue water and Bob pointed to oil slicks on the surface. "Something's been eating here," he said.

We passed through the "old whale zone," where another part of the Chatham fishery had once taken place. Bob and Brooksie had spent many days here, working among the whales. In the mornings they followed small giants and mediums, chasing them to the east as far as Georges Bank, as the fish swam into the sun and warmer water. The big giants didn't make this daily migration, preferring to stay in one area, to conserve energy perhaps. They tended to be more territorial. In the afternoons the big giants would come up and work with the whales. Bob tried to time his return to the zone with this rise of the giants. Late in the day the large mediums and small giants would follow the sun back to the west, and the next morning Bob and Brooksie chased them once again.

Trip Wheeler's voice came again: "Some action here, Bob."

By noon we'd reached the zone, in the Great South Channel between Nantucket and Georges Bank. Brooksie was still twenty miles away, so Bob cruised around the perimeter, watching the action. The area of activity was about two miles by two miles, and within it were thirteen harpoon boats and eight planes.

When Brooksie arrived, he coursed through the zone, and then found the boat. "The tuna thought they were safe out here," he said.

"Nobody's safe out here today," Bob replied.

"Ron just stabbed one," Wade said.

"I know that," Bob answered.

"I got a hundred fish here," Brooksie said. "Go south, to come in with the wind." The *Scratcher* looped around and entered the fray.

Many creatures were fattening up here. Pilot whales ran along the surface, spraying through the schools of sand eels. Humpback whales rose for breath. Some pitchpoled, bobbing up and down, and others breached, falling on their sides to stun the prey. Finback whales surfaced too, and some were bubble-feeding, blowing rings to herd mouthfuls of sand eels into the circle. The bluefin tuna were in schools of sixty to two hundred. They worked among the whales, and they ran through the zone, on tacks with and against the wind, or running north and south. Some schools followed a sequence in which they milled for a while and then ran downsea in the waves, looking for schools to feed upon. After reaching the end of the zone they milled again, turned, and ran hard upsea against the waves.

This was a show day, as it turned out. Bluefin were showing east of Nantucket, and jumping in the Gulf of Maine, from Cape Cod Bay to Ipswich to Grand Manan Banks.

"Off the tails of the blackfish," Brooksie said. Wade brought the *Scratcher* up behind a group of pilot whales. Bob looked into the water, saw a flash of silver, aimed, and threw.

"A hit!" he screamed. Wade hit the zapper. They started to haul the fish in, but it shuddered, came alive, and raced away. Out went a rig.

"I got two hundred fish for you here." They took the loran bearings of the rig, and raced toward Brooksie again.

The air was cold. Bob was wearing a snowmobile suit, but he had been hit by the spray off a wave when the pulpit dipped. The jouncing ride didn't do much for the pinched nerve in his left arm, either. On the second run he used both hands to steady himself, and held the harpoon against his side with the pressure of his right arm. Brooksie led him in on the bunch of two hundred, and Bob got a throw off, but it went wide. Immediately they were off on another run. Brooksie had never seen an area packed so tightly with boats and planes, but he had also never seen so many fish in one spot.

Billy Chaprales ran on the school of two hundred after the *Scratcher* lost it. Nick Nickerson turned hard and made a run. Eric Hesse got off a throw, and Ron Lein. Sonny McIntire stood with arms crossed on the cabin roof, his son steering from the mast.

Of all the activity in this whale zone, the most dazzling and the most dangerous was up above at levels of 400 to 900 feet. The whales were swimming, and the bluefin were swimming and milling, and up above them the planes were going a hundred miles an hour. In this two-mile space nine planes ran straight lines and veering arcs and figure eights and continuous circles, crossing paths above and below, flying side by side. This was the tuna hunt in the fourth dimension, the sea extended skyward, the perpendiculars in motion.

There were many close passes. Once four planes were coming side by side toward the *Scratcher*. Brooksie had been looking down, trying to find fish, when suddenly he saw another plane a hundred feet off his wing, just before it veered off. It put the fear of God in him, Bob said.

Some pilots took advantage of the danger, and tried to "work" others. Three times as Jonathan Mayhew circled, waiting for his boat to come in, another plane arrived, circled nearby, and pushed him aside, until he finally refused to budge. Trip Wheeler found a bunch and made a circle and was waiting for his boat when a plane came into his area and circled 200 feet above him. Trip called Jonathan, who had a Citabria, a stunt plane, and Jonathan came in and flew a circle inside and just below the other pilot, blocking his view. For Trip Wheeler, this day was the closest thing to combat he'd ever seen in his ten years of spotting. Trip liked that. He'd wanted to be a combat pilot.

Down below this zip and hum, the waves were rough. It was nearly impossible to walk around on the boat, and to climb the tower with the motion of six-foot waves was to risk getting tossed in. Before the day was done everyone on the *Scratcher* was seasick, except Bob. The *Scratcher* made one run after another, yet after that first hit, and the second missed shot, there were no more throws. The fish had been run so many times that they would dart away at the first sign of a boat, and boats were everywhere.

At two o'clock the zone began to thin out. Those fishermen who were unfamiliar with the area left first, wanting to get around Monomoy before dark. Ron Lein and Matt Comeau joked about the party poopers. Actually, Ron wanted to leave early, but he knew he couldn't when Trip was seeing hundreds of fish.

At three o'clock Bob looked around and said, "What do they know that we don't? Where did they go?" But he knew both what and where.

At four o'clock, even though the show was still going on, Bob went to the rig, and Wade hauled the line in, hand over hand. Bob told Brooksie to go off and take a leak, and Brooksie spoke of nature's simplest pleasures. The spotters used milk cartons. In years past, Wade said, Brooksie might pour the contents of a carton over a boat that crossed his circle. That sort of thing had been common among swordfish spotters before the 200-mile limit was set, when foreign factory trawlers worked Georges Bank and the Great South Channel. I must have looked shocked. "It's atomized by the time it gets there," Wade said. Brooksie made a pass at 75 feet to get a peek at the fish before he went off on his jaunt.

The boat tossed. Wade and Kip cut and cleaned the fish, while I was losing my breakfast over the rail. Bob climbed into the tower, and then Brooksie found another bunch. The *Scratcher* roared away, and with the charge water came spraying over the wheelhouse roof. Wade had put on a complete set of rain gear and had the hood up, but Kip had put on only a jacket, and the water poured down his back. This didn't stop him though. After they lowered the fish into the tank Kip, who had asthma, ran into the wheelhouse, pulled out an inhaler, and sucked away. "I got really hot doing that," Kip said.

The school dispersed before the *Scratcher* got there. Bob couldn't believe that on a day like this—so clear, with so much activity, and so many fish about—he would only get two throws. At 5:30, after another couple of runs, he decided to head in. There were only four boats left in the zone by then. One of them was Ron Lein's, and he wanted to ride in behind the *Scratcher*. Another boat was the *Kembe*. Eric Hesse wasn't ready to go in yet. He had found it awkward to work on the *Kembe*, with its pulpit fourteen feet above the water. Eric was used to throwing from nine feet, which allowed him to lean into the belly rail and touch his dart to the water. From the *Kembe* he had to throw four feet through the air, but this may have worked to his advantage, because he'd had his best day ever, catching three fish, one of which would bring $43 a pound. Eric, fishing one thousand hours in the 1992 season, caught thirty-three fish in all. Ron Lein got two fish that day, and for the season, working four hundred hours, he would get thirty-six.

Bob had said it would be an ugly ride. He was right. As the *Scratcher* headed east it banged up against the waves teased up by the southwest winds. These waves were about six to eight feet high, and the boat shuddered as it hit the big ones. Nevertheless, Bob didn't spare the horses.

"This is a comfortable seventeen and a half knots," he said, as we raced forward, blasting through the walls of water.

124

Before darkness, while it was still light out, you could brace for the biggest waves, because you could see the black sides coming on. But after dark you had to wait blindly for each wallop. Except for Bob, who had a good hold on the wheel, we fell back and bounced off the walls and tumbled about. The best way to ride these blasts was to stand with knees bent and feet apart, hands spread. This way there was a chance to land standing up, as if you'd just jumped off a fence. Kip Lewis was standing behind me, and many times when I went flying back he caught me and set me upright. Water streamed over the cabin roof and through various bolt holes, so there was a steady drizzle on us.

Bob was intoxicated with the power in his new Volvo 380. "She'll be broken in now!" he called out after one vicious hit. Ron Lein had lost all chance of staying behind the *Scratcher*, though he would break a motor mount and damage his pulpit trying. Ron called to remind Bob of the time he had towed him in when he ran out of fuel, but Bob waved it off. To him, this was just another day on the water, if an ugly ride, and he was steaming to port. And it was something of a boat race, too—no longer could the *Sandra C.* outpace the *Scratcher*. "He's probably waiting to get me on the calm!" Bob said, with a laugh.

"You bastard!" Bob yelled, after a hit that thrummed every timber and bone on the boat. At 10 knots these collisions would have been one thing, but at 17 to 19 knots they were something else entirely. We ran into these walls again and again, and the engine would rattle in its housing, the stringers would shake, and everything would clatter.

"Bastard!"

Maybe Captain Sampson had been up too long. This work day was pushing twenty hours.

We approached Monomoy. Wade told Bob the compass was off by twenty degrees, and that the radar wasn't working quite right. We stood and tossed in the drizzle. Wade had seen this kind of weather four or five times the previous year. The day had been like this the first time he went cod fishing with Bob, fifteen years ago.

Then, as we crossed Stone Horse Shoal just south of Monomoy, there was a ferocious hit and the sound of an explosion, and we all went flying. It felt as if we'd hit a buoy or a sandbar. Wade had run over a sandbar on the *Rush* the week before. A year ago the *Peggie B.* had run up on a bar at Monomoy and been filled by the next wave—the crew had put on survival suits and been picked up by the *Mooncusser*, which was in the area and heard the call.

But this wasn't a sandbar. We had crossed a rip, moved from one body of waves to another, and in the transition the *Scratcher* traveled about fifteen feet in the air before it was hit broadside by an oncoming wave. The explosion had been the sound of the hoist breaking loose from a cotter pin. A box of rope had fallen into the water.

Wade went to the stern to refasten the hoist. Bob yelled at Kip to haul in the rope. This seemed like a sand-in-your-ears-before-morning situation to me, and I thought we'd be taking on water, so I looked for Ron Lein, but he was nowhere in sight. Then Bob started the engine and we shot off again, rounding the corner and heading toward Harwich. The boat was pushed broadside by the waves now, with the pulpit swinging in circles and the tower dipping so wildly it seemed it would pull the boat over. At times the boat skidded side-ward down the waves. Then, as we approached the channel, and Bob let off, and the trip began to end, the speed—it all seemed worth it.

Inside the channel, it was so calm, with so little wind, and the lights on in the houses of the peaceful neighborhood. Fishermen, who came in from the edge after getting their brains beat out, as Bob put it, knew things that others didn't.

Bob cruised up to a dock to meet the manager from CQB, and they unloaded the fish. This done, he swung around and headed for his berth at Saquatucket. We were all red-faced, tousled, and dazed.

Wade and Kip stayed on the *Scratcher* and went about cleaning up. Bob walked over to the unloading dock to ask Ron Lein how the day had gone for him. On his return, passing where I stood, Bob called out to me:

"Just now when Ron came off his boat and shook my hand, he looked at me like I was the devil himself! Really! I'm not kidding you! The devil himself!"

The 1992 Season

• • •

ELEVEN FISH had been caught on Friday, October 2, all by boats from CQB. The following Tuesday the harpooners got out again, and those from CQB caught twenty-six fish. Bob caught four bluefin in one day. Ron Lein got five one day, three the next, and two the day after that. Ron said he was flying high.

That Friday, October 9, was another tight day, with about sixteen boats at work in the whale zone. Brooksie refused to fly among the pack of planes this time. Bob and Wade ran four bunches all day long and harpooned two very fat fish.

Bob left the next day for Colorado, this time for an elk hunt. He took a case of lobsters along to cook for his friends there. Jonathan Mayhew's brother, Greg, a commercial fisherman from Martha's Vineyard, took Bob's place on the *Scratcher*. On Monday the 12th, Greg Mayhew and Wade Behlman caught two of the five fish taken in the whale zone, and Eric Hesse got one. The harpoon category closed at midnight, and the 1992 season was over.

During the final two weeks of the season, 108 fish were landed in the harpoon category, 35 percent of the total number for the year. The average weight per fish during the last week of the season was 419 pounds, the culmination of a steady increase from the 350-pound average of July 10.

PART TWO

Winter

KAREN ANNE

❦

AT 5:30 one January morning Peter Atherton and Joe Jancewicz left Newburyport in the *Karen Anne*, and headed for the mouth of the Merrimack River. From there they would go six miles offshore to drag for shrimp. The temperature was about ten degrees.

Though in the summertime Peter Atherton used the *Karen Anne* to chum for tuna, it was not a sleek or fast boat. It was stubby, deep and buoyant, built for pulling long cables attached to heavy nets, built to support the gallows frame and the net winder at the stern, built for working with and cleaning fish on deck in a heavy roll. We cruised upriver at eight knots.

"Off like a herd of turtles," Peter said. "Off like a prom dress."

Peter was built like his boat—low to the ground and solid. He had straight red-blond hair, reddish eyebrows, the bluest of eyes, and experience written on his face, which was weather-burned, and deeply lined around the eyes.

I'd last seen Peter at TriCoastal Seafood one afternoon in August. Two fish were brought in that day, the first by a member of Tri-Coastal's board of directors, a fisherman who owned a dockside business in the off season and fished avidly for tuna in the summer. He'd been doing well, and had caught about fifteen fish at that point of the season. When he got the price that day, $12 a pound, he left in a huff. After getting similar prices from other buyers in Newburyport, he loaded his fish on a pickup truck, marched from his boat with clenched fists, and went to Gloucester, where he got $16—a victor for the day. The second fish was Peter Atherton's. He unloaded it, took a $12.50 price without question, walked along the dock saying hello and smiling to his friends, got his free ice, which the workers shoveled onto his boat, and left a happy man. Peter used only one buyer, and he thought it paid to do so—as it had that day, when his fish got fifty cents more per pound, or about $300.

Peter had grown up around Newburyport, and he'd begun market fishing for striped bass when he was ten. He dug seaworms for money, and later, after serving in Vietnam, he worked on various commercial boats, putting in an apprenticeship with a tuna fisherman. He got a boat of his own, and tried gillnetting for a while, then abandoned it after draggers twice ran through his gear, a $25,000 loss each time. The *Karen Anne* had been built four years before, the year after Peter got married. Normally in the winter he dragged for cod, but they hadn't yet arrived in Ipswich Bay, where he worked, so he was trying shrimping. In the springtime he caught cod and flounders. In the fall he caught cod, flounders, and lobsters. Summers he switched over to tuna.

Groundfishing was a consistent fishery, Peter said. If you got a hundred pounds an hour towing, and you put in ten hours a day, that was a thousand pounds of fish. The average price was ninety cents per pound, so a day's work could amount to $900. But it wasn't always that neat. Some days amounted to more, others to less. Peter got out groundfishing about 150 days a year, and his average gross income was approximately $150,000. Ten thousand of it went for fuel, nearly forty thousand for help.

Up to a third of that $150,000 came from bluefin tuna, depending on the success of the season. In 1992 Peter had caught six fish and averaged $15 a pound, for a total of $43,000. A decade earlier, back when bluefin were going for $3 a pound, he had made a name for himself by catching a tuna every day for twenty-eight days—using herring on the first baiting and squid on the second. He'd been running a skiff then, and when he hooked a fish he just let it pull him around until it tired.

Tuna fishing was like playing the lottery. There was always a chance you would catch a fish worth $40,000, so why not try it? He tried it about sixty days a year. Tuna fishing wasn't merely a sport to him—it was an important part of his livelihood, a crucial segment in the rhythm of his season. And with the National Marine Fisheries Service's new measures to protect groundfish stocks—closures of areas, increased net-mesh sizes, and limits on the numbers of days at sea—Peter Atherton and other draggers would depend more and more on the bluefin tuna fishery.

IT WAS warm inside the cabin as we moved out from shore, and the sky began to lighten. There was the ever-present aroma of fish oil, too. On the shelf in front of the windshield was a bank of electronic instruments, which enabled Peter Atherton to chart his course and find fish with the precision of a whale or dolphin. The irony was that these instruments had helped to bring about the depletion of New England cod and haddock stocks, and they were a reason why certain men, families, boats, and whole communities were now threatened with failure. Among Peter's electronic tools the most impressive was a scanner that allowed him to see underwater far away from the boat—a fifteen-degree swath 900 feet out and 250 feet wide. On the surface he could do the same thing at 360 degrees with his radar set. He had loran, a network of radio beams that allowed the fisherman to know precisely where he was located. He had several radios, a video sounder that showed the water column and the bottom condition, and a video course plotter, into which Peter could program the tows he ran and the places to be avoided. Green dots on the plotter screen represented wrecks, rocks, and hard bottom. Among the green dots floated a blinking yellow dot, the *Karen Anne*. Peter navigated among the hazards as if he were playing a video game. If things got tight, he could phase in for a close-up.

At 6:30 they made their first set, and the net rolled out from behind the boat.

The season for northern shrimp (*Pandalus borealis*) had begun in mid-December and would run until the end of April. The shrimp were migrating inshore to lay eggs now. Peter thought they came in on the westerly winds, moving against them somehow, then went out again on the easterlies and the tides—millions and millions of them finding some olfactory cue in the force of the water. To give the shrimp a break, no fishing was allowed on Sundays. The NMFS also required a Nordmore grate, or "finfish exploder." Shrimp and small fish passed through the grate and deeper into the net, but anything wider than an inch or so went flying up through the roof in a jet stream of water.

The shrimp fishery was another relatively small but important segment in the yearly scheme of certain draggermen. Annual landings in the Gulf of Maine had declined from 11,400 metric tons in the late 1960s to 400 tons in the late 1970s, then increased to 5,000 metric tons by 1987. In 1992 landings were 3,400 tons, and the 1993 catch was forecast as 2,100 metric tons. Two-thirds of the landings were by Maine boats, 15 percent by boats in Massachusetts. The number of vessels in the fishery was three hundred to four hundred yearly. The average daily catch was 750 pounds, and the shrimp were worth about $1 a pound. Peter expected to get about 400 pounds on this day.

He stood in his cabin, watching the course plotter, and the boat moved along at slightly less than three knots, with the sound of a slow hum, the deep growl of an engine at work. Joe watched the morning news on the TV set at the end of the bank of electronic gear.

A dragger resembles a large, mechanical fishing pole—a boat, a long line, a bag at the end. The reel was on the gallows frame at the stern, and onto the spool wound two cables 750 feet long. The reel was powered by hydraulic winches placed at the fulcrum of the boat.

The net system was called an otter trawl. Set out and doing its work, this net resembled a big fishnet stocking. The net rode along the bottom, and was held open by chains at the bottom and floats on the top. The sides were pulled apart by two hydrofoils, "doors" that flew outward. The steel doors were heavy, and ran along the ground, creating a mud cloud that herded fish in front of the net. Moving along at two and a half knots, the cod and haddock and flounders grew tired and drifted back, collecting in the bag, or cod-end. Unlike finfish, shrimp didn't react to the mud cloud, but just fell into the trawl as it plowed by.

At 8:30 Joe sprayed the deck with seawater to wash away the ice, and they began to haul in. The cables wound and snapped around the spool. The doors rose from the water and were fastened to the stern. Up came the floats, and the chains, and the first parts of the net, all winding onto the spool. Gulls swooped in to pick at the trailings. Then the bag, round and bristling, swung over the deck and hung suspended until Peter hit the hasp and the catch spilled into a pen.

The net was swung back, the hasp fastened, and out it trailed from the stern. Peter worked the winches while Joe, in oilskins, wearing gloves, crouched and picked among the pile, sweeping the shrimp to one side and tossing the cull overboard, the small mackerel, herrings, and flounders, the sea robins and the stray starfish, scallop, or octopus, all to the screeching of diving gulls. He ran seawater through the catch, then shoveled the shrimp into bushel baskets. He filled seven of them. Thus, this first haul amounted to a catch of 350 pounds. It was one of the best tows of the season.

P E T E R W A S back at the course plotter, working a northerly curve along the forty-fathom line. Rockport and the lighthouses of Thachers Island were off to the south. Seabrook, New Hampshire, was ahead on the horizon.

One of the things Peter liked about being a fisherman was that he could see his accomplishments at the end of the day. He could have been working in a factory, putting in this part or making this widget, and at the end of eight hours he'd punch the clock and never see what he'd done. But with fishing you put something on the dock. Good or bad, at least you could see the results of your efforts.

He had tried other things. When he turned forty, just after he got married, Peter began to think he was too old to be splashing around in the water. So he quit for a while, and got a job with *The Boston Globe*, distributing newspapers to the carriers. He quickly saw that there was no future in it, but he did have some time to think, and decided to build the *Karen Anne*.

After he got back in the water there were some great runs. For three weeks, working within sight of his house on Plum Island, Peter had caught 1,800 pounds a day. His family sat out on beach chairs watching him. With money from that run he bought the scanner. Now, in all, he had about $120,000 invested in boat and equipment—though it wasn't the kind of investment that made money on its own. You had to go out and use it to make it work.

Peter was having a new boat built, a Maine lobster boat of classic lines, a design he'd long admired, and he hoped his sons would work on it someday. But he was using inherited money to do it. He didn't intend to invest in any new equipment for a while, not until after the new groundfish regulations came out.

"The problem with some people is that they don't know how to manage their money," Peter said. "They have a good day and they go out and get drunk and then don't go out for a couple of days. Or they go out and buy a truck, rather than put some away for when times are bad."

This brought up the subject of alcohol and drugs. Cocaine had ravaged some fishermen in the 1980s. It was especially attractive to fishermen who took four-to-five-day trips and worked watches around the clock—four hours of sleep followed by eight hours of work. Cocaine nearly eliminated the need for those four-hour sleep periods, but the problem was in keeping the nose packed. They would come to shore, unload the catch (40,000 pounds of pollack, sometimes), visit their dealer, run a few errands, and then head back out to sea with a supply worth several thousand dollars. Some of them spent $500 or more a day to keep the buzz going.

But those days were over, for the most part. Some of those men were out of fishing, some had died, others were clean. There was a group of fishermen in Newburyport who neither drank nor did any drugs. Joe Jancewicz was among them.

"I'm glad I didn't get into that," Peter said. "There was all that available in Vietnam, but I decided not to do it. I wanted to come back, I wanted to stay alive. I thank God that Vietnam gave me that."

•   •   •

T W O   H O U R S   after the first haul they brought the nets in again and another 300 pounds of shrimp spilled into the pen. Joe culled the catch, then settled into his bunk to watch TV. This was the part of the day when he watched *The Price Is Right*. He put on sunglasses so he could doze off more comfortably. Outside the window next to his bunk were blue sky and the rolling ocean.

"TV is important out here," Peter said. "This fishery takes patience. All these boats have TVs on them." There was a rotary antenna mounted on the gallows frame, operated by remote control, and it was necessary to adjust the antenna to correspond with the tack of the boat. Joe did that now, got the best picture he could, and then settled back. All up and down the Gulf of Maine, I assumed, other fishermen were doing the same.

Peter talked about his son, Adam. He was thirteen, and doing well in football. Peter didn't fish on Sundays during football season so he could go to the games. Adam had scored eleven touchdowns this season, and rushed for a thousand yards.

Peter's first wife had died when Adam was two. Adam's birth had followed four miscarriages. Peter's second wife, Karen Anne, was Joe Jancewicz's cousin, and Joe had introduced them. Her husband had also died. The two dated—they had something in common—and soon they got married. Peter brought Adam to the marriage, and Karen brought a boy and girl. Now they had a baby daughter.

In Vietnam, Peter had been wounded by a mortar blast. In the hospital, after he'd recovered a bit, they asked him to feed some of the men in the next ward, the guys with serious injuries. Seeing them, Peter decided that he wouldn't try to get medical compensation for his wound, that there were guys who needed it more.

After he got out of the hospital he was cleared to go back to the field. He asked for a deferment—there was shrapnel in his neck—but the doctor threw up his hands. Then a sergeant came along and asked Peter if he could swing a hammer, and after Peter built a hooch he was hired as a bartender. There were others attached to this sergeant, and when the commanding officer came in and ordered everyone back to the field it was time for Peter to ship out. He left

Southeast Asia on his twenty-first birthday. Because of time-zone changes it was his twenty-first birthday all the way back to Boston.

The hard part was when he got back to Newburyport. People kept saying, "Where the hell you been?" They didn't care about what he'd been through, that he'd had to wear the same clothes in the jungle for forty days, until they were falling apart from the heat and the sweat. He was still messed up from all of that, just like everybody else who went over there.

But there was an advantage, one of relativity.

"All these things that have happened to me over the years, the marital problems, the gear problems, fishing, all those things, when I think about them, I just think about Vietnam and I say, this is nothing."

Joe was dozing. *Family Feud* was on.

While talking, Peter had lost track of his course plotter. The yellow blinking light was very close to an ominous green dot.

He spun the wheel. There was a change in sound, a lowering of pitch from the engine and a vibration from the gallows frame and cables.

"Time to haul in, Joe."

Joe roused from his bunk.

"Sorry," I said, for the distraction.

Peter pulled on his boots. "That's all right," he answered.

"Shit happens."

THE THIRD haul brought another 250 pounds. The sun was at its strongest, there was little wind, the sky was clear, and it actually seemed warm while Joe culled the trash fish, even though the temperature was in the low thirties.

Joe washed the deck, and Peter sat at the chair by the wheel and watched.

"What Joe is doing isn't hard work," Peter said. "You've just got to be out here. You've got to put the time in."

Joe did watch a lot of television, but he also spent a good part of the day on his knees in the cold, pulling herring and other cull from

138

the net. He had also grown up in Newburyport and had made a business of catching striped bass in high school, and he'd been part of a crew of boys on a tuna boat owned by two brothers who ran a taxi company and used one of the taxis to transport fish. He'd worked on draggers and longliners, and for the fabled harpooner Herb Randall, who once hit seventy-four shots in a row. Joe owned a slender 34-foot Jonesport, one of the last wooden boats built by Vinal and Osmond Beal of Beals Island, Maine. In 1990, ranging from down east Maine to east of Chatham, he had caught fifty-one bluefin and was given an award as the best tuna fisherman in Newburyport. Dragging provided steady work and a saving income, and Joe liked doing it, but it wasn't his true line of fishing.

To relieve the drudgery, he took vacations in the winter. He'd be going swordfishing in the Gulf of Mexico soon. When Joe went to Florida one winter to play golf, Peter brought his sons out to work for Christmas money. They had been out during the summer before, but the boys didn't like fishing in the winter very much. It was blowing hard that day, and they spent a lot of time at the back of the boat getting sick. Even so, they split what would have been Joe's share and took home $250 each, which made them feel a lot better about the experience. Maybe they would take up fishing later on, but as Peter said, "they might not get as much out of it as I do."

Peter gave Joe a good share, much better than he'd give someone else, for fishing with him in the winter. Joe was dependable, so Peter didn't have to hunt around for other men. If someone without experience or with a hangover slipped and got hurt there could be a lawsuit. He had insurance, but it probably wouldn't be enough. He'd lose his house, maybe.

Sometimes when Joe took time off Peter fished alone. He had an automatic pilot and could clean the fish while the boat ran on its own. Of course, working alone could be dangerous. Two years ago another fisherman—someone who was on the bay this very day, Peter added—had gotten caught up in the net and was wound around the spool. The trailing part of the net got caught in the propeller, and that stalled the engine. By chance another fisherman was looking around with binoculars, saw it happen, and came over to help.

Ideally there should be two men aboard a dragger. "But one time out here working alone I got into some flounders and some big cod. I made eleven hundred dollars in one tow, and got to keep it all to myself."

THE LAST haul began at four-thirty. Up came the cables, snapping with the tension, up came the doors, the floats, the mouth of the net, and the bag. Joe hit the hasp and another 225 pounds of shrimp lay on the deck.

The total haul that day had been 1,175 pounds. "Not a bad day," Peter said, as Joe stowed the baskets in the hold.

He turned for shore, and called Karen on the radio. He told her he'd be in at seven or so. He'd eat, talk to his wife, talk to the kids, and within an hour or so he'd fall asleep.

"At the end of the day you've had enough," Peter said. "You're ready to head in. Then the next morning you can't wait to get out here again."

And so we headed in. The sky was dusty brown, with a band of yellow-green and then blue. A quarter moon grew large and red and set over Newburyport. The clock tower glowed above the buildings and cast a long reflection on the Merrimack. The *Karen Anne* made its way up the river to TriCoastal Seafood, where Bob Campbell was waiting, and together they unloaded the $1,175 worth of shrimp, the day's work.

140

(1 4)

THE QUOTAS

I N M A Y 1992, there was a public hearing in Plymouth, one of
several held by the National Marine Fisheries Service for the purpose of taking comments about the bluefin tuna fishery. The NMFS
had proposed a new set of rules and a new allocation scheme that
conformed to a 10 percent cut in the U.S. quota.

More than two hundred fishermen were present. Among them were
a half dozen armed federal agents in plainclothes—"men with good
haircuts," as they were described by one federal employee. Their
presence said something about the antagonism between the National
Marine Fisheries Service and some American fishermen.

Working from a list that gave their names in order of importance,
Dick Stone, head of the newly formed Highly Migratory Species Unit,
called the speakers up to the microphone. The governor's office had
a say, as did Massachusetts congressional and state representatives,
a state biologist, and a member of the fisheries commission. Rich
Ruais of East Coast Tuna spoke out point by point on nearly every
article in the proposal, to great applause. Then the fishermen made
their appeals. They spoke of their years in the fishery, of their economic dependence on it. One said bluefin had put his kids through
college. Others drew patriotic analogies, speaking of their contribu-
tions to the trade deficit and to American competitiveness in Japanese
markets. Others said the government assessments of a shrinking blue-

fin population didn't reflect what the fishermen were seeing on the water.

Some said that the recreational catch of small bluefin should be limited. This catch had gone unregulated during the expansion of a charter fishery, and now greatly exceeded its quota. It didn't make sense to catch a small fish worth a couple of hundred dollars when a few years later the same fish could be worth $5,000. Several of the fishermen at the meeting made comparisons with the lobster fishery— let the school fish grow large enough to spawn, they said.

Another suggestion that night, one that didn't appear in the lengthy accounts in the *Federal Register*, was that the NMFS replace its director, William W. (Bill) Fox, Jr. Some of the fishermen wore pins with the No sign—a red circle and a line—over a drawing of a fox.

The bluefin tuna had become a most politicized fish, and the reasons went back about three decades.

BEFORE THE National Marine Fisheries Service was formed in 1969, the Bureau of Commercial Fisheries conducted research cruises to study populations and develop fisheries. BCF research opened up the modern commercial bluefin fishery in New England, after articles called attention to the resource and after BCF-assisted ventures on the *Silver Mink* brought purse seining to Cape Cod Bay.

In 1963, the first year of large-scale harvests, the purse seine fleet took 5,447 metric tons of school bluefin—approximately 200,000 sixty-pound fish—and recreational rod-and-reel fishermen took 1,072 tons of bluefin of all sizes. American longline trawlers and commercial harpooners took 215 tons. Japanese longliners, fishing strictly for giants off the coast of Brazil, took 6,191 metric tons— approximately 27,108 giants, at 500 pounds per fish. The entire western Atlantic catch that year was 13,838 metric tons, about 30 million pounds.

That was just one segment of one tuna fishery. Bluefin were harvested worldwide, and there were significant catches in other tuna species—yellowfin, albacore, skipjack, and bigeye. Because of concerns about overfishing and stock depletion, international organizations had been formed to monitor the tuna fisheries, gather scientific data, and establish catch quotas. The Inter-American Tropical Tuna Commission (IATTC) was formed in 1949, and in 1966 it set a quota for the yellowfin fishery in the Pacific Ocean. In 1966 the International Commission for the Conservation of Atlantic Tunas (ICCAT) was formed to study and manage tuna and billfish in the Atlantic Ocean. Membership grew to twenty-two countries, including the United States, France, Spain, Japan, Korea, Portugal, Brazil, Morocco, Senegal, and the Ivory Coast.

In 1975 Congress enacted the Atlantic Tuna Convention Act, giving the Secretary of Commerce authority to carry out the recommendations of ICCAT, and this authority was in turn delegated to the Assistant Administrator of Fisheries, the director of the National Marine Fisheries Service.

The ICCAT conferences are usually held each November in Madrid. Scientific delegations, varying in number from year to year, arrive with their own studies, catch reports, and stock assessments, and during several days of meetings they attempt to make recommendations by consensus. The scientific meeting is followed by a political meeting, where final recommendations are made. The United States is represented at these meetings by three commissioners—one from the Department of Commerce, another with experience in commercial fishing, and a third with experience in the recreational fishery.

In 1974 ICCAT agreed that it was necessary to limit fishing and to set a minimum size. The conference produced a voluntary quota, an agreement to "limit mortality to recent levels," and a prohibition on catching bluefin under fourteen pounds. As a result, in the western Atlantic purse seining of the very smallest fish ceased. The Canadians stopped purse seining bluefin entirely. American seiners continued to take the twenty-five- to 100-pound school fish for the canneries until 1981, and they were harvesting giants for the newly developing Japanese markets.

Meanwhile, the Japanese longliners, pressured to reduce their catches in the Mediterranean spawning grounds, responded by increasing their efforts in the Gulf of Mexico. From 1975 through 1978,

Japanese longliners took an estimated 36,000 fish—18 million pounds, at 500 pounds per fish. Even when the Magnuson Act went into effect in 1977, establishing the 200-mile limit, the Japanese continued to take bluefin in the Gulf, because tuna were highly migratory and so were not included in the Act. In the fall the longliners would move north and fish off New England and the Grand Banks.

It was an alarming situation for American recreational fishermen, because the longliners were also catching species such as blue marlin, white marlin, sailfish, and swordfish. There was already animosity between recreational fishermen and commercial fishermen. Tensions increased when fishermen in the north began shipping bluefin to Japan for returns of fifty cents to $1 per pound.

Recreational organizations began to work to protect the resource, among them the Sport Fishing Institute, the International Game Fish Association, and the National Coalition for Marine Conservation (which also helped establish the 200-mile limit). In 1974 the Sport Fishing Institute attempted to list bluefin as a protected species under the Endangered Species Act. Until 1974 bluefin research had been coordinated at the NMFS Southwest Fisheries Center in La Jolla, California, but it was thought that the La Jolla lab was under the influence of the canneries and that an Atlantic species should be studied at an Atlantic station, so research was transferred to the Southeast Fisheries Center in Miami.

During the 1970s bluefin science and the understanding of tuna biology changed, as the open-seas study of life history gave way to the development of quantitative methods—population dynamics. From 1955 into the 1960s, Bureau of Commercial Fisheries boats roamed the Gulf Stream and the middle Atlantic, using longline sets to sample the tuna stocks, to chart movements through the eddies and currents, and to study life habits. Aboard the *Delaware*, Frank Mather did some of his work on the life history and migratory patterns of bluefin. Researchers found medium fish in pre-spawning and post-spawning condition in northern reaches of the Gulf Stream.

According to the chief scientist on several of these cruises, support began to diminish after the assassination of John Kennedy (who summered on Cape Cod and helped establish the National Seashore there), because the Johnson Administration was less interested in oceanography and marine studies. During the Nixon Administration, when the Bureau of Commercial Fisheries was moved from the Department of the Interior to the Department of Commerce and reformed as the National Marine Fisheries Service, support for fisheries science cruises had largely ceased.

Such trips were increasingly expensive, and yielded ambiguous data—heavy concentrations of bluefin here, post-spawners there, feeding grounds there. Life science produced data that enabled fishermen to range out and find fish. Computer modeling of fish populations yielded specific numbers, and was cost effective as well. Gradually papers with titles such as "Distribution and Migrations of North Atlantic Bluefin Tuna," by Frank Mather III (Woods Hole Oceanographic Institution, November 1962), gave way to papers such as "Sensitivity of Bluefin Tuna Virtual Population Analyses and Projections to Uncertainty Inputs," by S. C. Turner (NMFS Southeast Fisheries Center, Miami, Florida, 1991).

It was a heady notion—that the right data and the right formula could provide an answer to the age-old question of how many fish were in the sea.

To the field biologists who had traditionally spent a few years around the docks before doing their research, the new computer modelers seemed arrogant and stiff. The old-school scientists didn't understand the new systems and didn't know how to question them, and the new-school people seemed to have all the answers anyway, since in population dynamics it was necessary to anticipate all the questions, and cover the arguments in the way a trial lawyer prepared for a case. As a result, the whiz kids, the number crunchers, as they were called, tended to advance quickly to positions of leadership.

Old-school biologists who spent time on the water getting to know fishermen acquired an empathy for them, a human bias. Though the first population dynamics biologists tended to have some field experience, it was optional, and became even more so as the science developed. They tended to develop a bias toward the population, a sympathy with the resource. While the old-school biologists tended to manage fisheries for maximum sustainable yield, to support the fishermen, new-school biologists tended to manage fisheries to protect fish.

The first work on bluefin models for the western Atlantic was done during the early 1970s at the La Jolla lab by Bill Fox, Gary Sakagawa, and Brian Rothschild. They surveyed the literature and drew heavily from the work of Frank Mather and his associates. The first analyses recommended less fishing on the youngest bluefin, the pre-spawners, but this wasn't well received among recreational fishermen or among the seiners.

The virtual population analysis, or VPA, for bluefin begun at La Jolla continued at the Southeast Center after bluefin studies were transferred in 1974. In essence, the VPA is an accounting procedure that provides a trend history of a population. Annual catches are scaled against the work expended by fishermen—catch per unit effort. Catches of age groups, or "cohorts," determined by size, are also matched against "indices of abundance," which in the case of the bluefin include larval surveys conducted in the Gulf of Mexico, and effort surveys from the Gulf of Mexico to Canada. The products of these calculations are "tuned" by indicators of relative abundance, including the fish's natural mortality rate, to come up with the size of year classes. With the inclusion of the fishing mortality rate, estimates of the absolute population size are possible.

Wes Parks took over the bluefin VPA in Miami. In 1975 his model showed a declining trend in the stock, and calculated an absolute population that turned out to be lower than the longline catch in the Gulf of Mexico. At a meeting in Gloucester, Massachusetts, Parks told a group of fishermen that there were nine thousand giants left in the Atlantic Ocean. They hooted. It was clear to them that the analysis was wrong and it was also clear that they were looking at a new kind of scientist. Frank Mather had called for strict conservation measures and claimed that the European stocks were near extinction, but the Parks assessment seemed brazenly absurd.

Bill Fox was appointed director of the Miami lab in 1978. He was thirty-three, and had moved from fisheries biologist with the Bureau of Commercial Fisheries in 1967 to program leader with the National Marine Fisheries Service in 1973, and in 1975 to division chief of

Oceanic Fisheries at La Jolla, where in addition to developing the bluefin population dynamics model he had done significant work on the problem of porpoise mortality in tuna purse-seining fisheries in the Pacific Ocean. Fox had been a member of the ICCAT scientific delegation since 1972 and was also a member of the scientific committee of the International Whaling Commission. He was known as a population biologist who was willing to stand up for populations.

In 1979 Fox hired Mike Parrack, who had been working on shrimp at the NMFS lab in Galveston, Texas. Parrack was told there were bluefin troubles, problems with the regulatory process, and he took over the Parks assessment. His first effort in 1979 was a crude one, not much more than a rough guess. It was clear that the Atlantic stock was a fraction of what it had once been, but the data were weak, particularly from the eastern Atlantic countries.

One solution to the lack of data was to divide the Atlantic in half and run a VPA for each side. The two-stock theory had been developing through the 1970s, and had often been discussed at ICCAT meetings. There were, after all, two major spawning grounds—in the Gulf of Mexico and in the Mediterranean—which suggested two stocks, and tagging data showed many local migrations. But to Parrack and other biologists, the tagging data also showed that the fishery was a conglomeration of fish from both sides of the Atlantic, that bluefin traveled wherever they wanted to go. A two-stock assessment didn't make complete sense scientifically, but it did make sense politically—if you had two stocks you could at least manage one of them. The European countries weren't ready for any kind of management, but the west could be managed by the United States, Canada, and Japan.

Parrack was told to devise two assessments—one for the entire Atlantic and a two-stock assessment for east and west. Though he complained that there was no proof of separate stocks, Parrack was told to follow orders and complete the assessments. A kind of party line developed—two stocks, two spawning grounds, limited intermixing—and with this, bluefin science became politicized. The party line became more resolute as time passed.

By 1981 Parrack felt ready to take a firm stand at ICCAT. His one-stock assessment showed a severe decline over the entire Atlantic and indicated that immediate action was necessary. His two-stock assessment showed that, while in the eastern Atlantic fishing could continue at current levels despite declines, in the western Atlantic the stock was at dangerously low levels. Even with no fishing its recovery was uncertain. He recommended that catch levels be set as "near-zero as possible."

The assessment done by eastern Atlantic scientists in 1981 indicated that the eastern stock alone was 839,717 fish greater than the NMFS assessment for the entire ocean, but they accepted the two-stock hypothesis because it gave them autonomy over their own side. The Japanese delegation to ICCAT didn't understand what the United States was up to, and thought they were bluffing. Late one night the Japanese called the bluff, and said that if the U.S. assessment was true, the bluefin fishery should be shut down. To their surprise, the U.S. delegation agreed. The Japanese later tried to object, but it was too late. Acting on the American research, ICCAT voted to reduce fishing in the western Atlantic to a quota of 400 tons. Japan, Canada, and the United States would meet in Miami early in 1982 to divide up the quota.

The 1981 ICCAT meeting was a coup for the NMFS scientists. They gained reductions in the western Atlantic from a historical average of 5,500 tons to a quota of 400 tons, and got the seiners to agree to stop fishing on school fish entirely. They had effectively pushed the Japanese longliners out of the Gulf of Mexico. Parrack returned a hero, since he had supplied the data. Bill Fox, who oversaw the plan, got political credit.

Parrack was then told to attend graduate school to work on his Ph.D. and left for the University of Washington. He was replaced at the Southeast Center by Joe Powers, who had worked under Fox at La Jolla. Powers was joined by another scientist, Ray Conser, and during 1982 they worked on the bluefin assessment.

Neither Parrack nor Fox was a hero in New England, where the bluefin fishery had been all but shut down just when bluefin had become the most valuable seafood product in the Gulf of Maine. Jerry Abrams, whose seafood company had been among the first to ship fresh tuna to Japan, called a meeting in Boston, and the bluefin fishermen formed the East Coast Tuna Association.

ECT hired two scientists who had worked at La Jolla to analyze the Parrack assessment. They read the ICCAT reports, but were denied access to the computer programs. At a meeting in Washington in December 1981, NMFS agreed to provide the programs, but later it refused to do so. ECT sought congressional help, and finally obtained the programs during the February 1982 meeting in Miami.

At that meeting Fox and NMFS proposed a quota of 565 tons for the western Atlantic, recommending that the catch be limited to the rod-and-reel fisheries in the United States and Canada, which provided better catch-per-unit-effort data. To Abrams and East Coast Tuna, the NMFS proposal seemed to be not so much about conservation as about eliminating the commercial fishery, particularly the seiners. Heated negotiations followed, and the quota was more than doubled, to 1,160 tons, based on the distribution of catches in 1976. The United States would get 605 tons, Canada 250 tons, and Japan 305 tons.

The 1982 ICCAT conference was unlike any previous one. Despite some intrigue, and a few minor scandals, there had always been a feeling of camaraderie at the conference, with scientists talking and drinking late into the night. In 1982 the Japanese and American delegations kept their distance from each other, and the scientists hired by East Coast Tuna played games of intimidation.

ICCAT was a stage, and scientists arrived prepared to test their work upon it. After the 1981 meeting, the Japanese scientist Ziro Suzuki had to explain the reduced quota to industry leaders, and it had not been easy for him. He arrived at ICCAT 1982 exhausted but prepared to debate, and with an assessment of his own.

There was a lot of shouting at ICCAT that year. Joe Powers and Ray Conser had changed some of the dynamics in the Parrack assessment, but they soon discovered they couldn't answer Suzuki's questions. Mike Parrack was called at the University of Washington and ordered to join the delegation in Madrid, but because he'd been in school and hadn't worked on the assessment that year he didn't have a complete understanding of it either. Though the assessment had come from the Miami lab, the delegation leader, Gary Sakagawa, was from the La Jolla lab, and he didn't have complete supervisory powers or a complete understanding of the assessment. Because of this split, the thorough preparation, the anticipation of questions and resolution of uncertainties, that had been such an integral part of the population dynamics process was missing. Suzuki was demanding answers, stalling and huddling with his advisers. The ECT scientists were there, stirring up the pot.

It was pointed out that only seven fish had been used to determine the age of the catch, that mortality rates were too high and the decline of the stock had been overestimated, and that the relationship between spawners and offspring was an artifact. The entire analysis, according to Suzuki, was therefore invalid.

According to one scientist who was present in 1982, it was a bad year at ICCAT. According to another scientist who later took over the assessment, ICCAT 1982 was a good experience because it brought improvements in the assessment process. To another, it was an embarrassing situation in which the scientific delegation fell flat on its face. For Mike Parrack, hauled out of graduate school and called on the carpet at an international scientific gathering, it was a humiliation.

At the commission meeting Japan accused the United States of political manipulation of the science and asked that the western Atlantic quota be increased. Over the objections of the U.S. delegation the commission voted to accept neither assessment, and again the western Atlantic quota was more than doubled to 2,660 tons. The figure was approximately half the historical catch of the two previous decades.

Mike Parrack returned to graduate school. The bluefin assessment was reassigned. Bill Fox soon resigned from the Southeast Center to accept a teaching position at the University of Miami. The director of the National Marine Fisheries Service decided not to criticize the assessment, since it would imply a lack of faith in U.S. scientists and an unwillingness to restrict commercial fisheries despite evidence of stock depletion.

With the establishment of the 2,660-ton quota, ICCAT settled on a long-term plan of stock recovery allowing for a continued fishing industry and gradual growth in the stocks. Because of the substantial harvests of the 1960s and 1970s, and the long life span of the species (spawning at eight to nine years, a longevity of twenty years), it was accepted that populations would remain at low levels and perhaps decrease into the 1990s, as year classes already heavily fished moved through the population and as fish spawned after 1982 became spawners themselves. ICCAT projected 1995 as a turnaround year.

The 1984 assessment, taken over by Steve Turner, was optimistic, and the ICCAT commissioners considered raising the quota. In 1985 a new mortality rate was plugged into the VPA, and the population estimates were reduced by about half. A similar assessment was offered in 1986. In 1987 the assessment showed a declining population, and the U.S. delegates stated that they would seek a moratorium if the decline continued.

In 1988 Frank Hester rejoined the process on behalf of East Coast Tuna. A new means of calculating fishing patterns was plugged into the VPA, and the assessment showed signs of increased numbers of young fish. No changes were recommended in 1988 or in 1989.

In 1990 a report by Joe Powers indicated that if the smaller 1,160-ton quota set in 1982 had remained in effect, the population would have been 3.4 times greater and increasing instead of declining. In response, a report by Frank Hester stated that such a decision would have resulted in annual losses of $14 million to U.S. fishermen, and that if 1981 predictions were correct the bluefin fishery would already have collapsed.

In 1990 Bill Fox was named director of NMFS. Upon taking office he pledged to put resources into data collection and scientific advice, experiment with the privatization of fisheries as a means of conservation, and restore finfish stocks along the Atlantic and Gulf coasts in ten to fifteen years. Fox had continued to teach at the University of Miami, served as a member of the Florida Marine Fisheries Commission, chaired the U.S. Marine Mammal Commission, and received conservation awards from the Florida Audubon Society and the Billfish Foundation.

The appointment was good news for recreational fishermen and conservation advocates, but commercial fishermen were concerned. In New England, Jerry Abrams felt certain that Fox would initiate efforts to limit the bluefin fishery. His suspicions were confirmed a year later when a revitalized East Coast Tuna learned that a group of recreational fishermen called INTERCOM had visited the White House to discuss the bluefin tuna fishery. According to a Commerce Department memo, INTERCOM was represented by George Barley, a Republican fund-raiser who had served with Bill Fox on the Florida Fisheries Commission and was one of his strongest supporters; George Hommel, president of World Wide Sportsman, who sometimes took President Bush out fishing for bonefish in Florida; and John Morris, the owner of Bass Pro Shops, the leading supplier of recreational fishing tackle. After the INTERCOM group met with one of the President's economic advisers, a presidential intern called the Department of Commerce to state that the White House supported a 50 percent reduction in the bluefin tuna fishery.

MEANWHILE, THE environmental movement had become involved with bluefin, as well, spearheaded by the Audubon Society, which had been undergoing a makeover in order to compete with Greenpeace and other higher-profile groups.

Carl Safina, an Audubon ecologist, had been undergoing changes of his own. He had grown up on Long Island and fished for striped bass and for bluefin tuna with his father. He had sold a bluefin tuna in 1986, but decided it would be his last, since he believed the fish should be left for commercial fishermen, and wanted to distance himself from the greed he saw developing on the docks. Safina had what he thought was an enviable life, studying the relationships between seabirds and fish and their prey. He got to spend his days on the water, and because he was working with the roseate tern, an endangered species, he felt that he was doing something for conservation.

But he didn't think he was doing enough. Safina had seen several species of fish become scarce in the New York Bight during the 1980s. Marlin and swordfish no longer appeared. The yellowtail flounder was scarce. The giant bluefin was becoming increasingly rare. Safina felt it was time to publicize the dilemma of stock depletion, not only in the waters off Long Island but all through the oceans.

Safina read the scientific literature, seeking a species that would best exemplify the cause of fisheries conservation. As he later wrote, he "searched the charismatic megafauna to find a flipper with gills," an animal with the public appeal of whales. (He would later regret the "charismatic megafauna" phrase, as it would be used to characterize his ambitions.) Haddock and cod lacked appeal and were too closely identified as food sources. Sharks were charismatic, but the scientific literature was spotty. Bluefin tuna, however, were highly charismatic and, due to ICCAT, had a rich literature and a questionable political history. The Japanese markets, to the American eye— with the extreme prices, the airfreighted fish, the frenetic auctions— were alienesque and extraordinary beyond belief. All would provide good material for a "contentious campaign."

Audubon's campaign focused on ICCAT. It criticized the commission for having delegates with strong "industry ties," for ignoring its own scientific advice, for setting quotas that had long exceeded maximum sustainable yield, for ignoring the 1981 recommendation for a near-zero catch, and for setting the 1982 quota at 2,660 tons—a "scientific monitoring quota" that was never intended to be scientific. In the journal *Conservation Biology*, Safina wrote that ICCAT should actually stand for "International Commission to Catch All the Tunas."

The central strategy in Audubon's campaign (and those of other organizations) was to threaten ICCAT and the bluefin tuna fishery with a proposal for a CITES listing. Founded in 1973, the Convention on International Trade in Endangered Species met biannually to review issues governing international trade in wildlife and list species that needed protection. CITES had banned trade in rare birds, tiger bones, rhinoceros horns, and, most prominently, elephant ivory. CITES protected wildlife species by placing them on one of two "appendices." An Appendix I listing banned international trade entirely, while an Appendix II listing allowed trade but required monitoring. Safina's CITES strategy was to "hold ICCAT's feet to the fire" by threatening to obtain an Appendix I listing for bluefin, which would prevent American fishermen from exporting the fish to Japan.

At the same time, Audubon would actively work on getting the bluefin tuna into the news, and try to use the CITES proposal as a way to get the conservation community interested in fish.

Using ICCAT documents which stated that from 1970 to 1991 the bluefin tuna population in the western Atlantic had declined 90 percent to 27,000 adults, Safina wrote a proposal for a CITES I listing and submitted it to the U.S. Fish and Wildlife Service. On July 24, 1991, the *Federal Register* reported that the National Marine Fisheries Service and the U.S. Fish and Wildlife Service had recommended a CITES II listing for bluefin tuna. But a proposal for a CITES listing wasn't submitted to the conference. According to Safina, NMFS and Fish and Wildlife bowed to heavy pressure from tuna exporters. According to Rich Ruais, director of ECT, they held back because the United States was a member of ICCAT and a CITES listing would have undermined the work of an international fisheries organization.

Safina then sought help from the World Wildlife Fund, and his proposal was sent to Lennart Nyman, a member of the National Swedish Board of Fisheries and Director of Conservation for the Swedish arm of WWF. On Sweden's behalf, Nyman submitted a CITES I listing, and so bluefin tuna was placed on the CITES agenda for the conference in Kyoto, Japan, in March 1992.

At the ICCAT 1991 meeting the National Marine Fisheries Service proposed a 50 percent reduction in the western Atlantic quota. According to Safina, this position was a hard-won victory for conservation advocates over bitter lobbying by tuna exporters. (East Coast Tuna had hired a firm—partnered by Rich Bond, who would become chairman of the Republican National Committee—to counter the lobbying of INTERCOM.) Despite the threat of CITES, two of the three U.S. ICCAT commissioners decided against a 50 percent reduction. Instead, they agreed to a 25 percent reduction over a four-year period.

Japan submitted a statement at ICCAT criticizing the CITES proposal. Sweden had never before attended ICCAT meetings, despite previous invitations, the statement read. ICCAT was responsible for conservation of bluefin tuna, and there had been an understanding that recovery would occur over a period of perhaps thirty years. Ad-

Winter

ditionally, there was no basis to the statement in the CITES proposal
that the western Atlantic stock would be extinct in ten years. A CITES
listing, Japan argued, would undermine ICCAT and lead to a chaotic
situation in the world's fisheries.

A detailed response to the Safina proposal was prepared for ICCAT
by the Canadian scientist Jim Beckett and sent to the secretary general of CITES. Beckett argued that fish stocks had demonstrated they
could maintain themselves even when harvested heavily. Safina's
claim that the bluefin was "clearly headed for extinction" was incom-
patible with the population dynamics of fish such as bluefin and with
the 1991 ICCAT report, which showed a leveling off in the downward
trend of abundance.

JAPANESE PROTESTERS picketed outside the convention hall
in Kyoto, and American television networks aired footage of Japanese
businessmen at sushi bars eating bluefin at $75 a serving.

Inside the convention halls, according to Safina's account in his
journal article, a drama of international intrigue was unfolding. Japanese, Canadian, and U.S. delegates worked feverishly to force Sweden to withdraw its proposal. A Swedish delegate reported that "the
Japanese and Canadians were applying the worst kind of pressure—
we will have to do as instructed." A "paper debate" raged in the
lobby. A "peculiar" ICCAT briefing book was passed around, and it
did little to dispel impressions that ICCAT had conflicts of interest.
Floor statements on the bluefin issue were not permitted, and Sweden,
under severe duress, finally acquiesced.

Nevertheless, Safina's strategy had borne fruit: "Sweden advocated
the need for a 50 percent reduction, adding that they would withdraw
the proposal if the Commission's countries agreed to pursue quota
reductions. The U.S., Canada, Morocco, and Japan eagerly agreed,
and Sweden withdrew their proposal."

Bill Fox was also at the CITES convention, and in a curious position. Fox had been appointed to the U.S. delegation by Curtis Bohlen, an Assistant Secretary of State. In 1969, while at the Department
of the Interior, Bohlen had helped draft CITES. In 1981 he had moved

155

to the World Wildlife Fund as director of government affairs, and had played a key role in passing the elephant-ivory ban. After the 1992 CITES conference, a letter sent to Bohlen from John Turner, leader of the CITES delegation, reported that Bill Fox and others had "worked long and hard to avert a CITES listing on Appendix I or II," and that their strategy had been to substitute a resolution for a 50 percent quota reduction. "I know I can count on the National Oceanic and Atmospheric Administration to ensure that these commitments are carried out," the letter concluded.

To bluefin tuna fishermen in New England, Bill Fox's role at CITES seemed a kind of betrayal. To them it appeared he had been appointed by the World Wildlife Fund to get a 50 percent quota reduction. Many had long felt certain that the National Marine Fisheries Service was no longer working in their interest, and now they were convinced that Bill Fox was out to get them. Thus the buttons with the No sign at the Plymouth meeting in May, and the calls for new leadership.

A T T H E Plymouth meeting, discussion centered on NMFS's proposed reallocation scheme, which conformed to the call from ICCAT for a 10 percent quota reduction (to be followed by another 15 percent reduction in 1994, if necessary). Under the NMFS plan, determined by averaging the harvests from 1983 to 1991, the general-category quota would be cut 31 percent. The harpoon category and the incidental category for longliners would remain roughly the same. Seiners would lose 17 percent. The angling category for recreational fisheries, however, would be more than doubled, from 126 tons to 271 tons.

Though the seiners had stopped taking school bluefin in 1982, during the 1980s, from Virginia to New York, the recreational fishery for small bluefin had gradually supplanted them. The fishery was monitored for scientific data, but otherwise it was left largely unregulated. In 1990 alone, according to NMFS data, fishermen in the angling category landed 1,461,252 pounds of school bluefin, at an average weight of sixty-four pounds—30,201 fish. Of these fish,

3,633 were sold at an average price of $3.23 a pound, for a total of $1,284,000.

Fishermen at Plymouth argued that the young fish should be saved to build the ranks of the old, as in the lobster fishery. Why sell a fish for $180 when it could later be sold for $5,000? And why reward the angling-category fishermen with an increase when they had exceeded their quota by several hundred tons? If the United States couldn't enforce its own quotas, how could it ask other countries to conserve?

After consideration of the comments made at all the hearings from Maine to Louisiana, NMFS did alter the proposals. NMFS reasoned that the recreational fishermen had exceeded their quotas, but through no fault of their own, and they had broken no laws. Too low a quota would harm this highly capitalized fishery in the extreme.

An adjusted reallocation scheme went into effect on July 20, 1992, while the fishery was in midseason. The general-category quota was set at 531 tons, a straight 10 percent reduction. The purse-seine allocation was dropped further, to 301 tons, a 22 percent reduction. The angling quota was set at 219 tons, up from 126, an increase of 74 percent.

The World Wildlife Fund did some public relations work in 1992, placing an ad in *Salt Water Sportsman* that targeted the seiners: "Currently one giant bluefin tuna can bring up to $30,000 on the export market, a value that has led to their relentless pursuit by a small group of commercial net fishermen known as purse seiners . . . Seiners are allocated nearly 15 times their fair share based on total employment . . . The small commercial and sport boat hook and line fishermen and more importantly the bluefin itself are being hurt by a handful of people and their Washington lobbyists."

Five environmental organizations joined to form "ICCAT Watch": the World Wildlife Fund, Audubon, the Center for Marine Conservation, the National Coalition for Marine Conservation, and the Council on Ocean Law. A newsletter was issued in August 1992, with articles that told of the promises at CITES for a 50 percent reduction, that advocated a maximum rather than minimum size, that said the CITES proposal if passed would lead to a loss of only 1 percent of

Japan's total tuna imports, that reported a bluefin "Tournament of Extinction" in Newburyport, that said the environmental community was in the fight for the duration.

ICCAT Watch issued a brochure entitled *The Bluefin and CITES*. A quotation on the cover read, "The bluefin's status is worse than the African elephant, and the population data for bluefin are more reliable." A "Rationale" developed arguments under five headings: (1) "ICCAT has failed to properly manage the western Atlantic bluefin tuna"; (2) "Where ICCAT has failed the bluefin, CITES can and should act"; (3) "Under a CITES listing, fishing for Atlantic bluefin tuna would still be allowed"; (4) "Japan could continue to import bluefin tuna caught elsewhere"; and (5) "Recovery of the Atlantic bluefin tuna fishery is in the best interest of the fishing industry and conservationists alike." A caption under a photograph of a bluefin on a dock, hanging by the mouth, read: "Commercial fishermen often fish up to two weeks to catch a single giant bluefin."

No bluefin assessment was presented at the ICCAT meetings that November—the first time bluefin had been skipped. Instead, delegates agreed to develop a "Bluefin Statistical Document," which would record the origins of all fish entering Japan. The intent was to discourage increasing sales from non-ICCAT countries, to close an illicit market estimated at 200 to 700 tons in the western Atlantic, and to head off a CITES II listing.

Mike Sutton of the World Wildlife Fund requested observer status at the conference, but was given a place in the U.S. delegation instead. Afterward, he stressed that environmentalists and fishermen had shared interests and could benefit from cooperation. "We need to be responsible here," he said. "Unlike rhinos, there's industry here to consider." Then, in a press release, Sutton blasted ICCAT: "The fishing industry has always dominated the commission. They're scared to death of independent scrutiny . . . We cannot allow this type of irresponsible management to continue."

East Coast Tuna and other fisheries groups continued to call for Bill Fox's resignation. Before the inauguration of President Clinton in January 1993, Fox's appointive position as director of NMFS was converted to a career appointment as deputy assistant administrator of fisheries. News of the conversion brought protests. Fox, along with other Bush appointees, was accused of "burrowing," but a Government Accounting Office official stated that the action was acceptable since Fox had previously served in a career position as director of the Southeast Center.

In March 1993, Brad Brown and Steve Turner of the Southeast Fisheries Center appeared at the Maine Fishermen's Forum. Their position was that 20,000 to 22,000 giant bluefin remained in the western Atlantic, and that a 50 percent quota reduction was necessary.

THROUGHOUT THE debate about the accuracy of population assessments, no assessment of declining stocks had yet proven wrong. In all the world's oceans, particularly the northwest Atlantic, fish populations had plummeted due to overfishing. The Newfoundland cod fishery, five centuries in existence, had been completely shut down, and the coastal communities there were in a state of shock. The cod and haddock stocks on Georges Bank had decreased by 90 percent, and fishing at that ground, one of the richest in the world, was also about to be severely cut back. The bluefin tuna, it was argued, was another example of a thoroughly overfished species. The evidence, in the stock assessments, was clear.

But in 1993 Rich Ruais and East Coast Tuna increasingly drew attention to the growth in the bluefin fisheries in the eastern Atlantic and the Mediterranean. Adversaries claimed this was merely a smokescreen to divert attention away from problems at home, but Ruais argued that catch statistics showed that each time the United States implemented new regulations the eastern catches increased. In 1974, reports had declared that the eastern stock was near commercial extinction, but in 1993 it was estimated to be twenty to thirty times that of the west. The documented harvest in 1992 was 27,000 metric tons, and that harvest included, Ruais estimated, between 2 million and 3 million young of the year. Despite minimal efforts at conservation, the eastern harvests had grown to ten times the western Atlantic quota. Why was it, Ruais asked, that U.S. fishermen, who accounted for only 4 percent of the Atlantic catch, were being asked to make further cuts? Conservation in the west was feeding the east, he claimed.

And in his view the assessments were inaccurate. The two-stock theory was not viable, and the VPA data were not adequate. It was one thing to build a VPA on cod by repeatedly towing a net over the grounds, and it was another thing to build a VPA on a highly migratory fish from effort data based on dockside interviews.

Repeatedly in the past, fishermen had insisted the stocks were strong and that regulations weren't necessary, and then the resource had been fished out. Fishermen were predators by nature, conservationists said, and couldn't stop catching fish. Advocates of quota reductions maintained that bluefin fishermen were no different, that they would say there were plenty of fish until they were all gone.

During the winter of 1993 East Coast Tuna announced it would conduct an aerial survey in conjunction with the New England Aquarium. Photographs taken by spotter pilots, they hoped, would disprove the stock assessments. ECT held a raffle to raise the $35,000 needed to outfit nine planes with cameras and to analyze the photographs.

(1 5)

C Q B

CONSIGNMENT PROGRAMS became widespread in 1989—once one buyer started offering them, others had to follow. When a fisherman sent his product to Japan for a share of the auction price rather than accepting a flat rate at the dock, he took a chance at a loss, but he also took a share in the marketing. Information came of this. In 1989, when Bob Sampson's medium bluefin returned $42 a pound on consignment shortly after he'd gotten a flat rate of $4, he learned something about the Japanese market. When he read the auction reports that were available with the consigned deals, he learned a bit more.

On Cape Cod that winter Bill Mullin stopped by Billy Chaprales's workshop at Barnstable Harbor. Mullin had just finished building the *Look Out*, and he wanted to take a more active role in the fishery. He was a builder, not a fisherman, but he had grown up next to Sesuit Harbor in Dennis, and he had worked on charter boats through his school years. Mullin knew fishing and he knew fishermen, and he was a good communicator and negotiator. Visiting with Billy Chaprales that day, he asked what they could do about the buyers, about the inequities of the situation.

Billy Chaprales had already figured this one out. There was only one thing to do, he said. Get the top producers on Cape Cod together and form a company. Put their differences aside. Stop worrying about who's catching the most. Stick together. Pledge all the fish as a group.

It was surprising to hear this coming from Billy Chaprales, one of the most competitive and aggressive of fishermen. Chaprales had been harpooning tuna since he was a boy for his father's restaurant in Cambridge. He was a pure bluefin tuna fisherman, though he had branched out into cod fishing in the winters. He had been the first harpooner to use a spotter plane, and for several years he was the only one to do so. During that period so many people followed his boat that he built a wooden decoy, an image of himself, and fastened it to his pulpit so other fishermen couldn't tell for sure if he was out there.

He'd had his share of adventures. Chaprales once ran his boat aground and watched it sink under the tide while waiting for the Coast Guard to arrive (they called a salvage operator who came the next morning). In a race to a school of tuna his boat crossed pulpits with a boat from Maine and he was tossed in the air as if flicked from a spoon, landing in a narrow space between the two boats. Another time, when he was steaming hard in rough weather, his tower snapped and he and his mate were thrown into the water. They would have drowned if another fisherman hadn't spotted the boat, its rudder turned hard, circling about Chaprales as he held up his unconscious mate. Once while trolling he had caught a bluefin in the shallows off Sandy Neck. To keep the fish from going under the boat and cutting the line he ran his boat aground, and when the fish tail-walked Chaprales jumped in and charged at it with a harpoon. Some fishermen on the Cape thought that Billy Chaprales had been similarly intense with them, and they were a bit wary of him because of it.

Mullin asked Chaprales if he thought it would be possible to get all of those guys to sit down in the same room together. Chaprales said it would be worth a try. They had East Coast Tuna as a model.

Their first meeting was in January 1990, at the Barnstable fire station. It seemed to Bill Mullin that the fishermen sat as far away from one another as they could. They'd been long-standing competitors and all had had some ugly moments riding the prow, with their harpoons in hand, but once they started talking everyone seemed to loosen up. They were the best harpoon fishermen on the Cape, and together they covered the areas. Bob Sampson and Brad Sampson had worked Nantucket Sound and around Martha's Vineyard and Cape Cod Bay. Nick Nickerson had developed his skills in the waters off Chatham, where the fishery was fast-paced and tightly packed and required athleticism. Chris VanDuzer was the best Cape Cod Bay harpooner—his patient manner served him well there. Billy Chaprales knew the waters from Cape Cod to Maine. Others were becoming more experienced all about, too—fishermen such as Eric Hesse, Ron Lein, Chris Woods, the Sullivan family, Ron Menard, Mike Unda, and Jeff Sullivan.

Mullin would function as moderator and mediator, since he could smooth out the differences among the various men. Chaprales would play a leadership role. He could be a forceful speaker.

We're all good fishermen, Chaprales told them. We catch a large amount of fish between us. Why don't we have a little fun? These dealers who come around while we're getting ready to go tuna fishing and tell us how nice our boats look, and ask us if we need anything, let's put the ball in their court. Let's get them to dribble around for a while. Let's form a company and let them know we've come together as a group of fishermen, that we're gonna sell our fish collectively to the buyer that gives us the best deal.

Let's do this now, in January, Chaprales said. Let's make a list, and specify everything, right down the line. We're gonna know what all these prices are, trucking, ice, airfreight, Japan costs, the percentages. In other words, let's ask the dealers what they're gonna do for the fishermen, instead of what the fishermen are gonna do for them. We've been real stupid in the past, because we've never done this before. We just brought our fish to the dock, the guy hauled it off and put it in his truck, and a week later he comes back with a check and says here, you did good.

We trust ourselves to these guys. Let's trust ourselves as a group of fishermen. Fishermen don't generally trust each other as a group because they're very independent, but we're more than fishermen here. A lot of people in this room are businessmen, too, and we've gotta start thinking about that. We've got to join together, because divided we're weak. Let's stick together as a group.

Everyone was saying yeah. Bob Sampson was among them, but he wasn't sure he believed what he was hearing. Bob and Billy had been like magnets on the water—magnets that repel. They rarely greeted each other. Bob was the Scratcher, a loner, but he always felt that he was part of a group of fellow fishermen. Sometimes, though, in his relationship with Billy Chaprales, when envy or greed came into play—when they'd crossed harpoons, so to speak—Bob had felt isolated, alone on the water.

You could be alone on your boat out on the ocean, but to feel mentally and spiritually alone too, that could be unbearable. You needed to have someone out there to talk to, to joke with, to share your successes with. Only other fishermen could truly understand what it took.

Tuna fishermen were egotistical, Bob knew that. He thought that his own ego, relatively speaking, was at the bottom of the scale, and he tried to keep it there, but he also knew that his egotism was probably greater than normal. It had to be that way. You had to have confidence in yourself out there, that your decisions were the right ones, that you were making the right moves at the right times. Otherwise, you watched other people and made your decisions according to what they were doing. You started second-guessing yourself. You sacrificed your individuality. You became a blend of what others had thought and decided.

In Bob's mind, individuality was made up of all the experiences you had over the course of your career. Some things made you successful, while other things made you unsuccessful. The good fisherman came to know his strengths and weaknesses, and molded his outlook accordingly. It was this self-knowledge, this individuality, that brought the capacity for independence. If you didn't have to watch others to know what to do, you were independent. Then, ironically, you could be part of a group. One among a group, you could have your best days, your greatest successes.

Independence and egotism were not the same. Independence made it possible to work together. Egotism, the kind that measured one person against another, doomed cooperative ventures from the start because there was a lack of trust. As a result, in a way that he explained as mere stubborn superstition, Bob Sampson didn't keep a tally of the fish he'd caught, and he told Brad not to tell him, because he didn't want to compete. He didn't want to say he was having a good season because he was doing better than Billy Chaprales or anyone else.

Bill Mullin had told Bob Sampson that Billy Chaprales had seen the light, that he had mellowed, that he wanted to work together. And Billy did seem to want CQB to work. After sitting there at the fire station, listening to Billy Chaprales, wondering what he wanted, Bob figured, what was there to lose—why not pledge his fish? If Bob had to work with the person who had sometimes been his antagonist in order to get leverage on the buyers, so be it. He'd do it.

Thus Cape Quality Bluefin was born: Bill Mullin, president, Billy Chaprales, vice president, Eric Hesse, secretary, Bob Sampson, treasurer.

The entire group was the board of directors, all twelve of them, and they met frequently. That spring they rented a conference room at a motel in Hyannis and interviewed five buyers. Three were from the Cape, one was from Long Island, another came from New Jersey. It was an instructive process, and the fishermen learned things that had been kept from them for years. They studied the proposals and took notes ("Hogwash," Bob Sampson wrote after one explanation about airfreight), and they played one buyer off another. They saw that each buyer had a different way of hiding profit, but the truly gray area appeared to be the airfreight costs. When they made their final choice of a company that year they specified that there would be no profit on airfreight.

The 1990 season was a successful one. Cape Quality Bluefin handled more than 100,000 pounds of tuna and grossed $2,153,000. They knew they had something—the idea had worked. Many people had told them they would fail, that one person would walk away and the rest would follow, just like so many of the other fishing co-ops that had come and gone. There were disagreements that first year, and they did come close to fracture, but they didn't want to go crawling back to buyers as individuals, knowing what they knew, doing what they'd done. They'd heard that even the Japanese buyers didn't think a group of New England fishermen could stay together. And so ego, as it worked out, kept them together—they wanted, more than anything, not to fail.

With a successful season, the lines of communication opened up, because other fishermen wanted to know how they were doing, and that winter they found out that the company they'd done business with in 1990 had made $84,000 on airfreight costs. They also learned of Bill Cort, an American in Japan who brokered fish to the auctions.

They decided to take the next step. Though it was April, and the 1991 season was only two months away, Bob Sampson, Bill Mullin, and Billy Chaprales left for Japan to make a deal with Bill Cort.

After they arrived and took the train into Tokyo, Cort asked if they'd like to go to a party. Some Japanese buyers from Tsukiji market had invited the American fishermen to be their guests at the Cherry Blossom Festival. The flight had taken seventeen hours, and Bob Sampson had worked at ComElectric the night before, and Billy Chaprales had the flu, and they were all tired, but they said sure— what the heck, we'll try it, raw fish. They wanted to make the broker happy, and he wanted to make them happy.

They went into the center of Tokyo, to a place of gardens and concrete walks and cherry trees. There were tents and tarps on the ground, and cardboard for kneeling on. In the center of the tent were coolers full of beer, and wine, and fish. The CQB men took off their shoes, knelt down, and joined the party.

They hadn't eaten raw fish before, not in this way, but they wanted to be the perfect guests. The Japanese, it seemed to Bob, wanted to be the perfect hosts to the American fishermen who had come to make a deal with Bill Cort. Everybody was trying to be perfect for everybody else.

Bob had been up for more than twenty-four hours, and his stomach wasn't in the best of shape, but he tried everything. There was raw salmon, and yellowfin tuna, and bluefin, pieces of shrimp, and fluke. There were small octopus and squid. There were even little eels with big eyes, served in clumps, and eaten raw. Most intimidating of all was a kind of fish that had been marinated in fermenting dead fish, that looked and smelled, Bob thought, like horseshit. But he tried it.

Even after he noticed that there were things the Japanese fish buyers wanted them to try, and things that the Japanese were eating themselves, and that the two didn't necessarily coincide, Bob and his fellow officers were sports and tried everything—including the fish that looked like horseshit and left a taste in your mouth for two days.

Billy Chaprales and Bill Mullin had beer to wash theirs down, but Bob had given up drinking several years ago, and all he had to drink was mineral water. The Japanese buyers were drinking. Bob had never seen people drink in such a way before, to the point of going off to vomit and then coming back to eat and drink more. They were all getting a big charge out of seeing the Americans try the raw fish that was traditional to the Japanese. A television crew even came by and interviewed the American fishermen. It was fun, and interesting.

They went back to their hotel to sleep, and after a breakfast of dried herring and tea they went with Bill Cort on a cruise to an island and discussed business. Upon returning to Tokyo, they went to Tsukiji market at midnight to watch the arrival and unloading of fish. They wanted to see the whole process, from unloading to the sale at auction. Tsukiji was an enormous place, acres in size, with every kind of fish imaginable, from bluefin tuna right down to the little eels with the big eyes. There were even live fish, transported in plastic bags in a truck that looked like an aquarium. The CQB men watched hundreds of thousands of pounds of fish being moved, uncrated, and displayed. Then they returned to their hotel, had a few hours of sleep, and went back to Tsukiji for the morning auction.

Bill Cort wanted them to observe a company that specialized in high-quality fish. It was a family operation, and had been in business at the Tsukiji market and its predecessor for three hundred years. They hadn't met American fishermen before, and they knew little of how the Americans caught bluefin, but they did know they had received fish from these Americans and wanted to meet them.

That day there was a bluefin at Tsukiji that the family was excited about, and they wanted the CQB men to see the auction. They arrived at 5 a.m., saw the fish taken out of the box and laid out on the floor. The son who did the bidding showed them some of the things he liked about the fish, though he did it discreetly. He didn't want to make a display of interest and drive up the price, but he did want to show the Americans that the fish was very special.

And so the fish went on the auction block, and the company bought it for the equivalent of $42,000. At a dressed weight of 350 pounds, the price per pound came out to $120.

The fish was carried to the booth the family rented at Tsukiji. Inside the booth was an elderly man, the grandfather of the family. He was in his eighties, and frail. Bob watched the two sons conferring with the old man after the fish had been lifted onto the table. For fifteen minutes, they assessed the fish, as if they were about to cut a diamond.

The company had bought thousands of fish, but this one was special, and they had paid $42,000 for it. They ran their hands along it, and looked at it in all ways. The sons talked at length with the old man about how to cut the fish. Then, finally, one of them took a long knife and made a single cut along the side.

This, Bob thought, was a cultural difference worthy of attention. He thought of the way things were done in American companies, where the ethic tended toward a period of usefulness followed by a period of uselessness—when Dad got old, in the American way of business, it was time for him to step aside. Not here. Maybe it was because of tradition, or because tuna hadn't changed. But these sons not only had faith in the old man's wisdom and accepted his advice, they asked for it. For Bob Sampson, this was refreshing and affirming.

They sampled the meat close to the backbone and gave some to the CQB men. Bob didn't have much to go by, but he had tasted some raw tuna at the Cherry Blossom Festival and he could tell the difference. This meat was sweet, and it didn't leave an aftertaste the way poor-quality tuna could—the jellybean effect, it was called.

Cut, packaged, and served at a restaurant in Tokyo, the fish would be priced roughly in this way: The price doubled immediately because of cutting and trimming, which amounts to a 50 percent loss of weight. So, after trimming, the fish's worth rose to $84,000 and $240 a pound, or $528 per kilo. A 15 percent profit margin for the dealer would raise the price to $607 per kilo. At the sushi restaurant, with a 100 percent markup, the price per kilo would have risen again to $1,214. Figuring approximately twenty servings per kilo, the price per serving at a Japanese sushi restaurant would have been $60.

Mullin, Chaprales, and Sampson returned to the United States, having made a verbal agreement with Bill Cort, who would handle their fish in 1991. Between April and June they rented a warehouse, bought trucks, bought shipping equipment, office supplies, hired a secretary and a manager. Each person in the group contributed a few thousand dollars.

By July they were in business, but the season was a worrisome one. The fish were caught up in Maine in the early going, and in August a hurricane came along and the fish disappeared for three weeks. Then, in October, the fish showed up off Chatham, and the harpoon quota was filled in four fishing days. Red October, the CQB men called it. They'd gotten the majority of fish taken. What had looked like a losing proposition in September had suddenly turned successful. In 1991 CQB took in 111,733 pounds of bluefin for a total revenue of $2,190,000. They had come within $10,000 of their estimated costs.

The next spring Eric Hesse and Tim Malley, then the manager of CQB, went to Japan. This year, to further cut expenses, CQB decided to bypass Bill Cort and deal directly with the auction houses. In 1992, even though the quota had decreased by 10 percent and the total catch was down slightly, to 110,723 pounds, the average price went up more than a dollar a pound and the total revenue was $2,350,000.

It had been a good idea after all, a successful venture for twelve Cape Cod fishermen who three years earlier had come uneasily to a fire station to listen to a proposal that they stick together and have a little fun.

PART THREE

The 1993 Season

(1 6)

A SPOTTER PILOT

O N J U N E 16 harpooners working off the coast of Maine caught
a dozen fish. As in years past, some were lean and brought prices
of about $3 a pound, but others brought incredible prices. One fish-
erman who harpooned four bluefin on June 16 got $36.37 per pound
for a fish of about 400 pounds. A few days later, a fish landed at
TriCoastal Seafood weighing 271 pounds—the only Boston bluefin
at Tsukiji market that day—brought a price of 19,000 yen per kilo,
which at an exchange rate of 106 yen per dollar meant $81.31 per
pound, $22,033 for the fish.

In February the exchange rate was 125 yen per dollar, but then,
in response to a journalist's question, the Secretary of the Treasury,
Lloyd Bentsen, said he'd like to see a stronger yen to help reduce
the trade deficit. The exchange rate immediately shifted to 116 yen
per dollar. In April President Clinton made a similar remark, and the
exchange rate shifted to 109 yen per dollar. By June 10 the rate was
at 106 yen—the lowest level since World War II—and a statement
came from the Federal Reserve that open markets, rather than currency manipulations, were the best way to reduce trade deficits.

For the bluefin tuna fisherman, the fish that might have brought
5,000 yen per kilo and $18 a pound in February brought $21 in June.
(In 1987, at an exchange rate of 240 yen per dollar, the same fish
would have brought $9.50 a pound.)

In other developments, in June a harpooner caught a medium

173

fish—250 pounds, seven or eight years old—with ovaries full of ripe eggs, which to them meant evidence of northern spawning grounds.

By July 9 the general category had taken 6.1 metric tons, or thirty-one fish. The harpoon category had taken 8.5 metric tons, or forty-nine fish—16 percent of the quota, a quick start for the season. Because dogfish sharks and bluefish were thick, chumming and trolling hadn't been productive. Most of the fish in both categories, seventy-one of the eighty taken as of July 9, were caught by harpoon.

After July 15 market conditions became less promising, because of large catches of Pacific bluefin by Japanese fishermen. Trolling and chumming picked up a bit, and by July 22 the general category stood at 35.85 tons, or 167 fish, 7 percent of quota. The harpoon-category quota on July 22 stood at 18.45 tons, with ninety-four fish taken, and was already one-third full.

ON JULY 24, I was at Plymouth airport, a passenger in Jonathan Mayhew's Citabria. Spelled backward, Citabria read Airbatic, and it was a stunt plane, light, narrow, and maneuverable. After seeing that I was a big guy, he decided to go short on the fuel, to put in only fifty gallons. Molly Lutcavage, a biologist at the New England Aquarium who was coordinating the aerial survey, arrived after Jonathan finished fueling. She installed two cameras in the plane, a Nikon for photographing the fish and a synchronized pocket camera set up to take photographs of the loran set, so as to get locations.

We taxied out to the runway. I was in the backseat, folded up like a cricket, with a life raft in my lap, which Jonathan had given me to hold "just in case we ditched." Ready to go, he gunned the engine, the propeller hummed, and we hurtled along to a liftoff.

Up we went.

"We cleared the trees," Jonathan said. "That's the hardest part of the day. The rest is a piece of cake."

We soared over Plymouth Harbor. Down below was the *Mayflower*, and a sprawl of sailboats. We passed over Gurnet Point, and then up over the northern reach of Cape Cod Bay. To the south the green arm of the Cape stretched around, white at the edges, with yellow-green sand flats feathering under the flat blue water. Below were the plea-sure boats plying threadlike wakes. In fifteen minutes we'd passed by the dunes of Provincetown and were headed toward Wilkinson Basin, water 700 to 900 feet deep, some of the deepest water in the Gulf of Maine.

Bob Sampson came in on the radio. Jonathan was flying for the Sampsons that day, and he'd be paired with Brad. "It's gonna be a nice day," Bob said. "I've got high hopes. This weather is as nice as it's been so far."

Bob thought I was in for a day of torture. He told of the time he and Brooksie had gone skydiving. When it was time to jump, the plane turned and the door opened and out they went. Brooksie said it was the last time he'd ever jump out of a perfectly good airplane.

Bob didn't like flying with spotter pilots—none of the fishermen I'd talked with did. Bob was fine while they were going straight along, but as soon as they started flying around in circles he began to get queasy. The first time he went out, after a few circles he'd told Brook-sie to take him right back in. Now he talked about the possibility of my deciding I "didn't like my lunch."

Jonathan reached back and handed me the microphone.

"It's a beautiful view up here," I said. I'd taken my daughter to an amusement park and ridden a roller coaster the week before in prep-aration for this ride.

"Not as beautiful as that little red spot six hundred feet down." My lunch, he meant. That wouldn't happen, though, because I hadn't brought a lunch, and I hadn't eaten breakfast. Nor had I drunk much of anything. So I wouldn't need the two toiletry items Jonathan had told me to pack for this trip, a garbage bag and a milk carton. I didn't want to use either, but most of all, I didn't want to use that milk carton, scrunched up in the back seat, flying around at a hundred miles per hour.

And I didn't. Next to seeing a parabolic school, and the opalescent light of milling fish, it was the achievement of the day.

Jonathan flew a circle over a whalewatch boat. He had told another biologist at the New England Aquarium that he would photograph right whales, but none were there, so he straightened out and flew on. He flew over a blue shark, and pointed to the triangular shadow below. Chummers were anchored up, their slicks fanning out and merging. A humpback whale glided below the surface, and then blew. The whale was a good sign, Jonathan said, because humpbacks fed on the same bait as bluefin. A harpoon boat made a run.

When we got near the zone, he opened the windows and let down a flap on the right door. This was so he could see better, so he could stick his head out and look down—like someone looking out a six-tieth-story window at the street below. The air came slamming in, and deep in the pocket, in that back seat, I got the full force of it. My jacket pushed against my chest, my sunglasses against my face, and my sleeves thrummed. It was a convertible ride, way above the speed limit.

Jonathan was lean and agile. As he began to look for fish, he bounced back and forth in his cockpit, looking out one window and then another. The wing tips dipped left and right too, but only slightly. Jonathan was in control. It was a steady ride, except when he hit some dirty air roiled up on a previous circling, and we dropped ten or fifteen feet. Hand on the wheel and foot on the pedals, rocking this way and that, ears cupped by headphones, Jonathan looked like a kid on a bicycle doing zigzag turns. For a while, the responsive back-seat passenger, attentive to the balance of the thing, I tried to stay with him and we rocked side to side together, but then the beat of the wind got to me, and I settled for hugging up close to one window to get out of the way.

The real work of the day began when Jonathan spotted a school of bluefin. Then we snapped to the side, dove a hundred feet, and flew a tight circle. Wing dropped down, as if pointing at the prey, Jonathan snatched the radio and called Brad.

My stomach lost its connection with gravity then. Jonathan had said his plane would be "spongy" until three in the afternoon, when he'd burned off some fuel, and that then he'd be able to turn on his wing tips, but it felt to me like we were already there. Eyeballs peeled downward, our bodies were nearly parallel to the water surface as we went round. I could see the tiny tuna boat making a vigorous wake as it headed our way, but I couldn't locate any fish in the shifting water.

Going round, there was clear water when the sun was behind us, and the rays penetrated deep, but at the back half of the circle, furthest from the sun, there was glare, white light. Going round this yin-yang, clear to glare, clear to glare, it seemed impossible to keep an eye on anything. But Jonathan did it. In and out of the glare, running an oblong orbit—climbing against the wind, riding down with it, to maintain altitude—talking on the radio ("one o'clock, five boats, twelve-thirty, twelve-fifteen," working in quarter hours), Jonathan kept his eyes pinned on the fish while he spun around. They settled before Brad got there, however.

Brad's slump hadn't continued into the 1993 season. During the early run in Maine he had gotten four fish, and in the last week he had harpooned three in one day. He had nine in all. There had been some rough-weather days. On the way back from Maine, Brad and Matt had run into a storm just after dusk. The waves got up to eight feet, and were quartering the stern, pushing the boat from behind, sideward down into the troughs. Brad steered from the tower because he couldn't see out the wheelhouse windows, and he couldn't hand the wheel over to Matt all through the night. They got into Cape Cod Bay just after dawn and the storm died down. The boat had sprung a leak in Maine too, but they stayed calm, and found the source in the stuffing box.

But the most difficult experience of Brad's life, he said, had come during the past winter when he taught at a middle school near Pittsburgh. The relationship with the resident teacher had soured over methods, and he hadn't been able to patch things up. Teaching, he found, was harder than fishing sometimes. You had to think about so many things at once, and it was emotionally draining. Brad had tried to work things out with the other teacher, but couldn't, and he nearly quit. But then he thought about fishing, that he'd never thought about quitting during his slump of 1992, that he'd been lucky to have such good teachers, to have worked with the best harpooners and the best pilots. He finished out the term, did substitute teaching in Barnstable in the spring, and tried to avoid any major responsibilities until the tuna season started.

Round we went.

Round and round.

Round and round. We passed over a smashing bunch that quickly darted away.

"Generally bunches don't stay up, first part of the day," Jonathan said. "Lot of feeding going on today. Hopefully, after they get done they'll act right for us. They're going into the sun now, up and down. Mostly down."

JONATHAN MAYHEW was a pilot, a flier, a guide, a fish-finder. In imaginative moments he saw himself as a sea hawk. But a fisherman?

Jonathan had always thought of himself as one. As he saw it, he was part of a team that shared in the rewards of a catch, like the crew of a dragger. If you looked at his past you could say that he was meant to be here, at this point in the evolution of New England fishing.

He had grown up on Martha's Vineyard, in a fishing family. The Mayhews had been in the harpoon swordfishery since it began in the mid-nineteenth century. Jonathan's father, Benjamin Mayhew, had harpooned swordfish from dories in the schooner fishery on Georges Bank. Jonathan's grandfather had been a fisherman and farmer, and so had his great-grandfather. When Jonathan was growing up, it was a family tradition to go swordfishing on the Fourth of July, and any of the children who spotted a swordfish got $10.

Jonathan went to Massachusetts Maritime Academy in 1969. During his senior year he and his brother Greg went to Maine, bought a hull, and built a 42-foot fishing boat. After graduating with a degree in nautical science and a third mate's license in the Merchant Marine, Jonathan shipped out for three years, going to sea four months at a time. Between voyages he fished for swordfish and for lobsters along the continental shelf.

In the early 1970s there were about thirty-five boats and twenty-five planes in the swordfishing fleet working Georges Bank, and soon after joining it Jonathan and Greg decided that one of them would have to fly. They both took lessons, but when Greg pitched from the back to the front seat during a stall maneuver, they decided he'd be the striker and Jonathan would be the pilot. Greg was the more athletic of the two anyway, better suited to throwing. In 1973 Jonathan flew with an instructor in a student plane, and the next year he was on his own.

Sometimes pilots "went in." One time a friend of Jonathan's was working for a purse seiner. While he was flying low to scare the fish to one side of the pursing net, the wing touched the water, the plane hit the boat, and the pilot died. Jonathan had gone in once, in 1979. He was flying a Super Cub (the other plane of choice for swordfish spotters) south of Martha's Vineyard when he had engine trouble. Going down, he saw a dragger and headed for it. He hit the water, and thought he was twenty feet down, but then bobbed up. He climbed out and sat on the plane for a few minutes while the dragger finished hauling back, not even bothering to inflate his life raft. When the dragger came up close he swam over to it. As they were pulling him aboard Jonathan dropped the raft. He'd just bought it, so he dove back in. Seeing this, the captain yelled, "Keep that kid on board."

Swordfish were worth from $1,000 to $2,000 each in the 1980s, and the fishery provided about half of Jonathan's yearly income. But with an increase in American longlining the swordfish stocks declined, and when Georges Bank was sectioned off Canada got the best summer grounds on the Northeast Peak. By 1991 fewer than a half dozen American boats remained in the Georges Bank harpoon fishery.

Jonathan watched the market for bluefin tuna, and he began to fly for Bob Sampson occasionally. After Bob introduced him to Leonard Ingrande, Jonathan became one of Leonard's seiner pilots. Now Jonathan's busiest time of year was from August 15 until the seiner quota closed. He also owned a fishing boat called the *Quitsa Strider*. Though a hired captain usually ran it, Jonathan sometimes worked the boat himself, going for cod, flounder, squid, tuna, and swordfish.

For the Mayhews, public service on Martha's Vineyard was also a family tradition. Benjamin Mayhew was a member of the Massachusetts legislature, representing Dukes County, and when he died in 1969 Greg Mayhew, just back from Vietnam, ran for and won his father's seat. By Jonathan's count, twenty-three Mayhews had served in the Massachusetts legislature.

They were descendants of Thomas Mayhew, who came to Massachusetts in 1631 to look after the interests of a London merchant. Mayhew built a lumber mill, and helped set the boundaries of some of the towns around Boston, and served as the selectman of Watertown. In 1641 he built the first bridge across the Charles River, though it was quickly taken over by the colony. In 1641 he bought Nantucket and Martha's Vineyard for forty pounds, and then sold Nantucket for the same amount. He moved to the Vineyard in 1646 and served as governor until he died in 1682. Thomas Mayhew, Jr., born in England in 1620, was a missionary to the Indian tribes on the island, and after he died at sea in 1657 his site of departure became a cairn monument. His great-grandson, Jonathan Mayhew (1720–66), was the pastor of the West Church in Boston from 1747 to 1766, and was known for his defense of the colonial cause.

In 1993 Jonathan Mayhew the fisherman, a twelfth-generation Vineyarder, was also active in public life, serving a third term as selectman for the borough of Chilmark and as a member of the shellfish board.

THE CONDITIONS of the day changed with the conditions of the light, as the sun moved across the sky and the angles shifted. Sometimes the water seemed to be full of clouds—the effect of sunlight on the backs of waves, Jonathan said. Sometimes it looked like black orange peel. At other times the surface was white and the tide rips were black, like rivers on ice. The largest tide rip, which looked like a tear in the surface, ran all the way to Provincetown, and Jonathan kept an eye on it, watching for fish swimming along the edges.

Then Jonathan spotted a school of giants. It wasn't difficult to see them. He was flying east, with the sun behind him, and the school was swimming west. There were about sixty fish, he estimated, three or four tiers of fifteen each, judging by the light. Moving along, they were a pool of purple and silver light, throwing off sporadic flashes as they turned and the sun glinted off them. The water around the school was yellowish, lit by the light reflecting off the fishes' silver sides.

There was a harpoon boat about a hundred yards away, and the school was about two or three times the size of the boat. The fishermen on board were certainly unaware of what was passing by.

Jonathan turned hard and tossed out a dye marker—a wax-paper bag that contained food coloring and a stone for weight, a visual reference and a claim to the space. Jonathan asked me to keep an eye on another plane that had come into the area, while he circled and took photographs.

The *Rush* came on, and Brad ran out on the stand. A toothpick of a harpoon flew out and made a little splash. The purple light vanished. The harpooner leaned over, and pulled in the line.

A few minutes later Jonathan found another smashing bunch stirring up whitecaps in the water. He directed the *Rush* on a loop around, and then brought the boat in from the direction of the sun. Brad threw, and the fish scattered. The other plane and boat were on the same school almost immediately when it came up again a few hundred feet away.

We passed over a line of five ocean sunfish, and one of them breached. We saw a basking shark, and Jonathan looked for bluefin trailing behind. We climbed a hundred feet to get out of the way of another plane. We had a lunch break, or rather, Jonathan did. He drank a Coke and ate some potato chips, not an easy thing to do at ninety miles per hour in swirling winds, and little pieces went streaming away. He found another school, and dropped a dye marker. Brad got a throw off, but again the fish scattered. "One of those days," came Brad's voice over the radio.

"Not an exact science," Jonathan said.

This was the "blue-water fishery," as Bob Sampson called it—fast-moving bluefin running deep in clear water. The mackerel schooner fishery had taken place a century ago on the same grounds.

As the sun moved, and the fish with it, the planes and boats began to work to the southwest. Jonathan got over a school of giants, and while he circled, waiting for the boat to come in, four other planes moved into the area and began circling. It was eerie to see them nearby, wings tipped, soaring like gulls. Then as quickly as they'd come they flew away, the action now off in another zone. Jonathan was relieved. "It gets like a cat on a hot tin roof, five or six planes, all circling and changing altitudes."

Then he found a milling school. Some of the fish in the ring were turning over, almost somersaulting. Again there was a purple and silver light, and the yellow cast about them, but because the mill was round the light was cylindrical. Jonathan turned above them and took a photo while Brad came steaming in. But the mill disappeared just before Brad got there.

Jonathan thought bluefin milled in order to stay in an area—by swimming around in circles they could stay in one place yet maintain the minimum speeds for respiration. Perhaps they milled over wells of warm water. He had found milling schools, flown away, and come back hours later to find them in the same spot.

He soon found a second milling school. Again we circled over the opalescent light. What a sight this was, this spectral cartwheel spin, this private glow. What interlopers we were, gliding above and peering down into it. Brad ran out on the pulpit, but the fish scattered like minnows.

Then, running over the edge of clear water, Jonathan spotted a basking shark just as a school of bluefin turned in behind it. He brought the *Rush* in from the path of the sun, pointing the bow just off the shark's tail, but the fish were gone before the harpoon hit the water.

Round we went. Round and round. The sun advanced into the western sky.

We passed over the *Sandra C.*, which Eric Hesse was then running for Ron Lein, who was building a new boat and hadn't quite finished. Eric had gotten eleven fish so far, and was the second-highest producer in CQB, after Sean Sullivan. He'd get his twelfth on this day. We also passed over Nick Nickerson, who during the past winter had outfitted an oversized tuna boat for an investor from Maine. This boat, the *Julie Ann*, was 48 feet long, had twin screws and could turn on

182

a dime, was powered by a 1,200-horsepower engine and could go 27 knots, had a tower with a transverse stairway rather than a ladder, and a 40-foot retractable pulpit. It looked like a floating fire escape. Nick thought the boat was overdone and had told the owner not to build it. Other fishermen had nicknamed it the "Tunaslayer." When we passed over, the big boat was idling, waiting for a call.

Jonathan found small bunches and big bunches, and another milling school into that afternoon. He pounced from window to window, he whirled like a fighter pilot, he held the microphone up close and gave his directions, he photographed one school then another.

Later in the day Jonathan thrust an arm out the window and pointed down. Below was a parabolic school, eight bluefin spread out along a curved line. The fish were about twenty feet apart, the blue-brown bodies staggered along the curve. The wing of the plane dropped, and hunters became hunted. The *Rush* came on and Brad made a throw, but the fish dropped down.

It was exciting to see the parabolic schools, because of the intelligence the form conveyed. "Each is in tune with its neighbor," Jonathan said. He had seen parabolic formations come upon schools of mackerel, and watched the ends of the line react simultaneously.

The sun's rays were penetrating the water more angularly. Jonathan found a second parabolic school, and then two more. Perhaps this was the afternoon show. First smashing schools, then mills, and then parabolas, punctuated with random bunches throughout the day.

"The thing about planes is you get to observe the fish in the wild state," Jonathan said, after one circling. "The fisherman is either harpooning or whatever, but we get to watch them. We get to see things scientists don't see. You watch them bunch up and spread out into hunter formation, going up and down. You get so you try to get into their sequence. You watch them, and you develop a sense for it. I don't know how accurate it is."

This had to be a most dangerous job, flying alone over the ocean in a single-engine plane. There were accidents, though they usually involved inexperienced pilots who lost control while doing stunts. ("There are old pilots and there are bold pilots," Jonathan said, "but there are no old bold pilots.") But to soar over the water like this, to see the opalescent millings, to see the tiered schools in their amethyst glow, the water a yellow aura about them, to see the hunter formations advancing, the smashers and the singles—there was a pleasure here, of the elemental dream of flight, and it made the vertiginous turns seem almost irrelevant.

Late in the afternoon, working to the west, Jonathan led Brad onto another hunter formation, but again Brad missed the shot. It was one of those days, he said again. You'd come upon a bunch and they'd take off. Bob said the same. They were just spooking too easy. They'd been run on too much. Neither of the Sampsons would get a fish that day.

Brad began to work toward Race Point and Jonathan kept ahead of him, crossing back and forth off in the distance. Then he made a beeline for Plymouth airport. As he came in, the gray sea was soft and majestic. Light streamed through the clouds and down over the Cape, and the Bay, and Plymouth.

Though Jonathan didn't tell me this until we'd landed, I'd hit a carburetor heat lever with my knee, and the plane had used more fuel than it might have otherwise. On his approach to the airport he stayed a bit higher than usual, and then, cocking the plane crossways, using the fuselage as a brake, he "dumped some air" and floated down on the runway like a goose dropping down on a pond. The selectman and his Citabria rolled up to the gas pumps and came to a stop, just in time.

SOUTH CHANNEL,
AUGUST 9

D URING THE last week of July and the first week of August, 506 bluefin were taken in the general category, and the quota stood at 24 percent. In the harpoon category, fifty-eight bluefin were taken for a total of 158 fish, 28 metric tons, 52 percent of the quota.

The second week of August was a big week in the harpoon category. Another fifty-eight fish were taken, and with 210 in all, the harpoon quota stood at 37 tons and 70 percent. A fall harpoon fishery seemed increasingly unlikely.

Large numbers of bluefin had been found east of Portland. Generally the fish were staying away from shore, feeding on the vast schools of herring and mackerel in deep water. The herring population in the Gulf of Maine, nearly depleted by foreign fishing vessels in the 1960s and 1970s, had regenerated to an estimated biomass of 2.5 billion pounds in 1990. Since the market for herring was limited, only 5 percent of the stock was being harvested each year. By one theory, the return of herring and a similar resurgence in mackerel had drawn the bluefin northward.

There were many schools throughout Wilkinson Basin, and on August 8 large concentrations appeared east of Chatham. Brooksie found a school that in his estimation was "a mile wide and a mile long." Several spotter pilots photographed schools that day. They were competing for the photo of the largest school, and the winner would get to keep his Nikon. John Betzner, who flew for Billy Chaprales, got a photo of a school of 1,290 fish (a surface count, made by the New England Aquarium). On August 8, Eric Hesse ran on bunches all day long and harpooned bluefins number 15, 16, 17, 18, and 19. One fish of 368 pounds dressed weight brought $19.25 per pound. A troller from Nantucket caught a fish weighing more than 1,000 pounds. On the *Scratcher*, Wade Behlman and Greg Mayhew got four fish.

Greg was on the boat because Bob Sampson had been told by his doctor to take a week off. In mid-July, Bob had reached out to lift a mooring and had crushed some tendons and muscle sheath in his right elbow, his throwing arm. He'd gone out a few times, but the arm had gotten worse. He didn't think it would heal in a week, but after hearing about the show on August 8 Bob had to get out on the water again.

The elbow injury had been the second setback of Bob's season. In May, Bob had gotten a call early one morning from the harbormaster at Sandwich Harbor, who said someone had run into the *Rush*, which was still on jackstands in the parking lot. Bob got Penny up, and they went to the harbor. A group of mackerel fishermen ("with a borrowed boat and a borrowed trailer, on borrowed time," Bob said) had come into the harbor driving too fast, and their trailer, which wasn't properly fastened, came loose and shot off across the parking lot. It hit the *Rush*, knocking it over on a jackstand, which narrowly missed puncturing the fuel tank. Bob spent two weeks repairing the hole.

There had been a close call recently when the engine in Cary Fitch's plane "popped a jug." or blew a valve, 38 miles from shore. Losing oil pressure, Fitch radioed Trip Wheeler and Norman St. Pierre. Norman was closer, so he found Fitch and flew alongside him to the airport at Provincetown. Fire trucks were waiting. Norman got survival gear ready in case Fitch went into the water. Six hundred feet from shore the propeller stopped, but Fitch had enough momentum to reach the runway and came safely to a landing. A few days later he was back in the air, flying for Eric Hesse.

•   •   •

The 1993 Season

"THE BOYS had a good day yesterday," Bob said. It was the morning of August 9 at Saquatucket Harbor, and he had just fueled up the *Scratcher*.

Brooksie had seen bunches of two hundred and eight hundred, and the mile-square school. "One-tenth of the entire population of bluefin were out there yesterday," Bob said, referring to the government assessments. "NMFS should have seen it. But even if they did they wouldn't have accepted it, because it wasn't done under their requirements and would have been anecdotal."

Eric Hesse was at Saquatucket, and made a trade with Bob, a few harpoon heads for a pole. "How'd you do yesterday?" Bob asked.

"Five," Eric answered, quietly, with a hint of pride, his eyes down. Bob gave a little nod.

Bob and Eric were taking their time getting out to the zone. The bluefin were feeding on squid during the morning (one fisherman had taken two buckets of squid from the stomach of a fish) and showing in the afternoon. Bob had tried to persuade the others to wait before going out, so as to arrive when the show began, but most of them had left Saquatucket already.

"A deer uses sight and sound," Bob said, "but smell is the most important sense. If a deer smells you, it's gone. A bluefin tuna uses its eyes. After you've run them a few times, as soon as the fish see a boat, they're gone. You run them in the morning, when they're active and feeding, and they're educated by the afternoon."

The *Scratcher* headed into Nantucket Sound, rounded Monomoy, and turned east. It would be a 65-mile trip from the harbor to the zone, but the day was beautiful, calm and sunny, and there was no hurry.

Wade Behlman was in the tower steering for the South Channel, and Bob was on deck, enjoying the early part of the ride. Monomoy had elongated and receded in the west.

Bob Sampson had a prodigious memory, and he recounted times past, even gruesome days, with care—they were his days, and they meant something. There was the day of the eye injury, for example. Bob was running a charter boat then. He made it a point to take his customers offshore, to the best bluefish and striper fishing spots. He had clientele who returned each summer, and one was a group of newspaper workers from Boston. They liked going out with Bob because they came back with all the fillets they wanted, and because they could drink and party. On this trip two of the customers were also repairing to the cabin to smoke marijuana. Bob thought there was a right time and a wrong time for that, and fishing was a wrong time, but he didn't say much. One of them hooked a bluefish and reeled it in, and Bob went to the stern to pull it aboard. He said to ease off, but the customer yanked the line. The hook and lead weight came springing up. Bob had his glasses on, and a lens shattered. He saw something come and he saw something go, and he thought what went was his eye.

He covered his face with his hands and lay down, and minutes passed while he writhed in pain and the passengers looked on. Finally he got up and asked one of them to see if he still had an eye. He did, but pieces of glass were embedded in it. Bob drank a few beers to dull the pain. He called the Coast Guard, and he called the captain of another charter boat fishing nearby. Then he put his head on the lap of a woman among the party, and eventually calmed down. The Coast Guard helicopter arrived in an hour and, hovering above, lifted Bob cleanly out of the *Scratcher*. He had been impressed with how they were able to do that, in 25-knot winds.

The charter captain who was bringing Bob's boat in had a reputation for going too fast and crashing boats into docks, and Bob was worried. The Coast Guard dropped him off at the hospital in Hyannis, and the glass was removed, and then Bob hurried over to Hyannis Harbor. He got there before the *Scratcher* did and, wearing an eye patch, docked it himself. The next day he took another party out.

The sea rolled gently as the boat headed east to the schools chasing squid.

Another time the boat had collided with a whale—or a whale had collided with the boat. Bob was in the pulpit when up came a humpback whale on a vertical ascension, pitchpoling. As Bob remembered it, the whale saw Bob just as Bob saw the whale, and it tried to get out of the way by contorting its body, but whale bodies contort slowly.

Bob wrapped himself around the pulpit. The boat rode up, slid down, tipped to the side, and then came sharply back. The whale swam off. Bob was hanging on. Everyone was okay.

The radio crackled with plane sounds.

And there was the time, in the days before he had an electric harpoon, when Bob hooked a fish and it towed the boat backward for ten miles, from Stellwagen Bank to Provincetown.

In the wheelhouse, light pouring in, Bob rubbed his elbow. He hoped the injury would work to his advantage, perhaps make him practice restraint. After working on the blue water he'd gone into Cape Cod Bay and gone at the schools too aggressively, missing all his throws. The injury had complicated his throwing, so on a blow day he had gone outside of Barnstable Harbor to throw at milk cartons. He'd never had to think about form before. And there were so many other things to consider—boat speed, waves, refraction, all playing into the throw adjusted to the placement of that image on top of the water.

"Today may be good," Bob said. We passed through a fog bank, a half hour from the zone. Then Jonathan Mayhew was on the radio— Brooksie had not yet arrived from Maine—and he had found fish.

Bob made his first throw just after noon, at a school on the surface coming at the boat. The boat was riding into the glare, though, and Bob missed, but he came walking back down the pulpit with a smile on his face. "Glad to be out here," he said.

A few minutes later he made another throw, on a school that had been milling but then broke toward the boat. Bob aimed at the largest fish, and hit.

"Yes!" he yelled. Brad came on the radio. He'd been listening to the approach, and asked if his dad got one. Wade told him. "Glad to hear the old man's still got it," Brad said.

"Yes he does!" Bob yelled, his fingers trailing along the guide wires.

The fish hadn't been stunned by the zapper, so the line went tearing out, and out went a ball and flag with it. A few minutes later Wade tried to pull the fish in, and Bob wanted to zap it again. He called to me to push the little black button up in the tower. I hesitated—I didn't really want to do any zapping. At the same time, Jonathan came on the radio and wanted to know how it was going and Bob asked me to talk to him. Then the manager of CQB called on the cellular phone—Bob asked me to answer that, too—to say that of the four fish caught the day before two had been overzapped and their spines had broken. Just then Bob yelled "Now!" and I pushed a button but it was the wrong button, and down went the fish again.

Brooksie arrived, and they sped off toward him. They came upon a school ten feet down and running hard to the west, and Bob missed. "There were so many fish in that bunch, Wade," Bob said.

On the next run they harpooned a second fish. Brooksie said the school was coming at the boat, a single fish running out ahead. Bob picked it out and tossed the harpoon. He howled. Out went a rig and off they went on another run. "That shows the advantage of planes," Bob said, coming down from the pulpit.

Though only three boats were off Chatham on August 8, twelve boats were out on the 9th. That was too many for Bob, and he wanted to get away into new territory. He was sure that he and Brad were beginning to run on the same bunches. Bob missed several shots in a row, and twice sat down in the wheelhouse to think about what he was doing.

During this string of tosses I went out on the pulpit and watched from a harpooner's vantage point. On one run the boat came upon a line of fifty to sixty fish, side by side, pushing slowly along and making water. As I stood over them, ten feet above the water, the cobalt streaks were vivid, the tail-let fins a bright yellow. They were such big, impressive animals, and it didn't seem that a fish could be of that size, or that nature, as it turned and swam sideways and looked up as Bob threw and the harpoon missed low. A patch of about fifty rings was left by tail beats. Bob couldn't believe he'd missed. Refraction, he figured.

In Bob's mind, missed fish began to accumulate on deck. Bob gave Brad a call. "I know that feeling," he said, "of not being happy, even though there's fish in the boat."

They tried to pull the rig on the first fish, but Brooksie found another bunch and called them off. "Forget it, Wade," Bob said, in a tone of frustration that masked pleasure. "He's not gonna let us pull it, not till six o'clock."

"Twenty boats," Brooksie said. "See the water?"

"Yeah." Wade went to the wheel, Bob to the stand. He missed.

They went back to the rig. This time as they were hauling it in a blue shark swam toward the boat, and seemed to be stalking the rising fish. Bob and Wade were wondering what to do, thinking about how to bat the shark away, when it abruptly turned and headed toward a milling school stirring up a round patch of water 200 feet away. Bob got on the radio and told Brooksie to leave them alone for a while, so they could get the rig in. The fish had been down wriggling in the mud. Wade sprayed it off, cut the head, gutted it.

Bob was off on a run. Before Wade finished cleaning the fish he got called into the tower. Blood and water dripping off his slickers, he said to me, "Just stick that hose in that cavity, will ya?" I smiled curiously. Wade smiled back in the same way. "Just stick it in there and leave it." He ran up the ladder.

Putting the hose inside the fish to cleanse it of blood, I was taken back to when I had worked on a tub trawler out of Chatham, twenty-two years ago. We worked these same grounds in the South Channel, early each morning setting a mile and a half of line with a hook every three feet, each afternoon bringing the line in. We caught as much as 7,000 pounds of cod and haddock a day, and my job was to gut the fish. The idea was to make a swift cut, reach in, twist, and toss the entrails overboard. This could be done in a clean motion, the way the captain's two sons did it, or it could be done in a herky-jerky way, the way I did it. On those sunny days, sweating in oilskins, pulling fish apart, I'd forget my hands were covered with gurry and reach up to wipe my forehead.

I never did really get used to all the blood and guts, and I never did get it right. But I did bring sweet, fresh codfish home for dinner, I saw a sperm whale open its jaws, and I got to know how fishermen worked, those people my grandfather had always spoken of with such admiration, as the strongest and most capable of people. I realized that I couldn't do it. I was happy to have tried it, and I was happy to leave the blood and guts behind.

At three o'clock the sea turned gray, and took on a feathery grain. Bob had missed three throws in a row. "They saw me move," he said.

Then I was called into the act again. Wade was cleaning the second fish, and I was in the tower with Bob, who was approaching a school under Brooksie's direction. Rather than interrupt Wade, Bob had me take the wheel while he went out on the pulpit. I listened to Brooksie saying "eleven o'clock, eleven-thirty," but I erred in that I didn't look for the fish and try to swing the pulpit over them. Bob threw six feet to the side and missed. He apologized to Wade for his haste, and he told me the miss wasn't my fault. Though I felt shanghaied, I now understood the skill of the wheelman, watching for fish while positioning the harpooner.

The sun was dropping toward the west. Cruising that way, Bob stood on the pulpit, suspended over the sparkling path. They ran on a bunch that was "kind of milling, kind of running." Wade talked about moving off to the northeast, as they'd done the day before, and Bob wanted to move off, too. The twelve stick boats were all too close to each other. Bob thought the fish were beginning to feed again. "The show is over," he said. Brad called. He had harpooned a fish, but it was two inches too short and he had to let it go. (The day before, Scott Laurie, the fisherman running the *Tenacious*, unwilling to take a chance on a $5,000 fine, dropped a fish that was a half inch too short. Not everyone was discarding the undersized "no-sale" fish below seventy inches. Some were taking them to shore for home consumption, but others were selling them to supermarkets and restaurants—along the coast many were running tuna specials.)

Bob said he was afraid of what he'd find at the dock. He didn't want to hear about those who got away from the pack and had a big day. (But only Eric Hesse did, with bluefins number 20, 21, 22, and 23.)

At 5:30 they ran on another bunch and Bob harpooned a third fish. He buttoned this one—the harpoon had hit below the pectoral fin and poked out the other side, so again the zapper didn't work. They set out a ball and flag and went off on another run, but the school was too deep. "Nothing but a bunch of pickles down there," Brooksie said. "Forget it."

They ran on a milling bunch but it, too, sounded. Brooksie circled and kept an eye on the mill while they pulled in the third fish. "Fifty feet down and rolling in the sun," he said. "Lot of light coming back. Wish I had a camera, impress the wife.

"Gotta catch a fish pretty soon. Gotta leave at six-thirty."

The third fish was broad in the middle, but thin at the tail. Wade took a tail cut, and looked at the meat. It was dark, without much marbling.

They made a run on another milling school and then started for shore. Brooksie flew lines ahead of the boat for a while, then doubled back and made a pass at 100 feet. Wade was cleaning the fish, but he stepped aside so Brooksie could see it. Brooksie waved and headed off for Hyannis Airport.

The *Scratcher* picked up speed and headed for Monomoy. Wade cut the fish's head off with a handsaw and threw it overboard without ceremony. He got on his knees, reached in and pulled out the heart, liver, and stomach, and with gloved hands scraped away other pieces of its organs. Blood was all over his arms.

These bluefin, these are not cod, I was thinking as I leaned against the wheelhouse door and watched. These are animals.

Wade was up to his shoulders, scraping.

Wade was a quiet man, but that day he talked about when he'd worked on a dragger. It wasn't the best time for him to be doing that kind of work, because his wife had just had a baby. She didn't like being left alone, but they had never seen money like Wade was making. They had started a savings account. Wade made eight-day trips, followed by two to three days onshore. He worked on a four-man crew, with watches of nine and three—nine hours on deck hauling the nets and cleaning fish, then three hours of sleep, round the clock, for eight days. It was especially hard work in the winter. The seas were rough, and it was difficult to sleep. In order to stay in the bunk he'd wedge himself against the wall with his duffel bag. Often they'd run out of food or, worse, fresh water.

On land, for a day or so he'd keep rolling with the boat, and for a night or two he couldn't sleep because the engine noise would still be in his ears and his bedroom was too quiet. Then it would be time to go out again. Wade wanted to quit, but the owner kept asking him to make one more trip, so Wade kept making one more trip for a year. When the owner of the boat hired another man to run it, they began making twelve-day trips. Wade went on one of those, and they spent most of their time running around looking, from the South Channel to Wildcat Knoll to Georges Bank. He quit after that trip and began potting black sea bass in Nantucket Sound.

Up to his shoulders in blood, wet with seawater, Wade was doing this for his family. This was his living. This was all he'd done, commercial fishing. Now, maybe, he had a little money in the bank. He had paid off the loan on the 31-foot lobster boat he'd bought from his grandfather, a commercial fisherman who had retired.

After he cleaned the fish Wade pushed it forward to the wheelhouse door, and he hosed the blood off the deck. This done, he filled a bucket and poured ice into the visceral cavity. Bucket after bucket, he poured and pushed the ice in with his hands. As he did this, there was a strange kind of transformation, and the bluefin was no longer an animal. It was a fish ready for market, seafood, with the ice cubes piled in and trailing out.

Wade covered the fish with a tarp, and the *Scratcher* steamed hard for Chatham.

(1 8)

A SUNDAY IN THE BAY

❦

THE LAST weekend in August, a lovely Sunday summer morning on Cape Cod, with a slight haze in the air. A fog had lifted when a high-pressure front came through and brought lower temperatures, but now warm air from the south was conjuring up another fog. An easterly of ten knots had driven most of the Cape harpooners into the Bay.

The *Look Out* had left Barnstable Harbor and was rounding Sandy Neck. Nick Nickerson was at the wheel. Peter LaRoche, his mate, was sitting nearby, and so was Scott Mullin, Bill Mullin's twenty-one-year-old son, who had been running the boat until Nick took over.

"I'm down a plane," Nick said. His pilot, Jack Wallace, was having his plane repaired, but he would be in the air. Nick had hired another pilot, a man who lived in Boston and owned a bakery and had a summer house in Chatham. It had been difficult for him to get away, because he had just hired some new people, and Nick was grateful that he'd come out for the day. He'd fly the plane, and Jack Wallace would do the looking and communicating.

Nick was not having one of his best years. In January, outfitting the 48-foot Duffy in Hyannis Harbor, he had been optimistic and full of plans. With the *Julie Ann* he'd be able to roam far outside, away from the pack, and in the first weeks of the season he had reached spots in the Gulf of Maine that other harpooners rarely fished, east of Wilkinson and north of Georges Bank. Nick and Peter had stocked

195

$60,000 worth of bluefin in July, but that hadn't been good enough for their backer in Maine. Suddenly, without warning, they'd been ordered to tie the boat up and remove their gear. Now, back in Barnstable Harbor, Nick was running the *Look Out* for his friend Bill Mullin. He wasn't saying much about what had happened, other than that he'd been a poor judge of character and was looking forward to the end of the season.

Willard Nickerson III was a Cape Cod fisherman through and through. His father had run the fish market at the Chatham pier for thirty-five years. His grandfather had been a commercial fisherman, and Nick had gone out with him many times, jigging for cod when they could be found inshore, "before draggers tore up the bottom and it could no longer hold the fish." Nick's great-grandfather, Rufus Nickerson, had worked on schooners and introduced the halibut fishery to Cape Cod. Rufus worked from a big catboat called the *Nickerson*. Often Nick was compared to his great-grandfather, because they both had wild ideas and were innovative in fisheries. It was strange, Nick thought, how traits could be passed down over the generations.

Nick was a twelfth-generation descendant of William Nickerson, a weaver from Norwich, England, who came to Yarmouth in 1641. In 1656 Nickerson traded a boat to the sachem Mattaquason for a thousand acres of land in Monomoyick, but made the deal without permission of the Colony Court, and the land was taken away from him. During the next two decades, after disputes with the authorities and some clever business deals, Nickerson regained the original parcel and then increased his holdings to about four thousand acres. The settlement he founded with his six sons, three daughters, and three sons-in-law became the town of Chatham in 1712.

Nick Nickerson considered himself lucky to have grown up in Chatham during a time when there was so much diversity in the fisheries. He'd fished for cod with his grandfather. When he was at Chatham High he would go out in the morning before school started and fish for bass in Pleasant Bay. In the fall he'd go scalloping after school. He went quahogging in the coves and inlets around Chatham. In the summers after his last two years of college, in 1968 and 1969,

he fished for cod by tub-trawling—setting out a mile of line a day—
and caught as much as 10,000 pounds per trip. When Frank Cyganowski showed up in Cape Cod Bay in 1971 Nick spent a week fishing
with his sisters in the Bay and got five bluefin. In 1973 Nick took
two weeks off from cod fishing and harpooned eleven fish.

With brilliant blue eyes, and a big engaging smile, he was a tree
trunk of a man, six-five, close to 300 pounds, size-15 shoes. During
high school Nick had been an all-Cape basketball player for three
years, and he'd taken his high school, one of the smallest in Massachusetts, to the semifinals of the state tournament. That spring, when
he injured his hand and couldn't pitch on the baseball team, the Cape
Cod *Standard Times* released the story in bold print. Nick went to
East Tennessee State on a basketball scholarship, and then taught
physical education at the high school in Yarmouth. Fishing was always on his mind, especially during scalloping season, and during
open periods he'd sometimes run out to his car, drive to Brewster,
change his clothes, and drag up a few bags of scallops. In the summers he fished for cod, and with each passing season he tried something new. Eventually Nick gave up teaching and went fishing
full-time. There was no clock out there, no smoke-filled rooms, and
no program other than the one you set yourself. Risk was part of it,
but he'd take the chance on not knowing where the next dollar was
coming from, and go out and get it.

He avoided the two most conventional commercial fisheries—
dragging for groundfish and lobstering. Nick potted black bass, scup,
and conch. He jigged for cod with hydraulic reels. He developed a
rake for harvesting quahogs. He developed markets for the Icelandic
scallops that grew near Chatham. He fished for spiny lobsters in the
Caribbean. He raked, pumped, and dragged seaclams off Chatham,
then took the fishery to Long Island, investing his savings in a 55-
foot steel dragger—just before he and his fellow clammers, filling ten
trailers a day, 550 bushels to a trailer, glutted the market with a
supply that would last for years.

Nick was the first fisherman to harpoon bluefin tuna off Chatham,
and because he knew the tricky currents and tides he could predict
where the fish would be, and go out even in the fog to find them. Thus

Nick Nickerson developed his own niche as a Chatham harpooner, and for someone adept at clearing the boards it was the perfect niche—a tightly packed fishery where Nick could charge in and express himself and have big days. In 1988 Nick caught thirty-six fish in twelve days. In the fall of 1991 after the hurricane, Nick harpooned twenty-seven fish in six days for a gross of $250,000. Now and then, over the years, expressing himself, he'd snapped a pulpit or two.

It amazed Nick that he could have days of $60,000 or even $70,000. No other fishery could produce like that. Now that so many of the fisheries around Chatham had been diminished or depleted, the winters on Cape Cod had become long and boring. It took too much work to get too little product, and Nick was looking around the world for other pastures. He and Norman St.Pierre had gone to Greece to look at the bluefin fishery, but with the wars going on along the Adriatic Sea, Nick was afraid he'd end up as target practice. He investigated possibilities in Sierra Leone, which had good stocks of bluefin, but then there was a military coup. Nick made contacts in the Azores, and even got fishing licenses, but he needed the capital to get things moving.

Nick thought of himself now as an international fishing consultant, and he had some business cards printed up. He had thought that the backer in Maine would want to take the bluefin fishery to other parts of the world, but that relationship had fallen through. It had happened at just the wrong time, just as Nick was getting back on his feet after the losses in the seaclam fishery. Maybe he'd go to a bank after the season ended and get the funding to build a 42-foot boat—the ideal length—but he talked about that without much enthusiasm, without the big smile that had come so easily in January.

THE *LOOK OUT* passed by Billingsgate and Great Island and then stopped off the Wellfleet shore, away from the yellow dunes covered with wild cranberries. Though the other harpoon boats and their planes were a few miles to the north, near Provincetown Harbor, Nick wanted to hang back until he'd made contact with his plane.

Then he'd move into the action. High tide was approaching. The slack tide and the show would be coming soon, Nick thought.

Everyone was looking at the sky, and toward Provincetown, when a smashing bunch hit the surface fifty feet in front of the *Look Out*. Momentarily they forgot about the radio and charged ahead. Nick climbed down and went out on the stand, but before he had raised the harpoon the bunch disappeared and the water settled.

Two planes began circling off Truro, and their boats rushed at them. The show had begun. Nick was worried. His plane was in the air, and it had flown by, but still there had been no word.

Nick called into the microphone. "Fish?" he said. The plane passed overhead, and he tried again, louder this time. "FISH?"

"Should we go that way?" Nick asked, meaning toward Provincetown. No answer. "SHOULD WE GO THAT WAY?" Nothing, though the plane headed that way, to the north.

"I'll come to you!" Nick declared. "You got fish there? I'll be over that way!"

Things were moving quickly. Outside Provincetown Harbor, five planes were now circling. Three more moved overhead. To protect a spot, one plane left its circle, dove 400 feet, and started circling again. Nick's plane threaded among them. "He'll probably never want to come back here again," Nick said of his pilot for the day.

"Should we come to you?" Nick called out. He waited, listened, tried again. "SHOULD WE COME TO YOU!"

Trip Wheeler moved from Provincetown Harbor to the south, and just off the Truro shore started circling. The *Sandra C.* came on. "YOU GOT FISH THERE?"

Norman St. Pierre ran into the area south of Trip Wheeler and found a bunch in water so shallow that Norman could see mussel beds on the bottom. Brenda Sullivan came on in the *Back Off*, and her son Sean went out on the stand. He hit, and out went a rig.

"JACK! CAN YOU HEAR ME! AM I COMING THROUGH!"

For Norman, flying in Cape Cod Bay was a cat-and-mouse game. He left the beach, ran along the deck, flew another circle, held it for a while, darted off and picked up another circle after a pilot aban-

GIANT BLUEFIN

doned it, flew that a few times, then darted back to his previous circle. On came Jackie Sullivan in the *Sean Jamie*, and his son Jamie went out on the stand.

Nick had put on polarized glasses with side shields, and a hat with ear flaps and a chin strap. "I guessed we missed that show," he said. He put the *Look Out* in gear and cruised toward Provincetown.

Other boats were cruising, too. This was Sunday in Cape Cod Bay, one of America's favorite boating spots. There were a few chummers, trailing slicks. There were troll boats, seeking tuna, bluefish, and striped bass. There were skiffs and pleasure craft out for a look at the Bay. An outboard zipped by, with a man standing at the bow and holding a harpoon. A schooner passed out of Provincetown Harbor, sailed to Truro, turned around, and headed back. Whalewatch boats rounded Race Point for Stellwagen Bank. Windsurfers crossed the waves, riding the east wind. Jet skis ripped along. Planes banked overhead. Harpooners rode the pulpits. From the lighthouse at the tip of the Cape, to Pilgrim Monument in Provincetown to the Provinceland parabolic dunes, to the green hills of Truro, all along the sand cliffs, houses perched on top, by Corn Hill on down to Great Island, with the blue sky and the cool water and the fresh breeze, this was the Bay.

At last a crackling came over the radio and a voice burst through. "YOU GOT FISH?" Nick yelled. They did. The school was deep, and turning. Nick scaled the pulpit and leaned out on the belly rail. A pursuit followed, with the fish coming up, going down, coming up again, making a turn. The *Look Out* rode up close, and then they were gone. Nick didn't get a throw off, but his spirits had lifted. The day had possibilities now.

"They're pushing into the wind," Nick said, back in the tower, "running onto the beach, chasing bait."

There were twenty-five stick boats cruising about, in an area of a mile or two, and there were eight planes in the sky. Nick's plane ran among the pack, darting in and darting out, and then on a run south of Provincetown Harbor found a bunch. Jack Wallace wanted to know how the approach should be made. "Heads or tails?" he asked. Since the fish were heading east Nick decided to go west and then run in

200

behind them from the direction of the sun. He got on the stand, but again the fish turned away and went down.

A boat was rushing in from the south, from the direction of Barnstable Harbor. It was Chris VanDuzer, on the *Sea Baby*, and his pilot had been circling while he crossed the Bay. VanDuzer steamed by the *Look Out*, white water spraying, and went on a bunch a hundred yards off the Truro beach. He crouched on the stand, his harpoon vertical, poised. A windsurfer sailed by. VanDuzer aimed and missed, hauled in his harpoon, cruised ahead on the same bunch and threw again. He missed and this time the school raced away.

VanDuzer's pilot flew out from shore, and a few minutes later found another bunch. The *Sea Baby* steamed by the *Look Out* again, passed by the bunch, turned and came in on the best light. The most successful of the Bay harpooners went out on the stand, threw, and hit. A few minutes later up came a thousand-pound fish. Three throws, an hour's work, and Chris VanDuzer headed back to Barnstable Harbor.

Nick lost contact with his plane again, but then the voice came through. They went on a bunch, which went deep, came up, and ran along the surface. Nick was in the stand and getting close when the plane passed over and the fish scattered.

"WATCH YOUR SHADOW, JACK!" Nick called out from the pulpit.

Scott Mullin got on the radio. "You shadowed them, Jack," he said. "Watch your shadow."

A mile to the south there was an incredible roiling in the water, a smashing bunch spread over an area of a hundred yards. The nearest boat was the *Back Off*. Brenda Sullivan turned toward the smashers and gunned the engine, and Norman St. Pierre raced in from a mile away.

In a fishery of few women, Brenda was the only woman I'd heard of who worked on a harpoon boat. Norman St. Pierre said that she was the "hardest thing on two feet." He also said she was very pretty, and at the age of fifty-three Brenda was sometimes mistaken for her son's girlfriend. She'd protected her skin during her many years on the water; if she hadn't, she said, it would have been like leather now. All summer long, riding up in the tower from morning till dark, Brenda wore a jacket with a hood pulled tight, or a scarf wrapped around her face, and a visor cap and sunglasses with blinders. She knew the fishermen made fun of her and talked about her turban, but she didn't care. Her skin had stayed fair. Sometimes she wore her hair up, and with her delicate neck, with the wisps of hair hanging down, she was indeed very pretty. Brenda had thin wrists, but beyond those wrists she had man's hands, fisherman's hands, thick at the fingers, and sunburned, since she didn't wear gloves. Brenda wondered sometimes why she had man's hands.

Brenda Sullivan had to be out there, and when she was on the water she rarely came out of the tower. She got her sons and her husband out of bed at five most mornings, at three when they were going off Chatham. She had told Jackie Sullivan long ago not to ever, ever, try to stop her from fishing—though he wouldn't let her go cod fishing in the winter because it was too dangerous. When Jackie had been doing carpentry Brenda would go to the building site and pull him off the job to go tuna fishing. Years ago, they had lots of "discussions" when they'd been fishing for lobsters, pulling traps in the morning, and Brenda could see the tuna boats going out. She knew she had driven her husband crazy at times over the tuna fishing, but she had to do it. She loved the ocean, and she loved the fish. She was going to fish for tuna into her seventies, if they were still around and the government didn't stop her.

Formerly Brenda Crowell, she grew up on a farm in Yarmouth. Her parents ran Crowell's Lawnmower Service, with Ruby working out front and Frank fixing the lawnmowers in the back. She was a descendant of John Crowe, one of three men who founded Yarmouth in 1639, and a Puritan of the strictest sect. Brenda got to know Jackie Sullivan at Frontier Valley, a Wild West tourist attraction in Dennis in the 1950s, the two shy teenagers making tentative conversations over the backs of horses.

They fished for striped bass, lobster, and codfish, and then, in 1973, bluefin tuna in Cape Cod Bay. Their sons, Sean and Jamie, were boys then, and spent most summer days on the boat. Brenda couldn't throw a harpoon, and Jackie wasn't very good at throwing either, but they towed milk cartons behind the boat and let the boys throw at them. At the harbor, Sean threw at pieces of Styrofoam in the water. When Sean was fourteen, Jackie decided to put him on the stand. Brenda wasn't sure she wanted him out there at that age, but she agreed, and Sean learned fast. He was deadly, as Brenda put it. He became a good javelin thrower in high school, and he also became, if Norman St. Pierre was right, the best harpooner in New England. His arm brought success to the Sullivan family business. When they added a second boat they formed pairs, Brenda and Sean on the *Back Off*, Jackie and Jamie on the *Sean Jamie*. Jamie, Brenda said, was becoming deadly, too.

It was a rare family enterprise, a mother-and-son team. One time after Sean harpooned a fish, in the excitement and chaos of getting a tail wrap on, Brenda's leg got caught in the line when the fish broke away. Her knee twisted, and she would have gone overboard, but Sean grabbed the line, and held on until the dart pulled free.

They were quiet, hardworking people, but there were legendary tempers in the family. Other fishermen could hear them from their boats. Sometimes Norman thought he could hear them from the plane. It gets intense out there, Brenda would say, and then with a laugh add that it got even more intense with a mother and son working together. One time in the fervor of the hunt on the *Back Off*, Sean turned and threw his harpoon in the wrong direction and it went through the wheelhouse window. Weeks later, in Portland, Maine, Brad Sampson and Sean Sullivan were having a beer at the dock, and Brad asked something he very much wanted to know.

"Sean," Brad said, "I know it's none of my business, but did you throw a harpoon at your mother?"

Sean looked at Brad with the confidence of a deadly harpooner. "Brad," he said, "if I was aiming at my mother, I would have hit her."

Such things were minor squabbles, part of the daily life of a family business. Brenda Sullivan would get everyone up in the morning and stay in the tower from dawn to dusk, and ride the swells until her legs turned black and blue, and sometimes sit still as a stone in the cabin if things didn't go right, and do the shopping and take care of the house, but her real concern was for the future of the fishery. She wanted Sean to have what she had. She wanted him to be able to do what he was good at, the only thing he'd done. Though Jamie had gone to college on a hockey scholarship, Sean hadn't. All he wanted to do was fish. Sometimes he said to Brenda, "If they shut this down, what will become of me?"

THOUGH TWO dozen stick boats had turned their pulpits toward the *Back Off* and the big smashing bunch, Nick told his pilot not to look that way. The *Look Out* was near Provincetown, off Wood End Light, and Nick knew that the fish were below. "They're moving off the beach," he said. He wanted his plane to stay in that area.

Nick's instincts were true. A few minutes later, just a hundred feet in front of the boat, mackerel began to jump out of the water. These were followed by the fins and tails of tuna. Then some big giants soared into the air. Nick ran out on the stand, and the fish were leaping as he moved up close to them. One fish was so big, about 800 pounds, that it couldn't get out of the water. Nick got off a long throw, but missed. "That was an aerial show," he said, coming back down the pulpit, smiling.

He climbed back into the tower. Scott Mullin had been watching from the wheelhouse. "There's fish here," he said. "Lots of fish." We nodded.

"The sun shines on a different dog's ass every day," he said. I took this to mean that though Nick hadn't harpooned a fish today he might tomorrow (actually it was a few days later, when Nick got a 600-pound fish that brought $22 a pound). Scott loved to throw harpoons. He'd hit his first fish at sixteen, and there was nothing so exciting, nothing. Scott had learned a few things by working with Nick Nickerson, but he missed throwing. He'd be going back to college soon. "There's only a few select people who can make a living doing this."

The sky emptied when several of the planes went off to refuel. The "high-sun feeding frenzy" was over, but Nick thought something might pop up. There was a run on a milling bunch, but the radios were shorting out and they didn't get close. They cruised to the south, off the Truro shore, down along Wellfleet. Billy Chaprales passed by on the *Easy Does It* with his family aboard. The planes seemed to gain altitude, to be flying straight lines, the pilots relaxing like Sunday drivers.

As the sun dropped into the west, the late afternoon light softened the water, which turned lavender and peach. The houses in Provincetown, and along the cliffs in Wellfleet, glowed. The sand on the cliffs turned gold, the marsh grass a brighter green. To the north, as the shadows lengthened, the white dunes in Provincetown dimmed and turned gray. A mist hovered over the green land curling around to the south and to the west. The air, pushed in over the ocean, warmed by the land, was full and fresh.

Just before six o'clock Nick's pilot decided to head into Chatham. Four planes remained then, and twenty harpoon boats. The *Look Out* made another sweep along the hook of Provincetown. "It's amazing," Nick said, "that you can catch an 800-pound fish in a place like Cape Cod Bay." Even with a lot of pressure, only two fish had been taken.

The sun descended over Plymouth, and the *Look Out* steamed toward Barnstable. The sky turned orange, the water purple, gold and gray.

"We saw fish," Nick said on the way in. "That gives you the courage to come back out the next day, even if you're the only one here." Nick didn't intend to return to the Bay, though. A northwest wind was forecast, and they'd be going outside, off Chatham.

(1 9)

A DAY FOR TROLLERS

ॐ

O N S E P T E M B E R 3, the Friday before Labor Day weekend, the general-category quota was at 313 tons, 54 percent full. A week later, with 347 more landings reported and a grand total of 2,010 bluefin, the general quota stood at 372 tons and 64 percent. As of September 10 it appeared that the general category would last into the fall.

The harpoon category was about to close. On September 10 the quota was 90 percent full, and though NMFS had added seven tons from a reserve category to extend the season they'd also announced a closure of midnight Friday, September 17. There was some chance that it would be reopened in October if the other categories went unfilled. This, of course, gave the Cape Cod harpooners hope for a fall Chatham fishery, a repeat of the 1991 and 1992 seasons.

Harpooners in Maine were having a good year. They'd been favored with calm weather, and big schools of herring and mackerel drew the bluefin to the north and kept them offshore. Though harpooners could get on them, chumming and trolling were slow in some places into the first week of September. As Joe Jancewicz put it, why should a fish go for a dead mackerel on a spreader bar when it could get forty live ones with a swipe of its tail?

The purse seiners worked those schools off the Maine coast and nearly filled their quota in two weeks. All five boats could have been done by Labor Day weekend, but Leonard Ingrande held back for some fall fishing in Cape Cod Bay.

Sonny McIntire had a good run harpooning in a pocket of warm water off the Maine coast. He took eighteen fish in two weeks, but then, as far as he could tell, a purse seiner caught the assemblage he'd been working on and his run ended.

Joe Jancewicz had some good runs, but he was not having a good season. When some new schools moved into Jeffreys Ledge after Labor Day weekend and the bite picked up, Joe got a fish three days in a row. He had another run of one fish a day for four days, but otherwise Joe felt like he was "zigging when the others were zagging," that he was always in the wrong spot thirty miles away from the action. Peter Atherton got five tuna on his new boat, the *Amanda* (named after his youngest child), and another fisherman running the *Karen Anne* got three.

Bob Campbell had been seeing fish coming into places where they hadn't been traditionally, and he'd seen good areas gone bad—there was hardly any fishery off Platts Bank in 1993, for instance. The chum fish coming into Newburyport in late August were "larger than life," dressing out at from 650 to 700 pounds. Troll boats were getting smaller fish of better quality, and after Labor Day the trollers began to produce. On the afternoon of September 9 seven boats were lined up at TriCoastal Seafood. Prices were averaging about $10 to $12 a pound.

The trollers working off Chatham had been doing well all summer, and over Labor Day weekend approximately forty troll fish were landed at the harbors around Chatham. Fish caught by the Chatham trollers were averaging about 250 pounds, while those taken in Cape Cod Bay and at Stellwagen Bank were coming in at about 600 pounds.

On the Sunday before Labor Day the Cape harpooners worked in the Bay and most of the CQB boats caught at least one fish. The schools were feeding on bluefish that day, and stayed close to the surface, though they weren't easy to get on. Trip Wheeler circled over a school of about two hundred fish for five hours, following it from Sandy Neck to Plymouth and back again, but they didn't take a fish from it. Eric Hesse did hit at two other times in the day, though.

Bob Sampson had aggravated his elbow again and taken another three weeks off. He'd been given electric shock therapy, physical therapy, and ice treatments, and was considering a cortisone shot to get through the season. During his rehabilitation, rather than pace around the house, Bob had gone to Colorado to hunt for elk with bow and arrow. He hiked eight miles into the mountains, slept on spruce boughs, and though he didn't shoot an elk he got close to several. The appeal of bow hunting was in the approach, in the interaction with the animals. Though this trip refreshed him, Bob kept thinking that everything had gone wrong in 1993—the accident in the parking lot, the elbow injury, the early harpoon-category closure. The blown engine in the *Scratcher* was still a fresh memory too. His rest period over, Bob would give the arm another try on Sunday, September 12, and then make a decision.

Brad Sampson was having his best season ever. He had moved over to the *Scratcher* when Bob took time off, and harpooned three fish his first day. On the Sunday of Labor Day weekend he got two fish in Cape Cod Bay. The next Wednesday, scouting on a cloudy day, Brad found a bunch, called for a plane, and got the only fish taken in the Bay.

Though Brad liked being on a harpoon boat he didn't like being the lead harpooner, in his father's place, because of the responsibility he felt for Wade's and Brooksie's incomes. One day after he'd already harpooned one fish he steamed seven miles and missed an easy shot. That night he felt dejected and it seemed that the season was a failure, but then he realized he'd caught five fish that week. Of the thousands of boats that fished for bluefin tuna, only seven hundred caught one, and only a hundred caught more than one. With twenty fish for the season, Brad was in the top one percent, among the most successful of all bluefin tuna fishermen. Nevertheless, the pressure was hard to take, and Brad wanted to see his father back in the pulpit.

ALTHOUGH IT was only the second week of September, summer was over. A cold front had come through, and the temperature on September 12 was in the fifties. But it was an ideal day for fishing, because a high-pressure front was passing over. The center of this front would pass over the grounds that afternoon, and a northerly wind should taper off to a flat calm. The sky would be clear.

"They should be up and numb as boots," Bob said. "This should be a good day. It'll whet our appetite for two weeks of one fish a day." Working in the general category, he meant. With the harpoon-category closure Bob would move over to the *Rush*, which was registered in the general category, and Brad would have to find another boat. Eric Hesse would leave the *Sandra C.* for the *Tenacious*. Nick Nickerson would be looking for a general boat, too. There would be similar displacements throughout the fishery.

The *Scratcher* was crossing Cape Cod Bay. They'd had to decide whether to fish in the Bay or to go outside, to make the long run around Provincetown and to the waters east of Chatham and Nantucket. In the Bay they'd be going for weight, chasing the big giants, and it would be a short trip home. But Brooksie had been watching the schools of large mediums and small giants off Chatham and they looked irresistible. This might be the last chance for multiple catches, with the closure five days away. Brooksie wanted to go outside. And so they would.

Brooksie was unhappy, Bob said. He wanted more money, an increase from 25 to 30 percent of sales. He had compared himself to Wade, Bob's mate, who got 20 percent. Brooksie argued that he brought a plane to the job, while Wade brought his lunch. He was risking his life.

Bob had told Brooksie they all risked their lives. And after deducting Brooksie's 25 percent and Wade's 20 percent, and boat expenses, fuel, ice, and dockage, there wasn't all that much left over. They could sit down at the end of the season and compare books, and discuss it then. Other captains had asked Bob not to go up, because their pilots would want raises, too. And then—who knows—they'd form a union, and then the mates would form a union, and then the boats wouldn't make money. Bob didn't want to lose his best friend over this, and he didn't want to lose his pilot, but he didn't want to raise the percentage, either. He'd told Brooksie not to quit his job with the commercial airline, but Brooksie had quit and worked the past winter on a dragger. Maybe Brooksie needed to go, but Bob couldn't imagine working with anyone else.

"In the end," Bob said, "it all comes down to the guy out on the stand." He made little passes with his hand, imitations of the throwing motion. He hoped the arm would hold up, but in truth Bob thought he was done for the season. He was on the water again, and he'd be out on the stand, and that was a cause for joy, but his mood was colored by frustration.

No one was having a great year, except Eric, maybe. Instead of ten or twelve people filling the harpoon quota, thirty people were doing it. "I guess that's the way it's supposed to be," Bob said.

Crossing the Bay, Bob reminisced about the summer of 1989, when the sand eels were six miles off the shore of the Cape. The whales were there all summer long, and so were the tuna. They'd catch a giant in with the whales in the morning and then chase mediums in the afternoon. They knew what they would be doing every day, not like now, chasing bunch after bunch in blue water, throwing at fish running deep and hard. That summer in the whale zone was the most fun he'd ever had fishing. And Brooksie had been happy then, too.

NEAR PROVINCETOWN Bob climbed into the tower. The *Scratcher* turned to the southeast, and the Cape receded in the wake. At about noon we reached the grounds, and troll boats came into view, boats of all kinds and shapes, from cabin cruisers to skiffs, all pulling baits. The *Scratcher* passed by the first of them at 20 knots, rode into the fleet, and then eased off and cruised at 8 knots. Wade counted forty-seven boats within his view. Bob kept cruising to the south, and soon we saw a fence of pulpits on the southern horizon, the little planes above them like kites.

Brooksie's voice came over the radio. "I got fish here," he said, and the *Scratcher* raced toward him. Running along, Bob looked down at the water. The waves were four feet high, and if the high-pressure area was to bring calm seas they were yet to come. "It's gonna suck on the stand," Bob said. He climbed down the tower, and went out on the dipping pulpit.

They'd decided to go for a head-on shot.

"Eighteen boats," Brooksie said. "They're running from port to starboard."

Then Bob changed his mind. Climbing down the rocking tower, he'd already reinjured his arm, and now he didn't want to take a hurried shot at a bunch coming straight at him. He gave a signal to come in from behind.

"Twelve o'clock and twelve boats," Brooksie said.

There was a 15-knot wind. Bob was riding in abrupt 10-foot plunges, holding the harpoon against his left side with his left arm, to protect his throwing arm.

"Eleven o'clock, eight boats. You gotta speed up to get with them."

Wade pushed on the throttle. The school, not yet visible, was seventy-five yards ahead. "These fish are flying," Wade said.

"Six-thirty. Come to port."

Wade wheeled the boat around.

"Twelve o'clock, and about eight boats, I guess. I'm going into the glare."

"Going awful fast," Wade said. Out ahead of the bow, Bob was jostling and shaking on the stand.

"They're going downsea now. Twelve o'clock. Seven and a half boats. Not a very good-looking school. All spread out. Give it a little speed."

Wade pushed the throttle. The boat was running at 12 knots now.

"Twelve o'clock, four boats. Less than four boats. Into the glare."

Then the school darted away. When Brooksie came round the fish had repositioned themselves.

"They're chasing some baits on a troll boat," Brooksie said. "They're schooled up on a squid rig."

Wade eased off the throttle.

"They went down," Brooksie said. "They took a look at those rubber squid, and didn't like what they saw. I don't think we're gonna catch those fish."

Bob tied the harpoon to the belly rail.

"They stopped and looked right at his baits," Brooksie said.

e *Sea Witch*."

ley swam right under his boat."

Bob climbed back into the tower and got on the radio. He needed information.

Amid the fleet of tuna boats, around the circle of the horizon, were the signs of whales—a humpback's long flipper smacking the water, tail flukes rising and dropping, black backs breaking the surface, pursed exhalations.

Some of the harpoon boats cruised, while others raced to their destinations. Trollers were doing the same. Many of them worked at an easy pace through the water, pulling their baits from long poles that looked like antennae, but other trollers were hurrying to get somewhere. Of the dozen planes in the air, one of them was working for a troll boat, owned by Peter Weiss, the president of a newly formed organization called the General Category Association. Though Weiss employed the pilot, his was not the only boat trailing the plane, which was "putting them in the area," Bob said.

There were occasions when troll boats chased the harpooners' planes. The last time Bob had been east of Chatham, Brooksie had put them on a vein of fish and eight troll boats had run with the *Scratcher*, four behind, four off to the side. Though the *Scratcher* kept passing over schools too deep to throw at, and left unapproachable bunches in the wake, the trollers kept pace, thinking they were headed for some destination. Bob, of course, hated to see other boats running along with him. They didn't have to pay for a pilot. "They force you to be a jerk," he said.

One afternoon on shore I'd talked to a troll fisherman about this. His name was Stretch. He was a tall man, about six-seven, with a gray beard. Stretch had been a treasure hunter before he became a bluefin tuna fisherman. "Why shouldn't we chase the planes?" he said with a smile. "They're out there, and the fish are underneath them. What should we do, go the other way?" Stretch didn't have an especially high regard for harpooners. "We call them Nazi boats," he said. "Look at the names. *Scratcher, Rush, Tenacious, Back Off, Look Out.*" Stretch was apparently unaware of the subtleties of these names—of what it meant to scratch for a living, of the mental rush of pursuing and catching a big tuna, of the need to be steadfast and unrelenting in the pursuit of one's goals, of the need to keep a respectful distance when coming upon a bunch in a crowded area, of the need to keep one's eyes peeled and to be ever aware when riding in a nodding tower on the open sea.

"We should have come out here earlier," Bob said after he finished talking on the radio. "Usually those fish don't show early but today they did. Brooksie was running bunches when we were coming out.

"Eric got two," Bob said (bluefin numbers 33 and 34). Eric had now moved off to the north with Trip Wheeler. Jonathan Mayhew was also in the air, and Roger Hillhouse. The seiners couldn't work in Cape Cod Bay on Sundays, but Mayhew and Hillhouse were out taking photographs for the aerial survey.

"Got fish here, Bob," Brooksie said. "A bunch of seventy-five or eighty." Bob had been massaging his arm. Now he climbed down and returned to the pulpit. A school of pilot whales surfaced ahead of the *Scratcher*, breathed, and went down.

"Coming head-on," Brooksie said.

He decided to bring the boat around behind the school. "Go nine o'clock to port." Wade made a left turn.

"Fish three o'clock and two boats. I'll get you up-sun of them."

But as the *Scratcher* was trying to find the path of the sun, the school suddenly turned and ran under the boat. Bob saw them fly by. He dropped the pole perfunctorily into the water.

They moved off to the west, to get on the edge of the fleet, but there were too many boats for that.

"Lot of warriors out here," Wade said. "It's the weekend."

The high tide was about to come, and the slack. "Maybe that will wake these fish up," Bob said. "At least we're moving in the right direction." West, he meant, toward shore.

Then came Brooksie's voice. "Got fish here, twenty-five fish. Bunched up kind of tight." The *Scratcher* steamed ahead and Bob went out on the stand and bounced along, but when he was a boat away the fish jumped, broke the surface, and were gone. "Spooky!" Bob called out.

"They keep changing direction," Brooksie said. "Next time, down-sun or what?"

With the movement into the afternoon and the changing of the tide, the wind died, and the seas calmed. The *Scratcher* kept making runs, three or four per hour, but Bob didn't get a throw off. It was just as well, he thought, since his arm was troubled. They chased a school, paused while a troll boat from New Jersey passed by, hit the throttle, and chased the school again, until it scattered. They raced after another fast-moving school, followed it for ten minutes, and then when the *Scratcher* was two waves away the fish shot off like swifts.

"Those fish didn't look like they hadn't seen a harpoon boat in two weeks," Bob said after he'd climbed back into the tower. "Looks like they've been run on again and again. They're trained."

"Can't work these fish," Brooksie said. "Very skittish." They began to wonder how things were going in Cape Cod Bay, whether they'd made the right decision to come to these grounds.

"I wouldn't have guessed in a million years that this would have happened out here today," Bob said. "A dying northerly. Glassy calm. September. I can't believe it."

The troll boats were faring better. Since the fish were down and running and hungry, they were more disposed to hitting the baits, pink or green squids and dead mackerel. Several trollers had taken fish, but the schools were nevertheless cautious. On yet another run, the fish swam up to a troll boat. "They're right on his starboard bait," Brooksie called out. "They came up to look."

"These fish won't straighten out," Bob said.

"Should I look off to the east?"

"I don't know. Seems they're like this everywhere."

Off in the distance, the *Back Off* ran ahead, then stopped. Brooksie found another bunch and the *Scratcher* made another protracted run behind fast-swimming fish. At one boat length they sounded.

"I'm not having fun today," Brooksie said.

Bob hadn't taken a single throw. "I can't believe this. They should be everywhere and numb as boots."

Nick Nickerson came cruising up in the *Look Out*. Bob sent Brooksie off to look at a zone east of Nantucket. The fishermen shouted to each other.

"Can you believe this!" Bob said.

"I hear they loaded up in the Bay!" Nick said with a big smile. "Someone got three! Junior VanDuzer got one!"

Nick had gotten two throws off, at fish down deep. They discussed the prospects of tomorrow. A southwesterly coming in, and clouds. Out here, or in the Bay? Bob didn't know. The *Look Out* drifted away.

Coming here today, Bob said, was the decision of someone who didn't really want to fish. They began to work to the west, to move toward Chatham. They made a run on a bunch too deep to throw at. A run on a bunch that sounded as the pulpit drew near them. A run on a milling bunch that scattered at two boat lengths. Then another long run on a parabolic school. Bob could see the tails moving, two waves away. But then they scattered.

"Let's go home," Bob said. "It's a waste of time here. These fish aren't going to let us play at all."

He had to go to work at ComElectric that night anyway, so at five they picked up speed and headed for Monomoy. They'd dock the *Scratcher* at Saquatucket that night. Bob called Penny, and she'd meet them there.

The sun was behind a bank of light clouds, and the sky was turning, but for a half hour, as was the custom, Brooksie worked back and forth in front of the boat, like a hunting dog sniffing the way back home. With the sky glowing orange, Brooksie disappeared from sight.

This had been a day of traveling—five hours of steaming to the grounds, five hours working them, and three hours steaming to the harbor. The wind and waves picked up. It was cold in the tower, and as we approached Monomoy, Wade came down to warm up. He didn't stay on deck long, because he didn't like to leave Bob alone up there. He tried to climb up the ladder to the south of Monomoy, but the boat was moving through the rips and he got sprayed. "I think I'll wait until we get round the corner," Wade said. Then he climbed up to freeze with the captain.

The seas were heavier in the cross-rips inside Nantucket Sound, and the boat was sliding, the tower tilting as the *Scratcher* steamed at 20 knots. Then Bob pulled back, and we glided into Saquatucket.

Penny was standing at the slip, smiling, her hands in her pockets. She already knew about Bob's day. She'd brought hot sandwiches, and walking down the dock, she had her arm around Bob, and somehow she made him laugh. She cheered everyone up. Shore support, I'd heard this called. Bringing the fisherman back to land.

Several troll boats were lined up and waiting to unload their catches. "It was a day for trollers," I said.

"Today," Penny answered. But this would be Bob's last day out for the year.

We got into Penny's car, left Harwich, and headed for the mid-Cape highway and West Barnstable. Within a few minutes, after some comments about the day, after describing how one bunch schooled up on a troll rig, Bob dozed off. It was Bob's sleeping time. He'd go in to work in two hours.

Penny and Wade talked about the year. In 1992 the CQB fishermen had averaged $16.50 a pound, $20 in the fall. This year's average would be even higher.

One fish got $34 a pound, Penny said. Another went for $26.

A fish got held up at an airport in Alaska for two days and still brought $16, Wade said.

"Good numbers this year," he said.

TAGGING

❧

THE HARPOON category closed on September 17, as announced, but on that day NMFS also reported a 24 percent increase in the general-category quota. A backlog of data had been accounted for, so that week's report listed 782 fish landed, 137 metric tons. The quota was at 88 percent and rising, and a few days later NMFS announced that the general category would close at midnight on September 23. Dock prices for bluefin shot up to between $20 and $25 a pound.

Those fishermen who'd been expecting a fall fishery were upset, of course. Though much of the problem had come from buyers holding back landing reports, the fishermen blamed NMFS, seeing the early closure as further evidence that the agency was inept and had little regard for their livelihoods. At the same time, they saw the increased catch rates as evidence that the bluefin stocks were getting stronger— and that they were getting better at catching them.

On September 24 about a hundred fishermen gathered at Barnstable Harbor for a demonstration. It was a quickly organized affair, but crews from three Boston television stations made the trip to Cape Cod, and their reports aired that night.

Bob Sampson was at the harbor with a placard that read "More Tuna for the General and Harpoon Categories." Ron Lein had arrived at Barnstable Harbor with his new boat, and told an interviewer that he'd expected at least two weeks of fishing, that if he'd known what would happen he would have put his other boat in the water. Eric Hesse, Nick Nickerson, Chris Woods, Bill Mullin, Trip Wheeler, Billy Chaprales, and others milled around the parking lot in a show of strength.

A producer told Chaprales that although a group of fishermen in a parking lot was an impressive sight, a speech would be much better for television, so Chaprales got Peter Weiss and Chip Bourget to climb on the back of a pickup truck with him. Weiss told the crowd that the government was for the fish and not for the fisherman. Chaprales was the more demonstrative. He waved a copy of an NMFS report and shouted, "Things have got to change! We want change!"

Afterward one of the television crews went to the Cape Quality Bluefin warehouse, where the manager, Andy Bailer, talked about grading and shipping and the effects of the closure. A reporter then stood over a bluefin carcass, held up an NMFS report card, and explained that every fisherman had to fill one out, but at a crucial point in the season when the tally was already ten days behind the NMFS recorder had taken three days off.

Brenda Sullivan stood watching nearby. She knew the fish were out there, and she was annoyed that she couldn't go out and get them. They had gotten a fish on the *Back Off* on the last day, she said, not by harpooning but by trolling. Nick Nickerson said he had also caught one trolling. Brad Sampson was standing with Nick, and Brad said that he and Wade had also caught a fish by trolling two days before the season ended ("What's so hard about this?" Brad had joked). Bob Sampson had been so pleased that he'd gone to the dock to take a photograph of his son. In 1993 Brad had "caught his age," twenty-three fish.

Later that afternoon some of the fishermen were at Barnstable Harbor—Ron Lein, Scott Laurie, Chris Woods, Eric Hesse, Billy Chaprales, and John Crompton, who ran a charter boat out of the harbor. Crompton was unnerved, because he'd just been interviewed by a federal enforcement agent about a Cape Cod Bay harpooner who had supposedly been videotaped passing a fish to another boat. The agent wanted to know if Crompton had witnessed the act, and told him he'd be committing perjury if he didn't tell the truth. Now the fishermen were speculating about what would happen to the offender. "He won't be fishing for a while."

They talked about the old days, when turning in another fisherman would have meant serious consequences for the informant. They talked about inept management of the fisheries. They talked about the seiners.

"They should put the seiners out of business," one of them said. "Divide up the quota and give it to the general people. Three people are getting three hundred tons." This was a common complaint, and recommendation, among general-category fishermen.

"You don't know what you're talking about," Eric Hesse replied.

"That's just what they want," Billy Chaprales said. "The fishermen fighting among themselves."

"We need the seiners," Eric said. "They support Rich Ruais." Ruais was the director of East Coast Tuna. Leonard Ingrande and the other seiners were major contributors to ECT. Ironically, at ICCAT and in Washington the seiners were protecting the others, the individual tuna fishermen who wanted to see them go. Without ECT, there might have been no fishery at all.

They talked about the one-stock and two-stock controversy. Eric asked Billy about tagging. Billy had tagged fish for an NMFS program. He'd worked out of New Jersey, under an arrangement in which he was allowed to keep one fish for every seven he tagged. You could still tag, Billy said, though you couldn't keep fish. All you had to do was call the Southeast Fisheries Center in Miami and they'd send a tag kit.

Eric's eyes lit up.

He went to his truck, got a notebook, and called Miami. He talked to someone who said it was true, he could tag bluefin. She took his address, and said the kit would be mailed on Monday. Standing at the phone, the receiver at his ear, Eric smiled and made a throwing motion.

"It'll be good practice," he said.

NEARLY TWO weeks passed before a group went tagging. By then there had been another protest, at the NMFS center in Gloucester, and this time the focus was not so much on the early closure as on developments at the ICCAT scientific meetings, where the U.S. delegation of seven scientists had recommended a 50 percent cut in the western Atlantic quotas. Rich Ruais helped to organize this demonstration. He argued that such an inordinately large delegation amounted to assault tactics on American fishermen, that a reduction to 600 tons for the United States would result in losses of $32 million, and that the aerial survey and visual observations indicated an abundance of fish. The two-stock theory was not credible, Ruais said, and the European fisheries were benefiting from American conservation efforts.

In a separate development, three environmental groups—the World Wildlife Fund, the National Audubon Society, and the Center for Marine Conservation—had jointly filed for a CITES I listing for the western Atlantic fishery, and a CITES II listing for the eastern Atlantic.

Now tagging seemed even more important to Eric Hesse and some of the other fishermen. If one or two bluefin tagged off Cape Cod showed up off Europe or in the Mediterranean, they would have further proof that bluefin moved throughout the Atlantic, that there was one contiguous stock, and this data would discredit and fend off attempts to eliminate their fishery. Tagging was one contribution they could make.

TRIP WHEELER wanted to be part of the battle, but he had another purpose in going out tagging. Trip wanted to try out a "live bait" method he'd come up with—live fish thrown in the water near bluefin schools, followed by baited lines. He would be working with two troll boats. They had left the dock at 1 a.m. to catch a supply of pogies, and by dawn were at the grounds east of Nantucket.

We left Chatham Airport in Trip's Cessna 172 at about 9:30. It was a perfect day for seeing fish, clear and sunny, with a high-pressure area passing through. The water would be a bit rough, due to northwest winds, and it was October, after all. We passed over Pleasant Bay and turned southeast over Monomoy. Off in the distance, cod draggers worked the South Channel.

Trip had come to Cape Cod ten years ago to work as a diver on the excavation of a pirate ship called the *Whydah*, which for more than two centuries had lain buried off Wellfleet. But he had soon become bored with pushing sand, and he got seasick living on a barge. After Trip met Nick Nickerson at Chatham Airport, he bought an old rattletrap of a crop duster in Louisiana and started spotting fish.

Trip had wanted to be a combat pilot, like his father, who had died in a plane crash, and his stepfather, who had flown fighter jets. But he had reading disabilities, and didn't test well. These disabilities, he thought, may have had something to do with what he called his "adrenaline addiction," his need to get "revved" and experience extreme states. As a boy, when his family was stationed in Libya, Trip liked to row out near the targets where the jets were lining up their sights, and listen to the shells hiss into the water. In California, on his bicycle, Trip had liked pedaling hard along behind the crop dusters. In college in Colorado he had flown his roommate's plane inside the narrow canyons. He had flown in some dangerous air over Nicaragua, all to get revved. Ultimately the adrenaline addiction had led him to become a speaker to school groups about the effects of chemical dependencies.

He had spent many hours, long into adulthood, flying model planes, and watching gliders soar in the currents off cliffs. Trip was a flying man—unable to deliver the country to the people, he delivered the fisherman to his fish. He felt himself a kind of guardian angel. And spotting fish, he thought, was the closest you could come to flying combat without getting shot at.

Trip got on the radio to the troll fisherman Bob Morgan. Morgan had already "doubled," caught and tagged two, with a troll rig. Another boat, the *Top Gun*, was with him.

Eric was an hour out of Saquatucket. Chris Woods was with him. They'd gotten a late start because they had to buy food and get film. "We're in sportfishing mode," Eric said. "Twenty miles to go yet, Trip. Be there in an hour or so. These tagging poles are a little short."

Norman St. Pierre's voice came over the radio. He had just taken off. Norman ran a gas station in Chatham. "When's the slack tide?" Norman asked.

"Ten o'clock, then again at four."

Norman would be photographing and spotting. "Betzner's got the best picture," Norman said. "Twelve hundred in a school." John Betzner's August 8 photo of 1,290 fish stood as the largest school photographed so far, and it appeared that Betzner would be the pilot who got to keep his camera.

Eric came on. "The last seiner dumped a big pile in New Bedford. Any whitecaps?"

"Little whitecap," Trip answered, "little bit of murky, but good visibility. We'll be able to see them. Got whales here, got slicks here."

Trip spotted a shark and circled a few times, but no bluefin were trailing behind. He reached Morgan's boat just as Morgan had hooked up, circled and took photographs while Morgan reeled in. It was a school bluefin, about 100 pounds. Morgan tagged and released the fish.

Eric said he was seeing shearwaters, often a sign of feeding bluefin. He told Trip to look along the tide rips, and Trip followed the lines. We flew over groups of minke whales, humpbacks and finbacks, a lone right whale, several blue sharks, and a basking shark.

It was nearly an hour later when the show began, and Trip spotted three giants, in a line and moving fast. "Screamers," he said. "You see fish like that, they're going somewhere." Migrating, Trip meant. He figured they'd be leaving soon (though dragger fishermen would see bluefin schools into December).

The three giants dropped down. Trip lowered a wing and coursed over a group of oily streaks. "Slicks everywhere," he said. "There and there and there. Lot of water to cover." He searched the slicks a while, until he came upon a hunting formation of six fish. He banked into a circle and called Eric. "Nice fish, 500-pounders," Trip said. Eric was a few miles to the north. Eric sighted the plane and steamed toward it, but he hadn't gotten far when the fish dropped down.

"Let's see if we can find some warmer water," Trip said. "Those fish are swimming like they're going somewhere. They'll be hard to stick."

Norman had a temperature-reading device in his plane, and soon found a warm spot, a sandy-colored pocket of 54-degree water within the cooler, green water surrounding it. Humpbacks and minkes had found the area, too. Trip circled and watched.

Then Eric arrived. "Lot of life here," he said.

Norman found a school of fifty fish, and called Trip over. They circled one above the other, Norman at 400 feet and Trip at 600, until Norman had taken a few photographs and flew off. Trip brought the boats in, but the school went down.

A few minutes later Trip found another school of fifty fish. These were 700-pounders, he guessed. Waiting for the boats, he took several photos. Norman came up and circled nearby, but then sped away. "I dropped my glasses," Norman said. After he found them he spotted a bunch, and led Eric in.

Trip brought the trollers on the school of 700-pounders. He'd reached a revved state.

"Turn left! Right! Now left! *Top Gun!*"

Another, larger, school rose to the surface nearby.

"*Top Gun!* You got a hundred fish a boat length away! *Top Gun!* Turn left! Get your baits in!"

The *Top Gun* turned, but the fish went down.

Trip then found a school of ten giants. He led the *Tenacious* in, and told the trollers to listen to the communications, the clock directions. Woodsie took the wheel, and Eric climbed into the pulpit. They made an approach from the path of the sun, and were about a hundred feet away when the school turned for the *Tenacious*. Eric leaned and threw, and darted a six-inch streamer into the body of a bluefin.

A school rose up near Bob Morgan. Trip grabbed a microphone.

"Come on, Bobby, and live bait those things!"

"You're in the warmest water around," Norman St. Pierre said as he flew by. "Fifty-four."

"If we don't hook up now we never will!"

The trollers heaved pogies into the water.

"You're gonna hook up any minute!" Trip said.

Morgan was about two boats away, the *Top Gun* a little further off. "Throw the baits out! Bobby! Off to your right!"

But these bluefin weren't much interested in chasing pogies, and the school began to drift away.

Norman had found another school and brought the *Tenacious* in. "Eric just tagged another one," Norman said.

Trip dropped one microphone and grabbed another.

"Good for you!"

Down below, the troll boats were turning haphazardly.

"Could be hooked up, Bobby! Are they hooked? Ah, they just went down!"

Trip was back and forth, window to window.

"They've spooked them! I think they know just where you are! My God, they're gone somewhere!"

Another bunch rose up and ran along.

"*Top Gun*! They're headed right for you! Off to your right-hand side!"

"You're in a hell of a hole," Norman said.

Trip then remembered his partner, something he'd meant to say. He switched microphones.

"Eric, you're hot!"

He reassured the trollers.

"These fish are too aware!"

He exhorted himself.

"Got to use the best light!"

THE FISH came up, the planes circled, the boats ran, and Norman said he was leaving, that he had to get back to his gas station. "Say hi to my dog," Trip said. Trip's old golden retriever, now sitting in his truck at the airport, had been his flying partner until the turning had become too much for him.

Trip sighted a hunting formation, spread out and running. "I'll bring you in if you wanna try," he told Eric.

"I wanna try, I wanna try, I wanna try."

They soon went down though—as hunters would, Trip said.

"I'm doing this more out of frustration than anything else," Eric said. It did seem quite an effort, banging out fifty miles in fall weather for this. The problems at ICCAT and with CITES, the need for political action, had played a part, and Eric wanted practice harpooning. But he had also come out for another day on the water. It was part of a fisherman's possession, his days. They remembered them, talked about them, mulled them over, savored them, reflected upon them. It took only a detail or two, something about the weather, a location, or the character of the fish, to bring back a particular day. Others in different walks of life had their rewards, but the fishermen had days. The most experienced of them were admired not so much for what they'd caught as for who they were as a result of those days. Fishermen possessed time, and it gave them breadth.

Trip spotted two schools lazily moving toward each other, and brought the troll boats in. But when the schools got close they both went down.

A school milled, formed two lines, ran ahead, gathered into a mill again, and then sounded.

A school of a hundred fish gathered and milled, gathered and milled, and Trip brought Eric in, but he couldn't get a throw off.

At about three, when Trip was beginning to talk about going in for fuel, he spotted an enormous milling school. The fish were spread a hundred yards wide, sparkling and flashing along the surface and down below.

"I got a big wad of fish here!" Trip called out, cutting hard.

Together they circled, two counterclockwise revolutions, one body up and making light, one pilot intent upon the silvery ring.

Round it went, round and round.

"Twenty boats!"

On came the tiny *Tenacious*, a comet of white water racing at the cartwheeling fish, a harpooner bearing upon a school near migration's end, gathering to disperse, a harpooner intent upon darting his bottled note into the Atlantic.

But then, a few boats away, the opalescent light flashed and was gone.

"It's like they can see you!" Trip said.

He told Eric he was going in, and that he might come out for the next slack tide.

"This is good therapy for me," Eric said. "We'll stay out if it's good. Call if you're not coming back." Trip angled away.

We ran along the Great South Channel, and Nantucket came up to the west. We passed over gliding humpbacks, their fluketips white under the green water. Balled schools of bluefish were heading south toward Nantucket Shoals, fall feeding grounds. We could see Monomoy, the long sand spit trailing off the elbow of Cape Cod.

Ahead were the ponds and bays of Chatham, off to the west the green land, the thin margin of beach stretching toward Yarmouth and Hyannis. To the north, the tall banks of the outer shore rounding toward Provincetown, and off in the distance, the curl of Race Point over the upper reach of the Bay.

Cape Cod, that beginning and extremity of the country.

A call came in. Bob Morgan had hooked up again, his fourth fish of the day. He'd taken it on a troll rig.

"How long?" Trip asked.

"Seventy-four inches."

"Congratulations."

Trip radioed the airport. We passed over lower Pleasant Bay. Cod boats were lined up by the Chatham fish pier.

"This was the last day of the 1993 season," Trip said. He cut the speed, turned, and descended in.

(2 1)

THE SURVEY AND
THE REVIEW

A WEEK later, four planes left Cape Cod and the islands for Washington, D.C., to attend an open meeting of the ICCAT Advisory Committee. Jonathan Mayhew was in his Citabria, with Kevin Scola in the backseat. Nick Nickerson flew with Norman St.Pierre, and Eric Hesse flew with Trip Wheeler. Pete Kaiser flew from Nantucket. Bob Sampson had intended to go with Mayhew, but couldn't get a replacement at ComElectric.

The committee had called the meeting to gather comments before developing the U.S. position for ICCAT 1993. During a morning session there were presentations on swordfish, sharks, billfish, yellowfin tuna, albacore tuna, and bigeye tuna. The afternoon session was devoted to bluefin, and the public commentary began at four.

Brad Chase, a Massachusetts state biologist who represented the Working Group on Bluefin Tuna, recommended improvements in the stock assessment, suggested further tagging studies, and questioned whether it was appropriate to make drastic quota reductions in the western Atlantic, if there was a single stock of bluefin.

Joe Powers, from the Southeast Fisheries Center, presented the results of the NMFS stock assessment. Over the past two decades, he explained, the stock had declined to between 6 percent and 12 percent of the size that could produce maximum sustainable yield. Even if there was only one stock, each year 2 percent of the fish would have to migrate from east to west in order to replenish the western

227

stock in any significant way, and such a level of migration was in-
consistent with catch-per-unit-effort data. The NMFS position was
that a 50 percent cut in the quota would result in a 50 percent chance
of stabilization of the population.

Dick Stone of the NMFS's Highly Migratory Species Unit, based
in Washington, presented catch statistics and summarized the four
major issues surrounding bluefin: (1) enforcement of ICCAT recommendations by countries fishing in the eastern Atlantic and Mediterranean; (2) the effects on the western stock of fishing by Japanese
longliners east of the 45'W boundary line; (3) implementation of the
ICCAT statistical documentation program; and (4) approaches to rebuilding the stock.

Twenty-eight people spoke during the public comment period. Trip
Wheeler said he was concerned about the way things were headed;
he was seeing more fish when the government was telling him there
was less fish, and if there was a cut in the quota he'd be out of a job.
Billy Chaprales said that just because they weren't catching the fish,
that didn't mean the fish weren't out there. Rich Ruais pointed out
that since the western Atlantic fishermen had taken a 65 percent cut
from 1981 fishing levels, Mediterranean catches had increased 42
percent. The U.S. catch was just 4 percent of the Atlantic catch, and
decreasing it to 2 percent wouldn't conserve the resource but only
destroy a fishery.

Paul Brouha, executive director of the American Fisheries Society,
an organization of fisheries biologists, read a statement, the product
of months of negotiations among members. After heated conflict about
whether it was proper for the group to engage in "the advocacy business," the AFS had concluded that recent quota reductions made by
ICCAT were inadequate and should be reduced to zero. If that action
wasn't taken, AFS would support a CITES listing.

A spokesperson for the Center for Marine Conservation essentially
seconded the position, and called for a recovery plan and timetable
as well.

Jonathan Mayhew made a presentation of photographs taken during
the aerial survey. At first the chairman of the advisory committee
objected, since such a presentation was outside of the five-minute

commentary frame, but Rich Ruais protested, and members of the committee said they wanted to see the photographs. So Mayhew was given his five minutes, and he took John Betzner's five minutes, and he stole another five minutes, and so spent fifteen minutes showing the results of the survey.

The first photograph was of the camera setup, the Nikon and the pocket camera aimed at the loran set. The second was of Mayhew's Citabria. The third was of a parabolic school of twenty fish, to show the viewers what to look for. The fourth was of a milling school of sixty fish. The fifth photo was of a large school of more than six hundred fish. The count was only of fish at the surface, Mayhew explained.

Then Mayhew moved to August 8. He explained the concept of a show day—that at certain times bluefin come to the surface, sometimes all at once through the Gulf of Maine. August 8 had been a show day. Though pilots other than Mayhew and John Betzner were taking photographs that day, their loran cameras weren't working, so their photographs were excluded from the count. Mayhew said he was working east of Chatham and that Betzner was north of Provincetown at Wildcat Knoll.

Mayhew showed Betzner's photograph of the school of 1,290 fish, and said it was just a surface count. In all, he and Betzner had photographed twenty-six schools on August 8. Six of the schools had more than three hundred fish. Excluding those with any hint of repetition, the two pilots' photographs from that day showed 4,984 fish.

In summation, Mayhew told the audience he was sorry he didn't agree with the NMFS scientists, but they were going to put him out of business—and if they did, they'd also lose the opportunity to photograph the fish. "Science is fine, and graphs are fine," he said, "but if you have the ability to hold it up to reality and check it, then you should."

With this, the tone of the meeting changed. Mayhew's point was clear: Just two pilots, working in two small zones of the Gulf of Maine, had photographed schools numbering a quarter of the estimated stock of giant bluefin in the entire western Atlantic. In doing so, they had cast greater doubt on all the existing bluefin-population science.

Also that year, without knowing it, the fishermen working with New England Aquarium scientists had initiated a return to the empirical field biology of the past. Though some participants at the advisory meeting said the survey proved nothing more than that big schools of bluefin were in the Gulf of Maine and that they could be photographed, Jonathan Mayhew's presentation brought a click in the wheel, a slight turn in bluefin science and bluefin fisheries, especially in the western Atlantic Ocean. The aerial survey, and to some extent the concept of the show day, had become credible.

The survey had been, as Molly Lutcavage described it, one of the first collaborative studies of its kind, combining firsthand knowledge of the fishermen with the analytical expertise of oceanographers. It allowed scientists to see the behavior of giant bluefin through a spotter pilot's eyes.

A MAJORITY of members of the ICCAT Advisory Committee supported a position of no further cuts in the quota. But at the ICCAT 1993 conference the U.S. delegation remained firmly committed to a 50 percent reduction. Some people believed the position had been determined long in advance. The U.S. commissioners arrived with a rebuilding plan that called for western Atlantic quotas of 1,200 tons in 1994, 1,000 tons in 1996, and 800 tons from 1998 to 2008. The U.S. share of the 1,200-ton quota would be 743 tons.

The plan didn't become public knowledge until the second day of the conference, when Carmen Blondin, one of the U.S commissioners, took Rich Ruais aside and showed it to him. Ruais saw quota cuts that ultimately would amount to 70 percent, and he became angry. He told Blondin the plan would destroy the bluefin fishery, and that it went against the recommendations of the Advisory Committee, and stated positions of congressional leadership.

Ruais and a number of fishermen in East Coast Tuna had been working their powers of constituency. Representative Gerry Studds of Massachusetts had passed a resolution calling on ICCAT to implement and enforce conservation programs in the eastern Atlantic and Mediterranean as well as in the western Atlantic. Senators

The 1993 Season

George Mitchell of Maine and John Kerry of Massachusetts had asked for postponement of quota reductions until the controversy over the science was resolved. Senator Ted Kennedy called for a one-year moratorium on further quota cuts. "Major doubts exist about the so-called two-stock theory," Kennedy's statement read. "The National Marine Fisheries Service needs to do a better job of working with the fishermen to obtain up-to-date information to resolve the complex scientific questions and settle these issues fairly."

Ruais also told Blondin that the plan would allow the Japanese fishery to "skate free." In the 1980s Japanese longliners had developed a central Atlantic fishery that began near the U.S. 200-mile limit in the fall and moved eastward across the Atlantic through the winter. Ruais said that if the western Atlantic quota were reduced to the levels proposed at ICCAT, the Japanese longliners would merely increase their efforts in the central Atlantic.

Ironically, however, it was the Japanese who brought a solution.

During ensuing rounds the Japanese delegation questioned the conclusion that the western Atlantic bluefin stock was lower than in 1991, despite the 10 percent quota cuts in 1992, and they doubted that a further 40 percent cut would result in improvements. Though the assessment showed that the spawning stock amounted to only 20,000 fish, the Japanese delegation pointed out that aerial photographs had shown 1,290 fish in a single school. What had been observed on the fishing grounds, they reasoned, did not support the results of the assessment.

The Japanese delegation stated that they meant no criticism of the scientists from the United States, but they thought it was time to examine the assumptions for the assessment. It would be important to examine migration, and perhaps work under the assumption that there was one stock. If the stock in the eastern Atlantic was twenty times greater, as reported, a mere 2 percent movement from east to west would result in an increase of 40 percent in the western stock.

Then, in a move that surprised many, the Japanese commissioner offered to reduce his country's share of the western Atlantic quota from 26.5 percent to 12 percent in 1994, and to limit the central Atlantic catches. The western Atlantic quota was then set at a level of 1,995 tons, which amounted to a 15 percent cut (25 percent from 1991 levels). But because of the Japanese concessions, the U.S. share would be 1,243 metric tons, about 5 tons less than in 1993. The agreement came with a promise from the United States for a comprehensive review of the science that determined the western Atlantic stock assessment.

The offer was a generous one, and there were Japanese fisheries representatives who were not pleased. But Japanese fishermen working in the Atlantic were perceived as outsiders in some way, and this gesture of goodwill would promote good relations with Atlantic coastal nations. Japanese officials also wanted a review of a population biology they had long questioned, and here was a way to achieve it. Most important, the Japanese wanted to avoid a CITES listing. They saw CITES as an organization driven not by rational thought but by political motives. If bluefin received a CITES listing, the way would be open for other species, and eventually, they feared, the Japanese food culture would be disrupted. Japan, the world's only major raw-fish importer, clearly wanted to keep this most revered food product from becoming a victim of the American environmental movement.

The fishermen had gained a victory in maintaining the status quo for 1994. But they stood to lose in 1995, when the western Atlantic quota would be cut 55 percent from 1991 levels, to 1,200 tons (nearly two-thirds of that for the United States) unless the review of the science indicated otherwise.

For the conservationists, the compromise was an unqualified victory. As the conference opened, Mike Sutton of the World Wildlife Fund issued a press release: "One of the ocean's top predators is being fished to extinction for lucrative markets in Asia and Europe," it stated. "The meeting in Madrid will be the last opportunity, prior to the 1994 Conference on International Trade in Endangered Species meeting, for ICCAT to live up to the treaty obligations to conserve this severely depleted species. Otherwise, CITES will shut the trade down."

After the conference, Sutton said he was "very pleased" with the results. "We've been calling for a 50 percent cut from the 1991 quota. Actually, ICCAT went even further, agreeing to a 50 percent cut from

232

the 1993 quota," he explained. "They took that action, in large part, because the 1993 stock assessment was the bleakest ever. It was impossible for the commission to ignore."

In his view, a 1,200-ton quota for 1995 was "very gratifying, but only the beginning. The 1,200-ton quota, according to science, will only stabilize the population at perilously low levels. If we're going to recover the stock, we're going to have to go considerably lower," he said, adding that WWF was willing to help minimize the pain to fishermen in any way it could.

The World Wildlife Fund also supported an independent review of the science, and because of the planned quota reductions Sutton announced that the members of ICCAT Watch—WWF, the National Audubon Society, and the Center for Marine Conservation—had decided not to seek a CITES Appendix I listing for bluefin.

IN JANUARY 1994, Doug Hall of the National Oceanic and Atmospheric Administration called upon the National Research Council, an arm of the National Academy of Sciences, to conduct an independent peer review of the bluefin science. The National Marine Fisheries Service called for comments.

In May the peer review committee—made up of accomplished fisheries scientists—met in Washington, D.C., to hear comments. Will Martin, the ICCAT commissioner largely responsible for working out the deal with Japan, said that NMFS stood behind its science but also welcomed the peer review. Brad Brown, director of the Southeast Fisheries Center, and Joe Powers explained their virtual population analysis and said their findings showed a continuous decline of the western Atlantic stock.

John Hoey of the National Fisheries Institute presented an alternative VPA which showed a higher population. Mike Sutton stated that the NMFS science was the best available and that he wanted good conservation practices. Carl Safina stated that he was the author of the CITES proposal and asked for objectivity among committee members, especially in regard to east-west mingling of stocks.

Rich Ruais made a presentation that included the aerial photographs, and a VPA with an alternative catch-per-unit-effort index composed not of the NMFS recreational rod-and-reel survey but of the "East Coast Tuna Captains Log," consisting of effort data taken from the logs of Bob Sampson, Eric Hesse, Lexie Krause, Brenda Sullivan, Nick Nickerson, and eleven other Gulf of Maine fishermen. This VPA showed a western Atlantic bluefin population of 56,000 spawning-age fish.

As CITES's November conference approached, Mike Sutton and WWF sought an Appendix II listing for bluefin tuna. The U.S. Fish and Wildlife Service refused to support a listing, so Sutton asked Sweden for sponsorship. This time Sweden declined. He tried Argentina, but Argentina also refused. Then he persuaded Kenya, a country with 300 miles of coastline on the Indian Ocean, only for Kenya to withdraw its sponsorship later on. According to a WWF press release, Kenya had bowed to the Japanese. According to an East Coast Tuna release, a new employee had unwittingly submitted the proposal without conferring with his government.

East Coast Tuna and the New England Aquarium continued the aerial survey in 1994. That year thirteen spotter planes were outfitted with cameras connected to laptop computers so as to utilize global positioning systems—any photograph would have an accurate placement reference within a few feet. The information obtained by spotter pilots would later be integrated with environmental charts obtained from satellite imagery, to determine how bluefin distribution relates to factors such as sea surface temperatures, oceanic fronts, and the presence of prey.

Fred Brooks was a highly productive photographer in 1994. On July 16, a marginal day, Brad Sampson and Matt Bunnell went out near Wilkinson Basin. As they steamed along, Matt saw a long patch of rippling water. Brad circled behind and called Brooksie, who flew over the school and said it was the largest he had ever seen. He couldn't get it all into the frame of the camera, and kept climbing higher. By his guess, the school numbered ten thousand fish. Molly Lutcavage's count at the New England Aquarium showed about 4,500 fish on the surface, and, she guessed, at least twice that below. Brad and Matt ran on the school for three hours that day, the silver sides turning and arcing ahead, and took two small giants.

Meanwhile, as a result of the ECT survey, the National Marine Fisheries Service released $30,000 to do its own aerial survey. The funds were used to lease a NOAA twin-otter plane with a high-resolution camera, and the plane flew transect flights (over a specified area, without preference for specific grounds) for eight days in the Gulf of Maine, beginning on August 30. On September 17, after flying transect flights in the morning, the NOAA plane contacted pilots and flew into a busy fishing zone. Spotter pilots got out of the way while the twin otter made ten circles.

THE NATIONAL Research Council released its report on August 30. To the surprise of many, the shock of some, the committee concluded that the bluefin tuna population had been stable since 1988. The low assessment by NMFS, the committee found, had resulted from data errors arising from the catch-per-unit-effort survey. Additionally, available evidence was consistent with a single-stock hypothesis with two major spawning grounds.

The committee's assessment (with corrected data errors, inclusion of the Gulf of Maine Captains Log data, and accounting for a 1 to 2 percent mixing of stocks) showed that the levels of giant bluefin in the western Atlantic were two to five times greater than in the NMFS assessment. The population was at about 20 percent of the 1975 level.

The committee recommended that NMFS conduct new assessments to include mixing from eastern and western fishing grounds, and use alternative methods of data management. Research should be undertaken, and the one-stock hypothesis should be rigorously tested. Spawning habits should be studied, and a comprehensive tagging program should be undertaken—especially with newly developed "archival tags" that recorded daily irradiance: sunrise, sunset, and day length, which could be used for global positioning. All work should be subject to external peer review.

"Given the results of reanalysis," the committee concluded, "further reductions in catch quotas in the western Atlantic Ocean from 1992–1993 levels cannot be based on a conclusion of a decline in western Atlantic stock abundance since 1988."

The National Marine Fisheries Service formed a task force to deal with the results, and East Coast Tuna protested that the task force consisted of the scientists whose work had been criticized. After ICCAT scientific meetings in September, ECT protested that NMFS scientists were attempting to discredit the peer review. A meeting in California followed, and the committee again explained and defended its work to NMFS scientists, conservationists, and fisheries professionals.

Meanwhile, fishermen called for a return to the 2,660-ton quota of 1983 to 1991. They claimed there was no longer a basis for the 25 percent reductions of 1992 and 1993. Certainly there was no basis for the impending reduction to 1,200 tons. East Coast Tuna appealed to Congress, and worked with the Japanese and Canadians (Canadian fishermen had caught their reduced 408-ton quota in record time) for a return to 1991 quotas.

When all was done, ICCAT 1994 brought "historic conservation measures," to use a phrase from a Department of Commerce memo released on the final day of the conference. The measures included: (1) a commitment to reduce the catches of bluefin tuna in the eastern Atlantic and Mediterranean by 25 percent by 1998, and to observe the 6.4 kilogram minimum-size limit; (2) an increase of 205 tons in the western Atlantic quota, to 2,200 tons, "in recognition of the positive impact of management actions in the western Atlantic"; and (3) the adoption of a provision for trade sanctions against nonmember countries that undermined ICCAT's bluefin conservation programs.

The U.S. share of the 2,200-ton quota was set at 1,311 tons, 76 tons fewer than in 1991. According to projections made by ICCAT scientists, a 2,200-ton quota would result in an 85 percent probability of a 20 percent increase in the stock biomass by 1998.

The 1994 bluefin fishery in New England got off to a slow start. By July 1, nineteen fish had been taken in the general category, fifteen in the harpoon category. By August 1 the general category was at 153 tons, and the quota was not quite one-third full. Then there was a flood of catches—120 to 150 fish a day—and NMFS abruptly closed the general category on August 15, nearly a month earlier than ever before.

Because 33 tons remained uncaught, NMFS reopened the fishery for three days on Friday, September 16. The first day had the look of a gold rush. As Bob Campbell put it, "Everyone with a bathtub that floats was out there." The fish were abundant, and in fall feeding mode. At one point on Friday, nine boats were lined up at TriCoastal. When the reports came pouring in that day, NMFS decided to close the category at noon on the second day. This brought confusion and bitterness, because some fishermen dumped their fish overboard after the noon deadline, while others brought their fish in and sold them. When the final count was taken, the general category had exceeded its quota by 85 tons, an overage that would be deducted from the 1995 quota.

More than ever, fishermen were bickering with each other. Reduced quotas, the shortened season, an increase in participants, migratory patterns that favored one region over another, and the abuse of the rules—all brought conflicts that seemed to overshadow the ICCAT problems. At an ECT meeting the day after the peer review was released, fishermen spent only a few minutes discussing the results, and two hours talking about such things as quotas for specific areas, limited entry, cheating over the minimum size, and delaying the opening of the season.

Because it was often cloudy or windy in 1994, the harpoon category wasn't even half full when the general closed, and harpooners fished until October 7. Occasionally they banded together and didn't go out, such as during the reopening of the general category, after some fishermen threatened to pass fish to harpoon boats and fill the category. (They accused harpooners of putting fish on the general quota to keep the harpoon category open into the fall.)

B O B S A M P S O N built another boat, the *Skilly*, in partnership with Jonathan and Greg Mayhew, and didn't finish until the season was under way. He got out for the first time on July 14. On his first throw, a head-on shot going fast, Bob tumbled over the belly rail. He reached back and caught hold, and came up hanging on, going up and down like a yo-yo.

By September 15, Bob and Wade had been out only seventeen times. To Bob's eye, there was a constant turnover of fish in 1994, with signs of new arrivals throughout the season. Because of the concentrated catches the prices were generally low (with exceptions), and one of Bob's domestic fish brought $1.75 a pound. Even in October some bluefin—lean, "racy" fish from destinations unknown—brought $5 a pound.

With the weather, the holdoffs, the early catches, and the "weird character of the fish," Bob had what he called a fair year—slightly under $200,000 gross. He knew that for some people that would have been a great year, but Bob figured he had the best pilot, and the best mate, and he expected more.

He would have had a great year, but he missed a day, on September 30. There was rain that morning, and a forecast for rain offshore. Bob and Wade and Brooksie met at a diner for breakfast, and they didn't even consider the possibility of going out. But four other CQB boats did—Brenda and Jackie Sullivan, Billy Chaprales, and Eric Hesse. The sun came out for three hours, and the bluefin showed. All four had their biggest days of the year. Eric harpooned seven fish.

"I painted the back of my truck that day," Bob said. "A $75,000 paint job. That bad call ruined me. We got five fish a week later, on the last day of the season. Five fish is a decent day, but I wasn't satisfied. When we got in, I didn't want to talk to anybody. I just wanted to get out of there."

Of course, money was only part of the disappointment. The Scratcher, the fisherman who always tested the weather, hadn't gone out at least a little ways.

Bob's most successful day of the year came on the Saturday of Labor Day weekend, when he and Wade went off Chatham. They got four fish, four of the five New England bluefin to appear at Tsukiji market two days later. Three brought from $30 to $40 a pound. The fourth, the fish of highest quality, brought 12,500 yen per kilo. In

June the exchange rate had slipped below 100 yen per dollar, for the first time. So on September 5, 1994, one of Bob Sampson's Chatham fish, at 99 yen per dollar, brought $57 a pound. It was his best price yet.

ACKNOWLEDGMENTS

I must thank Bob Sampson, first and foremost, for telling about his life, and for bringing me out on the *Scratcher*. And I thank Nelson Shifflett for introducing me to Bob Sampson, and for his stories about the bluefin fishery.

Many thanks to Brad Sampson and Penny Sampson, and to the Sampsons in Plymouth. To Eric Hesse for time on the water, documents, explanations, and the use of his log. And to those many other fishermen and family members who took me along and spoke with me and helped enlarge my vision—to Wade Behlman, Matt Bunnell, Joe Jancewicz, Keith Hudson, Peter Atherton, Sonny McIntire and the McIntire family, Fred Brooks, Jonathan Mayhew, Trip Wheeler, Nick Nickerson, Ron Lein, Matt Comeau, Billy Chaprales, Norman St.Pierre, Brenda Sullivan, Bill Mullin, Scott Mullin, Peter LaRoche, Lenny Hultgren, Joe Eldredge, Chris VanDuzer, Dave Linney, Jeff Tutein, Kip Lewis, St. John Laughlin, Steve Weiner, and Doug Gerry.

To Rich Ruais, executive director of East Coast Tuna Association, who took me to docks and introduced me to fishermen and led me to buyers, fisheries managers, government officials, and conservationists, and who provided accounts, and updates of events in the fishery and developments at ICCAT.

My thanks to Frank Mather, for his recollections of his tagging studies, for providing documents and videotape, and for the loan of his fascinating unpublished manuscript, *Life History and Fisheries of*

Atlantic Bluefin Tuna, which I drew upon in Chapter 2. And to Francis Carey, of the Woods Hole Oceanographic Institute, for copies of articles about bluefin biology.

My thanks to Dick Stone, director of the Highly Migratory Species Management Division, National Marine Fisheries Service, for providing documents and answering questions. To Kevin Foster, Northeast Fisheries Center, NMFS, for providing catch reports and statistics. To Steve Turner, Southeast Fisheries Center, NMFS, for providing documents and other information.

To Bob Campbell for his market updates and explanations. To Molly Lutcavage of the New England Aquarium for information about the aerial survey. To Frank Cyganowski for his recollections of the seine fishery and for lending his expertise on the stock question and the ICCAT and NMFS process. And to Leonard Ingrande and Roger Hillhouse for their recollections of the seine fishery and of fish spotting. To Gerald Abrams for his account of the early years of the fishery and of the ICCAT process. Thanks to Ted Bestor for information about the Japanese markets. Thanks to those others who explained the ICCAT process, recalled their experiences at ICCAT, and gave their views on the stock question, among whom were Ken Hinman, Carl Safina, Carmen Blondin, Gary Sakagawa, Frank Hester, Chris Weld, Gordon Broadhead, Ray Conser, and Peter Wilson.

Thanks to my daughter, Isha Whynott, for her research assistance. To Laura Templeton, Laurel Harris, and Valerie Jenkins for making tape transcriptions, and to Mount Holyoke College for a grant to pay them. To Chris Pyle for his Plymouthian suggestions and other advice. To Jay Neugeboren, for discussion and encouragement. And to K.L.

To Richard Parks, and to Jonathan Galassi and Paul Elie.